# Italian Yearbook of Human Rights 2017

P.I.E. Peter Lang

Bruxelles · Bern · Berlin · Frankfurt am Main · New York · Oxford · Wien

**Editors**
University Human Rights Centre
University of Padova
via Martiri della Libertà, 2
35137 Padua

tel. 049.8271817; fax 049.8271816

centro.dirittiumani@unipd.it
www.italianhumanrightsyearbook.eu
http://unipd-centrodirittiumani.it/en/

# Italian Yearbook of Human Rights 2017

Italian Yearbook of Human Rights

First Italian edition: *Annuario italiano dei diritti umani 2017*, Padova, Padova University Press, 2017.



1 avenue Maurice, B-1050 Bruxelles, Belgique
brussels@peterlang.com; www.peterlang.com

Printed in Germany

ISSN 2294–8848
ISBN 978-2-8076-0540-4
ePDF 978-2-8076-0541-1
ePub 978-2-8076-0542-8
Mobi 978-2-8076-0543-5
DOI 10.3726/b12015
D/2017/5678/74

Bibliographic information published by "Die Deutsche Nationalbibliothek"

"Die Deutsche Nationalbibliothek" lists this publication in the "Deutsche Nationalbibliografie"; detailed bibliographic data is available in the Internet at http://dnb.d-nb.de.

*Dedicated to Antonio Papisca*

# Table of Contents

## Part IV. National and International Case-Law

## List of Acronyms

| | |
|---|---|
| AGCOM | The Communications Regulatory Authority (Autorità per le garanzie nelle comunicazioni) |
| ANCI | National Association of Italian Municipalities (Associazione Nazionale dei Comuni Italiani) |
| C.l. | Constitutional law (Legge costituzionale) |
| CAT | Convention against Torture and other Cruel, Inhuman or Degrading Treatment or Punishment |
| CEDAW | Convention on the Elimination of all Forms of Discrimination against Women |
| CFREU | Charter of Fundamental Rights of the European Union |
| CFSP | Common Foreign and Security Policy of the European Union |
| CIDU | Inter-Ministerial Committee for Human Rights (Comitato interministeriale per i diritti umani) |
| CIE | Identification and Expulsion Centre (Centro di identificazione ed espulsione) |
| CJEU | Court of Justice of the European Union |
| CM | Committee of Ministers of the Council of Europe |
| CoE | Council of Europe |
| CPED | International Convention for the Protection of All Persons from Enforced Disappearance |
| CPT | European Committee for the Prevention of Torture and Inhuman or Degrading Treatment or Punishment |
| CRC | Convention on the Rights of the Child |
| CRPD | Convention on the Rights of Persons with Disabilities |
| CSM | National Council of the Judiciary (Consiglio Superiore della Magistrarura) |
| CSDP | Common Security and Defence Policy of the European Union |

| | |
|---|---|
| D.p.c.m. | Decree of the President of the Council of Ministers (Decreto del Presidente del Consiglio dei Ministri) |
| D.p.r. | Decree of the President of the Republic (Decreto del Presidente della Repubblica) |
| ECHR | European Convention for the Protection of Human Rights and Fundamental Freedoms |
| ECOSOC | United Nations Economic and Social Council |
| ECRI | European Commission against Racism and Intolerance |
| ECtHR | European Court of Human Rights |
| EP | European Parliament |
| ESC-R | European Social Charter (revised) |
| EU | European Union |
| FAO | Food and Agriculture Organisation of the United Nations |
| FRA | Fundamental Rights Agency of the European Union |
| GA | General Assembly of the United Nations |
| ICC | International Criminal Court |
| ICCPR | International Covenant on Civil and Political Rights |
| ICERD | International Convention on the Elimination of all forms of Racial Discrimination |
| ICESCR | International Covenant on Economic, Social and Cultural Rights |
| ICRMW | International Convention on the Protection of the Rights of all Migrant Workers and their Families |
| ILO | International Labour Organisation |
| IOM | International Organisation for Migration |
| L. | Law |
| L.d. | Law-decree (decreto legge) |
| Lgs.d | Legislative decree (decreto legislativo) |
| MIUR | Ministry of Education, University and Research |
| NATO | North Atlantic Treaty Organisation |
| NGO | Non-governmental Organisation |

| | |
|---|---|
| ODIHR | Office for Democratic Institutions and Human Rights (OSCE) |
| OHCHR | Office of the High Commissioner of the United Nations for Human Rights |
| OPCAT | Optional Protocol to the Convention against Torture |
| OSCE | Organisation for Security and Cooperation in Europe |
| P.l. | Provincial law |
| PACE | Parliamentary Assembly of the Council of Europe |
| R.l. | Regional law |
| SPRAR | Protection System for Asylum Seekers and Refugees (Sistema di protezione per richiedenti asilo e rifugiati) |
| TEU | Treaty on European Union |
| TFEU | Treaty on the Functioning of the European Union |
| UN-HABITAT | United Nations Human Settlements Programme |
| UNACLA | United Nations Advisory Committee of Local Authorities |
| UNAR | Office for the Promotion of Equal Treatment and the Fight against Racial Discrimination (Ufficio per la promozione della parità di trattamento e la rimozione delle discriminazioni fondate sulla razza e sull'origine etnica) |
| UNDP | United Nations Development Programme |
| UNEP | United Nations Environmental Programme |
| UNESCO | United Nations Educational, Scientific and Cultural Organisation |
| UNHCR | United Nations High Commission for Refugees |
| UNICEF | United Nations Children's Fund |
| UPR | Universal Periodic Review |
| WHO | World Health Organisation |

# Italy and Human Rights in 2016: the "Long March" towards Establishing Independent National Human Rights Institutions and the Ambiguous Addition of the Crime of Torture to the Italian Criminal Code

It was our Director, prof. Antonio Papisca, who chose the main theme for the Introduction to the 2017 edition of the *Yearbook*. This was just a few days before his sudden decease. During the latest meeting of the research and editorial committee, he had suggested focusing once again on the urgency of establishing national human rights institutions in Italy, specifically the independent National Human Rights Commission and the National Ombudsperson, in line with the Paris Principles, which were adopted by United Nations General Assembly resolution 48/134 of 20 December 1993.

The "Long March" – so far unsuccessful – towards creating an independent human rights institution had already set off in Italy back in the 1980s and grew in strength in the early 1990s. In those years, the pioneering initiatives of certain Regions, which had already established an Ombudsperson in earlier decades, were supported by a number of regional councils and found vital confirmation in innovative national laws on devolution and administrative procedures. The idea of moulding the mainly administrative profile of regional, municipal and provincial Ombudsmen's offices into independent, autonomous and authoritative human rights institutions proved the cornerstone for bringing the *real effectiveness* of human rights to the top of the agenda. A network of people and institutions, with a mandate solidly grounded in domestic and local legislation, yet closely tied to international human rights law, was to work alongside governments and other political institutions and civil society organisations to ensure that human rights remained a central focus in all areas of political, economic and social life. Human rights understood not as vague aspirations or ideological catchwords, but as a tangible and factual answer to the needs and demands of individuals and communities. Legality and effectiveness; participation and transparency; efficiency and accountability: these are the guiding principles needed to reinvigorate good governance at all levels.

Ten years ago, in an article published in the second issue of 2007 of the review "Pace diritti umani – Peace human rights", Papisca wrote:

> When implementing human rights, ignoring the institutions means depriving them of any valid guarantees. Taking this as a given, once and for all, it is equally important to stress the fact that a full guarantee – i.e. a solid and democratic one – of fundamental rights requires the existence of structures which are a direct expression of civil society and whose aim is not only to contribute to the development of policies, but also to promote and develop a culture of human rights, and to prevent their being infringed, through different routes from those preferred by governing powers. The Paris Principles provide an exhaustive list of the requisites that should characterise "national human rights institutions", precisely as independent civil society institutions. They must be established by a legislative act (hopefully, of a constitutional nature) and their members should be appointed, in principle, not by the Executive but by parliamentary bodies.
>
> International human rights law and its machinery are continuously evolving and becoming more complex, in their organisational aspects too, giving rise to an imperative which is now crystal clear: states which commit to observing international laws and principles must equip themselves with structures which are sufficiently specialised in promotion and protection of fundamental rights, distinguishing between strictly governmental apparati and independent structures.

And twenty years ago, in 1997, in writing about the Ombudsman (which at the time was expected to be established as an organ of constitutional status in the framework of one of the many constitutional reforms which failed to materialise), Papisca observed:

> Within a widespread statist doctrine, rife with abstractions and conservative and authoritarian hangovers, the social contract is emphatically invoked when discussing the safeguarding of supreme principles such as the defence of the nation's territory and keeping public order within its borders. Yet only rarely is the social contract brought up to specify the operational contents, *hic et nunc*, of the principle of promoting and respecting human dignity and the ontic equality of all persons. In short, social contract to emphasise the rights of the state, rather than to satisfy the equal, innate rights of the subjects by virtue of whom and for whom the state exists and is legitimated. Now, the Ombudsman is an "agent of the social contract" in the daily existential pressures people and families suffer; if a pension does not arrive punctually, if the door of a public office is slammed in Mr. X's or Mrs. Y's face, this is an issue concerning the dignity and the life of a person, of a family, of a human micro community; the social contract defaults on its everyday function, relating to the pursuit of community members' existential objectives, as distinct from the survival objectives of the community as a whole. For this painstaking task of articulating in detail the human promotion contents of the social

contract, the Regional Administrative Tribunals (TAR), the Council of State or the ordinary courts are not enough. Also needed are material behaviours, financing and dedicated budgets, efficient services, capable employees and officers, with human rights training and who are aware of the fact that their existence as 'civil servants' is based on their serving and not on giving orders". (Antonio Papisca, "Il Difensore Civico per la (ri)qualificazione costituzionale della difesa civica in Italia [The Ombudsman's office for the constitutional (re) qualification of the function of the ombudsman in Italy]", in Nino Olivetti Rason and Lucio Strumendo (edited by), *Il difensore civico. Tutela e promozione dei diritti umani e di cittadinanza*, Cedam, Padova 1997, p. 15–22).

Decades later, these observations are still relevant, not least because the situation they refer to is shamefully unchanged since then. While, both at the international level and in many individual countries, independent human rights institutions have developed in various shapes and have taken on ever more complex and advanced challenges, their course in Italy has been stalled. Officially because of cost-saving objectives – at least that was the reason given for the abolition of municipal ombudspersons in the 2010 budget act.

The failure to establish a National Human Rights Commission and/ or a national Ombudsperson's office is a structural shortcoming in the Italian legal system. It deprives the Country of fully independent and autonomous bodies representing the whole range of socio-cultural groups present in Italy, and which should be provided with sufficient means to actually protect all human rights (and not just a limited group of rights, or the rights of certain categories), and to open investigations to ascertain any infringement of human rights standards by public officials, both on their own initiative and in response to informal complaints by any individual or organisation.

Over the years, the fact that this institution is missing has been brought to the attention of the Italian authorities by several different bodies. In 2005 and again in 2009 the Council of Europe Commissioner for Human Rights requested it be established. The same request was made by the European Commission against Racism and Intolerance (ECRI) in 2002 and 2016, and by the Advisory Committee on the Framework Convention for the Protection of National Minorities (again, a Council of Europe body) in 2010. Of the human rights committees operating within the United Nations, the Human Rights Committee (civil and political rights) recommended the establishment of a national human rights institution in 2005 and reiterated its request in 2017. In 2008, 2012 and 2016 (i.e. all the most recent opportunities it has had to examine the report from Italy), the Committee against Racial Discrimination did the same. In 2011 the Committee on the Rights of the Child also made the same request; evidently it was not altogether satisfied by the introduction, in 2010, of the National Ombudsperson for the Rights of Children and Adolescents, precisely because this institution did not fall within the parameters of the Paris Principles. In 2015 came the turn of the Committee on Economic, Social and Cultural Rights, and in 2016 the Committee on the Rights of Persons with Disabilities added its voice in making the same recommendation.

A number of foreign governments have also contributed to this "siege". In the 2010 UPR, 15 countries requested Italy to take this major step, but by 2014 their number had swelled to 22, each one of them with words that made explicit reference to the Paris Principles, specifically, to the need to avoid sharing out the task of monitoring, promoting and protecting human rights over a mosaic of different institutions, but rather to concentrate this function in one body endowed with appropriate technical-legal and material resources. However, what is most shocking is to note that Italy accepted nearly all these recommendations, each time reassuring the interlocutor of the day that the establishment of this body, in line with the Paris Principles, was imminent. And indeed, between 1989 and 2017, all of 29 bills have been drafted to meet the commitment that Italy took upon itself, vowing publicly on several occasions to fulfil it, most notably when presenting the 2010 and 2014 UPR reports and in submitting its candidature as a member of the Human Rights Council in 2006 and 2010, as well as in the periodical reports to the series of human rights committees mentioned above.

Elaborated by the *2017 Italian Human Rights Yearbook* Research and Editorial Committee.

At the same time, there has been a proliferation of "independent authorities" in the field, with far-reaching functions and powers, designed to protect and promote certain fundamental rights (privacy and protection of personal data, combating corruption, protection of children, the rights of persons deprived of liberty, the right to information, etc.). However, bereft of a solid anchoring to the overarching paradigm of human rights (indivisible, interdependent and universal), these Agencies appear lacking in legitimacy and out of step with the suggestions from international and European organisations (Council of Europe, European Union and OSCE), and in their turn, at risk of "bureaucratisation". Other areas, equally appropriate for inclusion under the responsibility of an independent institution, are on the contrary entrusted to government-nominated offices, consequently undermining the guarantees of independence and autonomy in the protection they offer, with a negatively impact on the level of trust that citizens place in the efficacy of such mechanisms.

The contradictions of this disjointed and fragmented approach to the issue of non-judicial protection of fundamental rights are self-evident. These are at times exacerbated by further incongruencies, which may occur when a human rights institution is created with a specific mandate on an issue where the Italian legislative order is already lacking as far as the transposition of norms is concerned. The most strident case is perhaps that of combating torture and cruel, inhuman and degrading treatment. In 2016, the national mechanism for the prevention of torture (a body required by the Optional Protocol to the 2002 United Nations Convention against Torture, ratified by Italy in 2013) finally and happily began its work, represented by the National Ombudsperson for the Rights of Detainees and Persons Deprived of their Personal Freedom; however, this Office was created before the Italian Parliament approved a law introducing the crimes of torture and inhuman and degrading treatment. It is in no way being suggested that the failure to contemplate the crime of torture influences the actions of the Ombudsperson for the rights of Detainees (which is also the National Mechanism against torture). However, the current situation undoubtedly shows a lack of overall vision and strategic thought, both as concerns a consistent and holistic conception of human rights and as concerns the positive, negative and "systemic" obligations deriving from international human rights law.

Just as this edition of the *Yearbook* is going to press, the Italian Parliament has approved bill AC 2168-B, which at long last introduces the crime of torture. The new article 613-*bis* of the criminal code defines this offence as follows: "Whosoever, through violence or grave threats, or acting cruelly, inflicts acute physical suffering or verifiable psychological trauma to a person deprived of personal freedom or under their responsibility, entrusted to their custody, supervision, control, care or assistance and consequently less able to defend themselves, is punished with a four to ten year prison sentence if multiple instances of such behaviours occur or if they constitute inhuman and degrading treatment offensive to human dignity."

It is not feasible to provide a thorough appraisal of the new law at this point. However, even to the most cursory glance, it lends itself to much criticism, as already voiced in a letter expressing his concern sent by the Council of Europe Human Rights Commissioner to the Italian Parliament and published on June 21st 2017 (CommHR/NM/sf 027–2017). According to the Commissioner, the need for there to be multiple acts of violence before such behaviours constitute torture, and the limitation of psychological torture to cases where this is "verifiable" present significant discrepancies with the provisions of the United Nations Convention against Torture. The specific limitations added to the Italian law could lead to some instances of torture and inhuman or degrading treatment or punishment going unpunished, creating potential loopholes for impunity. Moreover, since the bill classifies torture as a common offence (that may be committed by anyone) rather than one relating to the behaviours of public officials, this risks weakening protection against acts of torture committed by State officials. Consequently, the *Yearbook* research and editorial committee is of the opinion that the problem of Italy's failure to bring its legislation in line with International standards on the question of torture has not been resolved.

The figures presented in this Introduction[1] show clearly that no further delay is possible in meeting the two commitments described above, in full compliance with the respective international standards.

Taking into consideration Italy's forthcoming candidature for the United Nations Human Rights Council for the period 2019–2021 and the celebrations for the 70th anniversary of the Universal Declaration of Human Rights, the Country must act promptly on the recommendations of the United Nations and the Council of Europe, by finally establishing an independent national human rights commission and fully aligning the crime of torture, just included in the Italian criminal code, to the definition contained in art. 1 of the 1984 United Nations Convention. At stake is Italy's credibility not only with the supranational human rights monitoring bodies, but also with the civil society organisations, government bodies at the local and regional level, and the Italian academic world, who have for years been asking the Government and Parliament to meet the commitments they have made at the international level.

---

1 The data on which the Introduction is based are shown in table format and available online at: www.italianhumanrightsyearbook.eu, in the section "Attachments".

# Italian Agenda of Human Rights 2017

As for past years, for 2017 too, the research and editorial committee of the *Italian Yearbook of Human Rights*, based at the Human Rights Centre of the University of Padova, has compiled an *Italian Agenda of Human Rights,* drawing on the analysis of the recommendations made to Italy at the international level and the most critical issues identified in the successive editions of the *Yearbook* itself. The Agenda is put forward as an up-to-the-minute instrument for choosing the main initiatives to be undertaken on the legislative, infrastructural and policy-making fronts in order to strengthen the Italian system for promoting and protecting human rights (Agendas from previous years are available online at www.italianhumanrightsyearbook.eu).

Comparing it to last year's edition of the Agenda, which had removed a total of ten items and sub-items (see *2016 Yearbook*, p. 15–16), the *Yearbook*'s research and editorial committee found that Italy had made little significant progress. Only one point has been removed completely in the new Agenda, and the wording of four others has been altered in the light of the most recent developments.

The item removed was on children's rights and legislation concerning the expulsion of children (point 28 of the 2016 Agenda): indeed, the provisions of l. 7 April 2017, No. 47 forbid the expulsion of unaccompanied foreign minors, whatever the circumstances, and also specify that in any case foreign minors may not be expelled if their expulsion exposes them to serious personal risk.

As regards the points from the previous Agenda which have been reworded in this edition, the first is on the normative level, specifically relating to the United Nations Declaration on the Right to Peace. Contrary to the Agenda recommendation in this respect, Italy abstained at the General Assembly vote which led to the adoption on 19 December 2016 of the text previously approved by the Human Rights Council. In this area, the research and editorial committee of the *Yearbook* hopes that the Italian Government will, at least, make a concerted effort to promote awareness of and application of this significant Declaration. The second point concerns the Extraordinary Action Plan against sexual and gender-related violence (2015–2017). The timeframe of the plan is coming to a close, and yet the systematic provision of information as to the state of implementation of the actions and interventions, as the plan required, has not taken place, although this data is necessary for the adoption of the next plan of action. The third point is on the issue of corruption. Although the Council of Europe's Group of States against Corruption (GRECO) found some areas of significant progress by Italy, considerable shortcomings remain, particularly as concerns bringing charges of corruption, the transparency of party funding and the prevention of corruption of members of Parliament, magistrates and public prosecutors. The fourth point concerns the crime of torture, added to the criminal code following the approval of bill AC 2168-b on 5 July 2017 but which, as illustrated in an earlier part of the Introduction, conforms only in part to the standards established by the 1984 United Nations Convention. Consequently, the rewording of this agenda item recommends aligning the definition of this crime with that contained in art. 1 of the Convention in point.

Compared to the previous edition, the 2017 Agenda has also been expanded with new recommendations. These include the need to adopt new action plans on certain human rights (for example, the Second Biennial Programme for the promotion of the rights and the integration of persons with disabilities, as proposed by the relevant National Observatory in autumn 2016), monitoring the implementation of recently-adopted plans such as the new National Action Plan on business and human rights (December 2016), or those in their final stages, such as the aforementioned Action Plan against sexual and gender-related violence. Another new recommendation is on the issue of migration and concerns the adoption of initiatives which can go beyond the inflexible parameters of the Dublin III Regulation. Finally, the Committee decided to add a new item emphasising the importance of providing the independent authorities operating in sectors directly relating to human rights with the necessary human and financial resources. Whilst awaiting the (hopefully imminent) establishment of at least one national institution in line with the Paris Principles, the committee considers that it is crucially important to guarantee the smooth functioning and the autonomy of the authorities responsible for the protection of the rights of children and of persons deprived of freedom, as well as the right to personal data protection.

## Italian Agenda of Human Rights 2017

| | |
|---|---|
| **Normative Level** | 1) Ratify the following legal instruments at the United Nations and the Council of Europe:<br>a. International Convention on the Protection of the Rights of All Migrant Workers and Members of their Families;<br>b. Protocol XII to the Convention for the Protection of Human Rights and Fundamental Freedoms;<br>c. Protocol XV to the Convention for the Protection of Human Rights and Fundamental Freedoms;<br>d. Protocol XVI to the Convention for the Protection of Human Rights and Fundamental Freedoms;<br>e. European Convention on Nationality;<br>f. Additional Protocol to the Criminal Law Convention on Corruption. |
| | 2) Deposit the instruments of ratification for the following legal instruments for which Parliament has already adopted the relative ratification and implementation laws:<br>a. Convention on Human Rights and Biomedicine (Oviedo Convention);<br>b. Additional Protocol to the Convention on Human Rights and Biomedicine concerning Transplantation of Organs and Tissues of Human Origin. |
| | 3) Promote awareness of and application of the Declaration on the right to peace adopted by the United Nations General Assembly on 19 December 2016. |
| | 4) Accept article 25 of the European Social Charter (revised), on the right of workers to protection of their claims in the event of insolvency of their employer. |
| | 5) Withdraw the declaration that excludes the application for Italy of Chapter C of the European Convention on the Participation of Foreigners in Public Life at Local Level and, accordingly, provide for the introduction of active and passive voting rights in local elections for foreigners who have been residing in Italy for a certain number of years. |
| | 6) Include hate motivation as an aggravating circumstance in article 61 of the Italian criminal code. |
| | 7) Align the crime of torture, introduced as art. 613-*bis* of the criminal code, so that it is in conformity with art. 1 of the United Nations Convention against Torture. |
| | 8) Expressly recognise representative non-governmental organisations within Italian jurisdiction having particular competence in issues regulated by the European Social Charter (revised) the right to present collective complaints pursuant to the 1995 Protocol. |

| | |
|---|---|
| | 9) Complete the adoption process of the parliamentary bill on defamation in light of the of United Nations, Council of Europe and OSCE standards. |
| | 10) Continue efforts to reform the system for the prevention and repression of corruption in both the public and private sector, with special reference to the most recent recommendations made by GRECO on the following issues: pressing charges of corruption, transparency of party funding and prevention of corruption of members of Parliament, magistrates and public prosecutors. |
| **Infrastructural Level** | 11) Complete within the shortest time the system of independent national human rights institutions in line with the Paris Principles adopted by the United Nations:<br>a. establish the National Human Rights Commission;<br>b. establish the National Ombudsperson. |
| | 12) Ensure the existence of a permanent parliamentary Human Rights Commission, in one or both Chambers. |
| | 13) Assign all Ministries an ad hoc human rights office. |
| | 14) Provide the necessary human and financial resources to the independent authorities operating in areas directly related to human rights. |
| **Implementation of International Obligations and Commitments** | 15) Complete the legislative process for the implementation of the Statute of the International Criminal Court as concerns substantive law. |
| | 16) Increase the timeliness and full execution of European Court of Human Rights rulings, including paying out compensation awarded, and improve Italy's capacity to conform to the standards defined by the same Court. |
| | 17) Address as a matter of urgency the issue of the excessive duration of legal proceedings, including those initiated to seek remedy for their excessive duration. |

| | |
|---|---|
| **Adoption of Policies** | 18) Hold an annual debate on human rights in Parliament. |
| | 19) Adopt the following national action plans, providing them with suitable tools for monitoring and assessment:<br>a. National Action Plan on the human rights situation within detention structures;<br>b. National Programme on education for democratic citizenship and education and training on human rights;<br>c. new National Action Plan against sexual and gender-related violence;<br>d. second Biennial Action Plan for the promotion of the rights of and the integration of persons with disabilities. |
| | 20) Provide information on the implementation and impact of the following national action plans:<br>a. National Strategy for the inclusion of Roma, Sinti and Travellers – 2012–2020;<br>b. National Strategy for preventing and combating discrimination on grounds of sexual orientation or gender identity;<br>c. National Plan against racism, xenophobia and intolerance for the three-year period 2013–2015;<br>d. National Action Plan against the trafficking and serious exploitation of human beings (2016–2018);<br>e. National Action Plan on business and human rights (2016–2021);<br>f. National Action Plan on "Women, Peace and Security" (2016–2019);<br>g. fourth national plan of action and interventions to protect the rights and development of children and adolescents (2016–2017);<br>h. Extraordinary action plan against sexual and gender-related violence (2015–2017). |
| | 21) Formally extend the remit of UNAR to include all forms of discrimination, including those based on language, religion, nation of origin, disabilities, sexual orientation and gender identity. |
| | 22) Allocate sufficient public social spending in the various categories (illness, disability, family support, unemployment, social housing and combating social exclusion). |
| | 23) Continue with efforts to resolve the problem of overcrowding in prisons, making further progress on the structural measures and deflation mechanisms introduced. |

| *Initiatives in specific areas* | |
|---|---|
| **Women's Rights** | 24) Promote real equality between men and women in all aspects of public and private life, specifically through the adoption of policies and actions directed at:<br>• reducing the under-representation of women in the highest decision-making roles in public bodies, including Parliament and Regional Councils, public administration in general, including the diplomatic service and in the private sector;<br>• reducing the salary gap between men and women;<br>• fostering a more balanced sharing of family duties between men and women, both in running the home and care-giving;<br>• eliminating stereotyped attitudes towards the roles and responsibilities of women and men within the family, in society and in the workplace;<br>• supporting the integration process for foreign women;<br>• tackling and resolving the phenomenon of resignations without a justified reason ("blank resignation letters") for pregnant women and working mothers. |
| **Children's Rights** | 25) Adopt a general legislative measure which enshrines the right of children to be listened to in court, in administrative bodies, in the institutions, at school and in the family on every issue which concerns them directly and establish suitable mechanisms and procedures to this end, to ensure that the participation of children really takes place. |
| | 26) Amend the criminal code so as to explicitly forbid and criminalise the recruitment and the deployment, by either the armed forces or armed groups, of young people under the age of 18 in the course of armed conflicts. |
| | 27) Adopt legislation prohibiting and criminalising the sale of light and small calibre arms to countries which deploy child soldiers. |

| | |
|---|---|
| **Citizenship rights and the rights of Migrants, Refugees and Asylum Seekers** | 28) Address migratory flows as a structural phenomenon, the systematic planning for which must be assigned to instruments of an ordinary nature (rather than to emergency measures linked to a purely security-oriented viewpoint) and to multi-level governance with the involvement of the relevant Ministries, Regions, local administrations and civil society. |
| | 29) Respect the principle of *non-refoulement*, the right of asylum seekers to an individual examination of their case, as well as immediate access to asylum procedures and other forms of national and international protection, including where there are bilateral agreements for return or for cooperation in management of migratory flows. |
| | 30) Give substance to the initiatives designed to remedy the inflexibility of the parameters of the Dublin III Regulations in order to satisfy both the expectations of those requesting international protection and the needs of the communities in Europe which are most heavily impacted by the influx of migrants who are potential asylum-seekers. |
| | 31) Support the activities of the "Roundtable on the Legal Status of Roma", established on 30 January 2013 as part of the National Strategy for Inclusion of the members of these communities, with the objective of finding solutions to the situation of statelessness of large numbers of Roma and Sinti originally from the former Yugoslavia, and of their children born in Italy (the so-called "de facto stateless people"). |
| | 32) Develop a more expeditious identification system, in order to reduce as far as possible the period that migrants are detained while waiting for the identification procedures to be completed and ensuring that the rights of people held in repatriation centres are fully respected. |
| | 33) Re-examine laws on citizenship in the light of the principle of *ius humanae dignitatis*, continuing in the direction taken by the simplification of the process for acquiring citizenship status pursuant to art. 33 of l.d. 21 June 2013, No. 69. |

# Structure of the 2017 Yearbook

As it was for the previous editions, the *2017 Italian Human Rights Yearbook* aims to provide a snapshot of the human rights situation in Italy, both from the legislative and "infrastructural" point of view and from that of the practical implementation of policies and initiatives to promote and protect them. The reference timeframe of the book is calendar year 2016. The level of detail and further background provided in the various sections allow for crosscutting and targeted reading, which can also be developed by consulting the analytical indexes.

The information presented in the first three Parts of the *Yearbook* comes from documents in the public domain, normally consultable via the official web pages of each body examined. For Part IV the databases of the courts mentioned were used (for Italian case-law the Giuffrè "De Iure" database was that used the most). The complete and updated lists of the international legal instruments adopted and Italy's behaviour in relation to them (ratifications, signatures, no action) are available online in the specific section hosted on the site of the "Pace Diritti Umani" Regional Archive (www.italianhumanrightsyearbook.eu, Attachments), managed by the University of Padova Human Rights Centre pursuant to art. 2 of Veneto regional law 55/1999.

*Part I* of the *Yearbook* illustrates the main developments in Italy's incorporation of international and regional laws into its domestic legislation. This overview starts from the global level (United Nations), moves on to the regional level, comprising legislation drawn up by the Council of Europe and the European Union, before presenting domestic legislation which has implemented international obligations through national and regional laws.

*Part II* illustrates the human rights infrastructure in Italy and is divided into three chapters. The first is on the structure, functions and activities of State bodies: Parliament, Government, the Judiciary and independent authorities; it also covers the activities of civil society organisations and academic institutions which operate at the State level. The second chapter considers the sub-national level of the Italian order and illustrates the variegated local and regional human rights infrastructure and the relative coordinating bodies at the national level. The third chapter is devoted to the "peace human rights infrastructure" and the local and international initiatives in this area developed by the Region of Veneto. The specific focus on this Region is explained by the pioneering commitment shown by Veneto, dating back to its 1988 regional law No. 18, in promoting a culture of human rights, peace and international solidarity.

*Part III* examines Italy's position with reference to the regional and international bodies and mechanisms for monitoring the implementation of human rights. It includes the assessments and recommendations that these bodies have addressed to Italy following specific missions to the Country and periodic monitoring activities. Italy's role within these organisations and the contribution of its diplomatic representatives for the promotion of human rights at the regional and global level are highlighted. This Part is subdivided into five chapters. The first focuses on the United Nations system, with particular attention devoted to the activities of the General Assembly, the Human Rights Council, the Treaty Bodies and the specialist Agencies. The second chapter is on the Council of Europe, and the third on the European Union. These two chapters complement the information presented in Part I (concerning legislation) and in Part IV (concerning case-law), relative to Council of Europe and EU activities in 2016. The fourth chapter is on the Organisation for Security and Cooperation in Europe (OSCE) and its bodies for the promotion of the human dimension of security. The fifth and final chapter is on international humanitarian and criminal law. In this area, in addition to providing updates on Italy's level of conformity, there is a list of the international peace missions to which Italian troops contributed in 2016.

Finally, *Part IV* presents a selection of domestic and international case-law concerning Italy over the reference period. It comprises three chapters, into which the cases are subdivided according to the subjects to which the various judgments refer. The chapters address domestic case-law (mainly the Constitutional Court, the Court of Cassation and the Council of State), case-law of the European Court of Human Rights and case-law of the Court of Justice of the European Union; in the latter two cases, only cases directly concerning Italy are recorded. A targeted reading of the case-law can also be made using the index of referenced case-law at the end of the book.

Information on the previous versions of the *Yearbook* – from 2011 to 2016 – is available online at the following address: www.italianhumanrightsyearbook.eu.

# Part I

# Implementation of International Human Rights Law in Italy

# International Human Rights Law

The first Part of the *Yearbook* is divided into two chapters. The first is devoted to updates concerning the major international human rights instruments that Italy has ratified, as well as to the identification of both those international instruments signed but not ratified by the Country and those adopted in 2016 that have not been subjected to any initiative of acceptance yet.

The framework of Italy's international obligations takes into consideration the universal conventions adopted within the system of the United Nations, the conventions of the Council of Europe as well as the European Union treaties and secondary law. Accordingly, the information provided are preliminary to the presentation of the national normative apparatus – the Constitution, national and regional laws – which is the subject of the following chapter.

The complete list, updated to December 2016, of the 114 international legal instruments on human rights considered into this publication (43 of the United Nations, 16 on disarmament and non-proliferation and 55 of the Council of Europe) and of Italy's acceptance status (ratification, signature, no initiative) is available online at www.italianhuman rightsyearbook.eu, in the section "Attachments".

## I. Legal Instruments of the United Nations

In 2016 Italy deposited the instrument of ratification for the following international instruments: the Optional Protocol to the Convention on the Rights of the Child on a Communications Procedure (4 February) and the International Convention for the Suppression of Acts of Nuclear Terrorism (21 October).

The complete list, updated to December 2016, of the legal instruments of the United Nations, and of Italy's acceptance status (ratification, signature, no initiative) is available online at: www.italianhuman rightsyearbook.eu, in the section "Attachments".

## II. Legal Instruments on Disarmament and Non-proliferation

In 2016 no changes were made to the status of Italy's acceptance of these legal instruments.

The complete list, updated to December 2016, of the legal instruments on disarmament and non-proliferation, and of Italy's acceptance status (ratification, signature, no initiative) is available online at: www.italianhumanrightsyearbook.eu, in the section "Attachments".

## III. Legal Instruments of the Council of Europe

In 2016 no changes were made to the status of Italy's acceptance of the Council of Europe's human rights treaties. No new legal instruments on these matters were adopted by this Organisation.

The complete list, updated to December 2016, of the legal of the Council of Europe, and of Italy's acceptance status (ratification, signature, no initiative) is available online at: www.italianhumanrightsyearbook.eu, in the section "Attachments".

## IV. European Union Law

### *A. Treaties*

As envisaged by the Treaty of Lisbon, since 1 December 2009 the EU legal framework has consisted of two fundamental instruments: the Treaty on the European Union (TEU) and the Treaty on the Functioning of the European Union (TFEU). Article 6 of the TEU attributes the status of primary law to the Charter of Fundamental Rights of the EU, and also refers specifically to the rights guaranteed by the European Convention for the Protection of Human Rights and Fundamental Freedoms (ECHR) and those deriving from the constitutional traditions common to the Member States, which are part of EU law insofar as they are general principles.

Furthermore, in the Preamble of the TEU, explicit reference is made to the 1989 Community Charter of Fundamental Social Rights of Workers and the 1961 European Social Charter of the Council of Europe (revised in 1996). Both these instruments are also mentioned in the TFEU in the context of Title X on Social Policy (art. 151).

## B. EU Law in 2016

During 2016, The European Parliament and the Council of the EU adopted directives, regulations and decisions with particular relevance for human rights. For its part, the European Commission presented significant communications and legislative proposals.

In 2016 in particular the following directives were adopted: on the strengthening of certain aspects of the presumption of innocence and of the right to be present at the trial in criminal proceedings (2016/343 of 9 March 2016); on procedural safeguards for children who are suspects or accused persons in criminal proceedings (2016/800 of 11 May 2016); on the protection of natural persons with regard to the processing of personal data by competent authorities for the purposes of the prevention, investigation, detection or prosecution of criminal offences or the execution of criminal penalties, and on the free movement of such data, and repealing Council Framework Decision 2008/977/JHA (2016/680 of 27 April 2016); on legal aid for suspects and accused persons in criminal proceedings and for requested persons in European arrest warrant proceedings (2016/1919 of 26 October 2016). Of the Regulations adopted in 2016 with relevance to human rights, the following are of note: Regulation 2016/1953 of the European Parliament and of the Council of 26 October 2016 on the establishment of a European travel document for the return of illegally staying third-country nationals; Regulation 2016/679 of the European Parliament and of the Council of 27 April 2016 on the protection of natural persons with regard to the processing of personal data and on the free movement of such data, and repealing Directive 95/46/EC; Regulation 2016/2134 of the European Parliament and of the Council of 23 November 2016 amending Council Regulation (EC) No. 1236/2005 concerning trade in certain goods which could be used for capital punishment, torture or other cruel, inhuman or degrading treatment or punishment.

Furthermore, some decisions have been adopted which have a particular significance for the matter at hand: Decision 2016/344 of the European Parliament and of the Council of 9 March 2016 on establishing a European Platform to enhance cooperation in tackling undeclared work; Council Decision 2016/590 of 11 April 2016 on the signing, on behalf of the European Union, of the Paris Agreement adopted under the United Nations Framework Convention on Climate Change; Council Decision 2016/1754 of 29 September 2016 amending Decision 2015/1601 establishing provisional measures in the area of international protection for the benefit of Italy and Greece.

Finally, regarding Communications adopted by the Commission in 2016 it is worth drawing attention to the following: Fourth Report on the Progress made in the implementation of the EU-Turkey Statement (COM/2016/0792); Proposal for a new European Consensus on Development (COM/2016/0740);

Enhancing security in a world of mobility: improved information exchange in the fight against terrorism and stronger external borders (COM/2016/0602); Assessing the implementation of the EU Framework for National Roma Integration Strategies and the Council recommendation on effective Roma integration measures in the Member States (COM/2016/0424); Supporting the prevention of radicalisation leading to violent extremism (COM/2016/0379); Action Plan on the integration of third-country nationals (COM/2016/0377); Lives in Dignity: from Aid-dependence to Self-reliance. Forced Displacement and Development (COM/2016/0234); Delivering on the European Agenda on Security to fight against terrorism and pave the way towards an effective and genuine Security Union (COM/2016/0230); Reform of the common European asylum system and enhancing legal avenues to Europe (COM/2016/0197); Launching a consultation on a European Pillar of Social Rights (COM/2016/0127).

Since the adoption of law 24 December 2012, No. 234, two instruments are employed to bring Italian legislation into line with European law: the European Law and the Law of European Delegation. While the former contains norms for the direct implementation of EU law, designed to remedy situations where European norms have been implemented incorrectly, the latter contains the authorisation necessary for implementing the directives and other acts of the Union.

On 12 August 2016 Parliament adopted the Law of European Delegation 2015. With particular reference to the protection of fundamental rights, the law empowers the Government to transpose: Council Directive 2015/637 of 20 April 2015 on the coordination and cooperation measures to facilitate consular protection for unrepresented citizens of the Union in third countries and repealing Decision 95/553/EC (deadline for transposition: 1 May 2018); Council Framework Decision 2003/568/JHA of 22 July 2003 on combating corruption in the private sector; Directive 2014/26/EU of 26 February 2014, on collective management of copyright and related rights and multi-territorial licensing of rights in musical works for online use in the internal market (deadline for transposition: 10 April 2016).

On 7 July law 122/2016 was adopted containing provisions for the fulfilment of obligations arising from Italy's membership of the European Union (European Law 2015–2016). In the context of this measure, actions concerning the protection of fundamental rights were: provisions on matters of maintenance obligations, matrimonial matters and matters of parental responsibility; adjustment rules for the granting of state-funded legal aid in cross-border cases relating to maintenance obligations and international child abduction; individual residence permits for foreign minors; the right to compensation for victims of intentional violent crime, in implementation of Directive 2004/80/EC (infringement proceedings

2011/4147); provisions relating to workers' rights following a change of contractor (EU Pilot case 7622/15/EMPL); provisions relating to funding for an Ombudsperson for the protection of personal data, and relating to the way in which the Arbitrator for Financial Disputes at Consob (the public authority responsible for regulating the Italian financial markets – TN) operates.

Data provided by the Department of European Affairs of the Prime Minister's Office show that as of 15 February 2017, 72 infringement procedures were pending against Italy, 9 of which were started in 2016. Of particular note in relation to human rights are proceedings of formal notice pursuant to article 258 TFEU No. 2016/0368 for failure to transpose Directive 2014/26/EU of 26 February 2014 on the collective management of copyright, and No. 2016/2095 for failure to transpose Council decisions 2008/615 and 2008/616/JHA on the stepping up of cross-border cooperation, particularly in combating terrorism and cross-border crime.

Finally, as regards the continuing evolution of infringement proceedings initiated in previous years, it is of note that on 8 December 2016 the European Commission again referred Italy to the Court of Justice of the EU while proposing financial penalties for failing to be fully and completely compliant with the Court's ruling of 12 July 2012 (case C-565/10). In the opinion of the Commission, Italian authorities are yet to ensure that urban waste water is collected and treated correctly in 80 agglomerations across the Country (compared with 109 in the previous judgement) to prevent serious risks to human health and to the environment (infringement procedure No. 2004/2034). On 22 July 2016, the Commission presented a supplementary reasoned opinion pursuant to article 258 TFEU in relation to infringement procedure 2013/0276 for failure to transpose Directive 2011/51/EU of 11 May 2011 to extend its scope to beneficiaries of international protection.

However, during 2016 the following infringement procedures were closed: No. 2015/2203 for the incorrect transposition of the Eurodac Regulation on recording digital fingerprints of asylum seekers; Procedure 2014/0134 for failure to transpose Directive 2011/93/EU of 13 December 2011 on combating sexual abuse and sexual exploitation of children and child pornography; and procedure 2011/4021 on the compliance of the landfill at Malagrotta (Lazio Region) with the landfill directive 1999/31/EC.

# Italian Law

## I. The Constitution of the Italian Republic

> "The Republic recognises and guarantees the inviolable rights of the persons, both as an individual and in the social group where the human personality is expressed. The Republic expects that the fundamental duties of political, economic and social solidarity be fulfilled" (article 2).
>
> "All citizens have equal social dignity and are equal before the law, without distinction of sex, race, language, religion, political opinion, personal and social conditions. It is the duty of the Republic to remove those obstacles of an economic or social nature which constrain the freedom and equality of citizens, thereby impeding the full development of the human person and the effective participation of all workers in the political, economic and social organisation of the Country" (article 3).
>
> "The Italian legal system conforms to the generally recognised principles of international law. The legal status of foreigners is regulated by law in conformity with international provisions and treaties. A foreigner who, in his home Country, is denied the actual exercise of the democratic freedoms guaranteed by the Italian Constitution shall be entitled to the right of asylum under the conditions established by law. A foreigner may not be extradited for a political offence" (article 10).
>
> "Italy rejects war as an instrument of aggression against the freedom of other peoples and as a means for the settlement of international disputes. Italy agrees, on conditions of equality with other States, to the limitations of sovereignty that may be necessary to a world order ensuring peace and justice among the Nations. Italy promotes and encourages international organisations furthering such ends" (article 11).

The whole of Part I of the Constitution (articles 1–54) is devoted to the fundamental rights and duties of citizens, which are grouped into four areas: civil relations, ethical and social relations, economic relations and political relations.

In 2016, the text of Constitutional Law "Provisions for overcoming equal bicameralism, reducing the number of Members of Parliament, limiting the operating costs of the institutions, the suppression of the CNEL and the revision of Title V Part II of the Constitution" was approved at the second stage of voting by an absolute majority of each Chamber of Parliament, but by fewer than two-thirds of members. The

Law went to a referendum on 4 December 2016, pursuant to art. 138 of the Constitution, where it was rejected.

## II. National Legislation

During the year 2016, Parliament and the Government passed a number of legislative acts (laws, law-decrees, legislative decrees) relating, directly or indirectly, to the safeguarding and protection of internationally recognised human rights. The list of legislative acts is structured on the ensuing classification:

a) general legislative acts;
b) legislative acts dealing with specific issues;
c) legislative acts concerning the protection of particular social groups.

### *a) General legislative acts*

*Cohabitation, marriage*

L. 20 May 2016, No. 76 (Regulating civil unions between persons of the same sex and governing cohabitation).

### *b) Legislative acts dealing with specific issues*

*Peacekeeping missions, civic service, third sector*

L. 6 June 2016, No. 106 (Delegating to the Government the power to reform the Third Sector, social entrepreneurship and regulating worldwide civic service).

L. 14 July 2016, No. 131 (Conversion into law, with amendments, of law-decree 16 May 2016, No. 67, extending international missions of the armed forces and police, development cooperation initiatives and support of reconstruction processes, and participation in the initiatives of international organisations for the consolidation of peace and stabilisation processes, as well as urgent security measures).

L. 21 July 2016, No. 145 (Provisions regarding Italy's participation in international missions).

L. 4 August 2016, No. 157 (Ratification and execution of the following Treaties: a) Agreement between the Italian Republic and Bioversity International relating to the organisation's headquarters [...]; b) Agreement between the Italian Republic and the European Space Agency on the European Space Agency's structures in Italy [...]; c) Amendment to the Agreement between the Government of the Italian Republic and the United Nations on the status of the United Nations System Staff College in Italy [...]; Protocol amending the Memorandum of Understanding between the Government of the Italian Republic and the United Nations regarding the use by the United Nations of Premises on Military Installations in Italy for the Support of Peacekeeping, Humanitarian and Related Operations […]).

L. 19 August 2016, No. 166 (Provisions on donating and distributing food products and pharmaceuticals for social solidarity purposes and to limit waste).

*Crime, Criminal procedure*

L. 16 June 2016, No. 115 (Amending article 3 of law 13 October 1975, No. 654, relating to the fight against and suppression of crimes of genocide, crimes against humanity and war crimes as defined by articles 6, 7 and 8 of the Statute of the International Criminal Court).

Lgs.d. 23 June 2016, No. 129 (Supplementary and corrective provisions to legislative decree 4 March 2014, No. 32 implementing Directive 2010/64/EU on the right to interpretation and translation in criminal proceedings)

L. 28 July 2016, No. 153 (Regulations for the fight against terrorism, as well as ratifying and executing: a) the Council of Europe Convention on the Prevention of Terrorism, done at Warsaw on 16 May 2005; b) the International Convention for the Suppression of Acts of Nuclear Terrorism, done at New York on 14 September 2005; c) the Protocol Amending the European Convention on the Suppression of Terrorism, done at Strasbourg on 15 May 2003; d) the Council of Europe Convention on Laundering, Search, Seizure and Confiscation of the Proceeds of Crime and Terrorist Financing, done at Warsaw on 16 May 2005; e) the Additional Protocol to the Council of Europe Convention on the Prevention of Terrorism, done at Riga on 22 October 2015).

Lgs.d. 15 September 2016, No. 184 (Implementing Directive 2013/48/EU on the right of access to a lawyer in criminal proceedings and in European arrest warrant proceedings, and on the right to have a third party informed upon deprivation of liberty and to communicate with third persons and with consular authorities while deprived of liberty).

L. 29 October 2016, No. 199 (Provisions combating employment in the black economy, exploitation of labour in agriculture and realigning remuneration in the agricultural sector).

L. 11 December 2016, No. 236 (Amending the Code of Criminal Proceedings and law 1 April 1999, No. 91, on trafficking organs for transplant, and law 26 June 1967, No. 458, on kidney transplants between living persons).

*Information, Culture*

L. 26 October 2016, No. 198 (Establishing a Fund for Information Innovation and Pluralism and empowering the Government to redefine the public support framework for the publishing sector and local radio and television broadcasting […]).

L. 14 November 2016, No. 220 (Cinema and audio-visual media).

*Environmental protection*

L. 3 May 2016, No. 79 (Ratification and execution of the following environmental agreements: a) Doha Amendment to the Kyoto Protocol to the United Nations Framework Convention on Climate Change [...]; b) omissis; c) Protocol concerning cooperation in preventing pollution from ships and, in cases of emergency, combating pollution of the Mediterranean Sea [...]; d) Decision II/14 amending the Convention on Environmental Impact Assessment in a Transboundary Context [...]; e) Decision III/7 containing a second amendment to the Convention on Environmental Impact Assessment in a Transboundary Context [...]; f) Protocol on Environmental Impact Assessment in a Transboundary Context [...]).

L. 28 June 2016, No. 132 (Establishing the National Network System for environmental protection and governing the Higher Institute for Environmental Protection and Research).

L. 4 November 2016, No. 204 (Ratifying and executing the Paris Agreement linked to the United Nations Framework Convention on Climate Change, adopted in Paris on 12 December 2015).

*Education*

L. 26 May 2016, No. 89 (Conversion into law, with amendments, of law-decree 29 March 2016, No. 42, containing urgent provisions on the functioning of the education and research system).

*Equal opportunities*

L. 15 February 2016, No. 20 (Amending article 4 of law 2 July 2004, No. 165, containing provisions ensuring gender balance in regional councils).

## c) Legislative acts devoted to the protection of special groups

*Migrants*

L. 21 March 2016, No. 45 (Establishing a National Day of Remembrance for victims of immigration).

Lgs.d. 29 October 2016, No. 203 (Implementing Directive 2014/36/EU on the conditions of entry and stay of third-country nationals for the purpose of employment as seasonal workers).

*Children and adolescents*

L. 20 January 2016, No. 12 (Provisions promoting the social integration of foreign minors residing in Italy through admission to sporting organisations belonging to national federations, associated disciplines or sports promotion associations).

*Persons with disabilities*

L. 22 June 2016, No. 112 (Provisions for assistance to persons with serious disabilities who do not have family support).

*Religious freedom*

L. 28 June 2016, No. 130 (Regulating the relationship between the State and the Italian Buddhist Institute Soka Gakkai, in accordance with article 8 (3) of the Constitution).

## III. Municipal, Provincial and Regional Statutes

Since 1991, after the adoption of law 8 June 1990, No. 142 (Local authorities system), the so called "peace human rights norm", originally contained in article 1 of Veneto regional law 30 March 1988, No. 18 (then updated by regional law 55/1999) on "Regional measures for the promotion of a culture of peace", has been included in the Statutes of several Italian Municipalities, Provinces and Regions. The original wording of this norm reads:

> The Municipality […] (the Province […], the Region […]), consistent with the Constitutional principles sanctioning the repudiation of war as a means of resolving international controversies, and the promotion of human rights, the democratic freedoms and international cooperation, recognises peace as a fundamental human and peoples' right.
>
> To this end the Municipality […] (the Province […], the Region […]) promotes the culture of peace and human rights through cultural, research, education, cooperation and information initiatives aimed at making the Municipality a land of peace.
>
> In order to achieve these goals, the Municipality […] (the Province […], the Region […]) will take direct initiatives and foster the initiatives by local authorities, associations, cultural institutions, volunteers and international cooperation groups.
>
> There are also many other local and regional bodies whose Statutes include a specific reference to international norms and principles relating to human rights, particularly to the United Nations Charter, the Universal Declaration of Human Rights, the International Covenant on Civil and Political Rights, the International Covenant on Economic, Social and Cultural Rights, the International Convention on the Rights of the Child, the Charter of Fundamental Rights of the EU, and the European Charter of Local Self-Government (see *2011 Yearbook*, pp. 65–69).

On 17 November 2016, Basilicata Regional Council adopted its new Statute through Statute Law No. 1, which includes the "peace human rights norm" and recalls the Universal Declaration of Human Rights. Article 3 (Participation) of the Statute states that the Region promotes citizens' participation, particularly in planning and programming decisions, as well as decisions affecting fundamental rights, the protection of health and of the environment. Article 5, dedicated to the person, to equality and solidarity, enshrines the concept that the Region shall contribute, among other action areas, to the protection of the rights of the person, shall work to overcome discrimination linked to all aspects of the human and social condition and considers peace to be the sovereign right of the people collectively and in the interests of each individual.

## IV. Regional Laws

This section lists the laws on human rights, equal opportunities, development cooperation, fair trade, minorities, migration, Ombudspersons and the protection of children's rights, workers' rights, the rights of persons with disabilities, solidarity, social advancement, family assistance, and citizenship and legality education adopted by the Councils of the Italian Regions and Autonomous Provinces in 2016. The laws are divided according to topics and listed, for each authority, in chronological order.

*Peace, human rights, development cooperation, fair trade*

R.l. Tuscany 9 February 2016, No. 11 (Institution for the management of the National Peace Park. Amendments to r.l. 38/2002).

R.l. Tuscany 29 February 2016, No. 19 (Extraordinary solidarity contribution to help the Saharawi people).

*Equal opportunities, gender*

R.l. Abruzzo 23 June 2016, No. 17 (Establishing and regulating the "Pink Code" in accident and emergency departments in Abruzzo).

P.l. Bolzano 24 May 2016, No. 10 (Amending provincial laws relating to healthcare, affordable housing, and social, labour and equal opportunities policies).

R.l. Calabria 23 November 2016, No. 38 (Establishing a Regional Observatory on gender-based violence).

R.l. Friuli Venezia-Giulia 10 May 2016, No. 6 (Amending r.l. 8 April 2005, No. 7. (Regional interventions for information, prevention and protection of workers from moral and psycho-physical harassment in working environments)).

R.l. Piedmont 24 February 2016, No. 4 (Interventions to prevent and combat gender-based violence and to support female victims of violence and their children).

R.l. Piedmont 23 March 2016, No. 5 (Regulations implementing the ban on any form of discrimination and equality of treatment in matters where the Region is competent).

R.l. Umbria 25 November 2016, No. 14 (Regulations for gender policies and for a new society based on relations between men and women).

*Ombudspersons, children's ombudspersons*

R.l. Calabria 23 November 2016, No. 36 (Amendments to r.l. 12 November 2004, No. 28 (Ombudsperson for Children and Adolescents)).

R.l. Marche 15 December 2016, No. 30 (Organisation and functioning of regional authorities).

P.l. Trent 26 September 2016, No. 16 (Integration of p.l. on social policies, 2007, relating to the charter on social services and the protection of minors).

*Persons with disabilities*

R.l. Abruzzo 12 January 2016, No. 3 (Interventions to help citizens with disabilities use self-service facilities at petrol stations).

R.l. Lombardy 5 August 2016, No. 20 (Provisions for social inclusion, removing barriers to communication and recognising and promoting Italian Sign Language and Italian Tactile Sign Language).

R.l. Veneto 26 May 2016, No. 16 (Amending r.l. 22 February 1999, No. 6 (Benefit for citizens of Veneto who have a psycho-physical handicap following the "Doman, Vojta, Fay or ABA Method" and subsequent amendments and transitional regulations)).

*Migration, Roma and Sinti*

R.l. Basilicata 6 July 2016, No. 13 (Standards for welcoming, protecting and integrating migrants and refugees).

R.l. Veneto 15 March 2016, No. 10 (Repealing r.l. 22 December 1989, No. 54 (Interventions to protect Roma and Sinti culture)).

*Workers' Rights*

R.l. Calabria 12 February 2016, No. 3 (Amending and supplementing r.l. 19 April 2012, No. 13 (Provisions seeking to protect work safety and quality, combat irregular work and favour the emergence of irregular work)).

R.l. Marche 25 November 2016, No. 26 (Amending r.l. 8 October 2009, No. 22 (Regional interventions to relaunch construction work to tackle the economic crisis, defend employment, improve building safety and promote sustainable building techniques) and to r.l. 4 December 2014, No. 33 (2014 budget consolidation)).

R.l. Sardinia 17 May 2016, No. 9 (Governing labour services and policies).

R.l. Sardinia 26 May 2016, No. 10 (Provisions relating to the Commission for auditing activities for socially-useful workers' job security. Amending article 4 (32) of r.l. 11 April 2016, No. 5 (2016 stability law)).

*Solidarity, social promotion and assistance to families*

R.l. Abruzzo 9 June 2016, No. 16 (Promotion and enhancement of active ageing).

R.l. Abruzzo 27 September 2016, No. 33 (Interventions in favour of people hit by the earthquake of 24 August 2016 and further urgent provisions).

R.l. Abruzzo 27 December 2016, No. 43 (Law recognising and supporting family caregivers (people who voluntarily provide care and assistance)).

R.l. Basilicata 2 December 2016, No. 25 (Arrangements for the humanitarian use of property previously held by healthcare agencies, hospital facilities and approved private facilities).

P.l. Bolzano 24 May 2016, No. 10 – see *Equal opportunities, gender* above.

R.l. Calabria 8 November 2016, No. 34 (Recognising the role played by mutual-aid associations operating in Calabria).

R.l. Emilia-Romagna 15 July 2016, No. 11 (Legislative amendments to social, housing, youth and early years education policy, following reforms of the regional and local government).

R.l. Emilia-Romagna 19 December 2016, No. 24 (Measures to combat poverty and support income).

R.l. Friuli Venezia-Giulia 10 May 2016, No. 7 (Urgent regulations relating to heritage activities and volunteering, as well as governing state-owned property).

R.l. Lazio, 24 March 2016, No. 2 (Regulating interventions to prevent and combat bullying).

R.l. Liguria 5 July 2016, No. 11 (Interventions to help victims of crime).

R.l. Marche 29 February 2016, No. 2 (Amending r.l. 13 November 2001, No. 27 (Interventions to coordinate towns' timing and to promote the use of time for social solidarity purposes)).

R.l. Molise 17 December 2016, No. 20 (Provisions to prevent pathological gambling).

R.l. Piedmont 2 May 2016, No. 9 (Regulations to prevent and combat the spread of pathological gambling).

R.l. Piedmont 16 May 2016, No. 10 (Implementing article 118 (4) of the Constitution: regulations to promote active humanitarian citizenship).

R.l. Apulia 14 March 2016, No. 3 (Regional living wage and active social inclusion policies).

R.l. Sardinia 2 August 2016, No. 18 (Social inclusion benefit. Regional fund for regional social inclusion benefit – "*Agiudu torrau*").

R.l. Tuscany 11 May 2016, No. 32 (Amending r.l. 25 July 2006, No. 35 (Establishing regional civic service) relating to employment sectors).

R.l. Tuscany 16 September 2016, No. 65 (Solidarity initiative of the Region of Tuscany in favour of the people of Central Italy affected by the 24 August 2016 earthquake).

P.l. Trent 26 September 2016, No. 16 – see above *Ombudspersons, children's ombudspersons*

R.l. Valle d'Aosta 25 January 2016, No. 1 (Amending r.l. 10 November 2015, No. 18 (Measures for active social inclusion and income support)).

R.l. Veneto 8 March 2016, No. 9 (Promoting communications and training on organ and tissue donation for municipal employees and others working in the field).

*Education for citizenship and legality*

R.l. Emilia-Romagna 28 October 2016, No. 18 (Consolidated text for the promotion of legality and to enhance responsible citizenship and economy).

R.l. Piedmont 28 January 2016, No. 2 (Amending r.l. 18 June 2007, No. 14 (Interventions to prevent crime, and establishing a Regional Day of Memory and Commitment in Remembrance of the Victims of Mafias)).

R.l. Tuscany 28 January 2016, No. 7 (New provisions on measures in favour of Tuscan schools and universities and civil society to contribute to the fight against organised and widespread crime and against hidden powers, through education on legality and developing democratic civic awareness. Amendments to r.l. 11/1999 and r.l. 42/2015).

R.l. Umbria 30 November 2016, No. 15 (Supplementing r.l. 19 October 2012, No. 16 (Measures for a coordinated implementation of regional policies to combat and prevent organised crime and mafia crime, and to promote a culture of legality and responsible citizenship. Supplementing r.l. 14 October 2008, No. 13 containing provisions on promoting the integrated urban safety system and policies to ensure citizens' right to safety – repealing r.l. 19 June 2002, No. 12)).

# Part II

# The Human Rights Infrastructure In Italy

# National Bodies with Jurisdiction over Human Rights

International human rights law requires States to set up structures that are adequately specialised in promoting and protecting fundamental rights. In this regard, a distinction shall be made between, on one hand, strictly governmental bodies, and on the other, independent structures directly emanating from civil society. The latter in particular, through channels different from those classically used by governmental powers, aim to participate in policy-making and to promote and develop a human rights culture, as well as to prevent violations.

In this Part the composition, mandate and activities of the following institutions will be illustrated:

- *Parliamentary bodies*: the Special Commission for the Promotion and Protection of Human Rights of the Italian Senate; the Permanent Committee on Human Rights instituted within the Foreign Affairs Commission (III) of the Italian Chamber of Deputies; the Parliamentary Commission for Children and Adolescents.
- *Governmental bodies*: Bodies established within the Prime Minister's Office: Committee of Ministers for Orientation and Strategic Guidance for the Protection of Human Rights (data are lacking on the actual functioning of this Observatory in 2014); Department for Equal Opportunities; Commission for International Adoptions; National Committee on Bioethics. Bodies established within the Ministry of Foreign Affairs: Inter-Ministerial Committee for Human Rights; National Commission for UNESCO. Bodies established within the Ministry of Labour and Social Policy: National Observatory for Children and Adolescents; National Observatory Monitoring the Condition of Persons with Disabilities; and other departments and bureaus of the Ministry of Justice which work specifically on human rights matters.
- *The Constitutional Court*
- *Judicial authorities*: the Court of Cassation, acting as the supreme judge of legitimacy.
- *Independent authorities*: the Communications Regulatory Authority; the Data Protection Authority; the Committee Guaranteeing the Implementation of the Law on Strikes Affecting Essential Public Services; the National Ombudsperson for Children and Adolescents; National Ombudsperson for the Rights of Persons in Prison or Deprived of Liberty.

Italy's national human rights infrastructure is completed by academic institutions promoting not only research, but also education and training in human rights issues, and by several non-governmental organisations, some of which function through networking.

# I. Parliamentary Bodies

## *A. Senate of the Republic: Special Commission for the Protection and Promotion of Human Rights*

The Senate's Special Commission for the Protection and Promotion of Human Rights was first set up during the 14$^{th}$ legislature (motion 20, 1 August 2001) and is the fruit of long experience by the Committee against Capital Punishment (1996–2001). Since the Commission is not permanent, it must be instituted formally at the beginning of each legislature, and the Senate did so during the 15$^{th}$ legislature (motion 20, 12 July 2006), the 16$^{th}$ legislature (motion 13, 26 June 2008) and the 17$^{th}$ legislature (motion 7, 26 March 2013). In the latter motion, the Senate decided to commence the proceedings for the establishment of a permanent human rights commission.

The Commission has the task of studying, observing and taking initiatives on issues concerning the protection and promotion of internationally recognised human rights. To this end, it can establish relations with institutions of other countries and with international bodies; carry out missions in or outside Italy, in particular with foreign Parliaments, even – if necessary – in order to establish agreements fostering human rights or to facilitate other forms of collaboration; it can carry out informational procedures and formulate proposals and Assembly reports; and provide its advisory opinions on proposed legislation as well as on matters deferred to other Commissions.

The Commission is made up of 25 members, present in proportion to the size of the parliamentary groups to which they belong. Among these members, the Commission elects the bureau, made up of the Chair, two Vice Chairs and two Secretaries.

In 2016 the Commission was composed as follows: *Chair*: Luigi Manconi; *Vice Chairs*: Riccardo Mazzoni, Daniela Donno; *Secretaries*: Giovanni Bilardi, Paola De Pin; *Members*: Bruno Alicata (until 21 July 2016), Silvana Amati, Anna Maria Bernini, Federica Chiavaroli, Franco Conte, Peppe De Cristofaro, Aldo Di Biagio, Enzo Fasano, Emma Fattorini, Elena Ferrara, Miguel Gotor, Sergio Lo Giudice, Emanuela Munerato, Venera Padua, Francesco Palermo, Maria Rizzotti (from 21 July 2016), Lucio Romano, Manuela Serra, Ivana Simeoni, Daniela Valentini, Guido Viceconte.

In the ambit of the survey of the various levels and systems of human rights protection currently in place in Italy and abroad, in 2016 the Commission held 18 hearings of representatives from associations, organisations and institutional bodies, and of individual experts, as reported below.

- 26 January: State Undersecretary for the Interior, Domenico Manzione, on the implementation of the European Agenda on Migration;
- 26 January: Elisabetta Zamparutti and Sergio D'Elia, treasurer and secretary of the association *Nessuno tocchi Caino* (Hands off Cain, anti-capital punishment advocacy – *TN*);
- 16 March: Paola and Claudio Regeni, parents of Giulio Regeni, and Alessandra Ballerini, lawyer;
- 6 April: Salvatore Fachile, member of the Association for Legal Studies on Immigration;
- 20 April: parliamentary advisor Daniele Piccione on "mechanical restraints";
- 4 May: Giovanna Del Giudice, Chair of the "Franco Basaglia and Vito D'Anza Permanent Conference for Mental Health in the World" of the Mental Health Forum;
- 17 May: Filippo Grandi, United Nations High Commissioner for Refugees;
- 25 May: Bernardo Carpiniello, Chair of the Italian Psychiatry Society on restraints;
- 8 June: Felice Romano, national secretary of SIULP, the joint Italian police workers' union, and Mario Deriu, SIULP secretary for the province of Bolzano, on migratory flows affecting Italy and the Brenner area in particular;
- 21 June: Gisella Trincas, Chair of the National Union of Mental Health Associations and Marco De Martino, lawyer, on restraints;
- 12 July: Barbara Mangiacavalli, chair of the National Federation of Professional Nursing, Healthcare Assistant and Childcare Supervisor Colleges, on restraints;
- 19 July: Salvatore Fachile, member of the Association for Legal Studies on Immigration, on the agreement between the heads of State or Government of the European Union and Turkey on managing migratory flows;
- 12 October: Stefano Canestrari and Grazia Zuffa, members of the National bioethics committee, on restraints;
- 19 October: Mario Giro Deputy Minister for Foreign Affairs and International Cooperation, giving an update on the Italian Government's proposed migration compact;
- 25 October: Francesco Martone, advocacy officer at "Un ponte per…" (an advocacy association promoting solidarity, peace and human rights

initiatives – *TN*) and Andrea Rocca, director of the international organisation Front Line Defenders' protection programme, on instruments for protecting human rights defenders;
- 8 November: Mauro Palma, Chair of the collegiate National Ombudsperson for the Rights of Persons in Prison or Deprived of Liberty, Emilia Rossi and Daniela De Robert, members, on restraints;
- 15 November: Antonio Marchesi, chair of Amnesty International, and Matteo De Bellis, researcher, on the report "Hotspot Italy: how European Union policies are leading to the violation of refugees' and migrants' rights";
- 16 November: Mario Morcone head of the Department for Civil Liberties and Immigration at the Ministry of the Interior.

Furthermore, in 2016 the Commission adopted two reports: the Report on Identification and Expulsion Centres (February) and the Report on the Special Detention Regime 41-bis (April).

## B. Chamber of Deputies: Permanent Committee on Human Rights

The international protection of human rights is one of the focal points of the activities performed by the Commission for Foreign and European Union Affairs (3rd Commission) of the Chamber of Deputies. As from the 10th legislature (1987–1992), the Commission set up within it the Permanent Committee on Human Rights, which, especially through hearings, ensures that Parliament is kept continually informed and up-to-date with regard to the status of international human rights. The Committee also has the task of following the course of individual human rights measures, performing preliminary tasks pertinent to the activities of the Commission. The Committee for the current legislature (17th) was set up on 16 July 2013.

In 2016 the Committee was composed as follows: *Chair*: Pia Elda Locatelli; *Vice Chair*: Gianni Farina; *Secretary*: Marta Grande; *Members*: Paolo Alli (until 12 December 2016), Maria Rosaria Carfagna, Franco Cassano, Khalid Chaouki, Edmondo Cirielli, Fucsia Fitzgerald Nissoli, Michele Nicoletti, Erasmo Palazzotto, Gianluca Pini, Lia Quartapelle Procopio, Mariano Rabino, Carlo Sibilia, Maria Edera Spadoni, Sandra Zampa.

In the ambit of the survey on the protection of minority rights to maintain peace and security at the international level, in 2016 the Committee held eleven hearings of representatives from associations and organisations, institutions and individuals, as reported below.

- 26 January: Khalil Almarzooq and Ali Alaswad, former Shiite members of parliament in Bahrain;
- 25 February: Isabella Peretti, co-author of the introduction to the book "*Stupri di guerra e violenza di genere*" ("War rape and gender-based violence") and editor of the series "*Sessismorazzismo*" (Sexismracism), Vittoria Tola, national officer of the *Unione Donne Italiane* (Italian Women's Union), Chiara Valentini, journalist and essayist, Simona La Rocca, editor of the book "*Stupri di Guerra e violenza di genere*" and expert in human and environmental rights;
- 5 May: Nadia Murad, human rights activist for the Yazidi people, Ismael Murad, executive director of the "Yazda" Association, and Luba Elias Sulaiman, doctor and human rights activist for the Yazidi people;
- 17 May: Peter Pierre Krähenbühl, Commissioner-General of UNRWA, and Tana De Zulueta, Chair of the Italian UNRWA Committee;
- 19 May: Ivano Carcano, president of the "Spirito della Pianeta" cultural association, Susan Simayiai Muteleu, representative of the Masai people, and Zakaria Yahaya, representative of the Tuareg people;
- 8 June: Antonio Marchesi, Chair of the Italian section of Amnesty International;
- 6 July: Franco Frattini, Chair of the Società Italiana per l'Organizzazione Internazionale, (a non-profit run by the Italian Ministry of Foreign Affairs which promotes international cooperation – *TN*), Giulio Terzi di Sant'Agata, member of the Governing Board of the Società Italiana per l'Organizzazione Internazionale, and Matteo Angioli, Laura Harth and Sergio D'Elia, members of the Round Table "SOS Stato di Diritto" (promoting human rights and freedom of conscience – *TN*);
- 20 July: Enrico Calamai, Spokesperson for "The Truth and Justice Committee for the new *Desaparecidos*" (an advocacy group against the drowning of refugees and migrants in the Mediterranean – *TN*), and Emilio Drudi, journalist and representative of the Habeshia Agency for Cooperation and Development;
- 5 October: Berta Isabel Zuniga Caceres, a human rights activist in Honduras, and Francesco Martone, human rights activist;
- 23 November: Myria Vassiliadou, the European Union's Anti-Trafficking Coordinator;
- 21 December: Noemi Di Segni, Chair of the Union of Italian Jewish Communities, David Meghnagi, Councillor for Culture of the Union of Italian Jewish Communities, Victor Magiar, Councillor of the Union of Italian Jewish Communities, Carolina Del Burgo, Representative of the Committee of Jews Expelled from Egypt and Vittorio Mosseri, Councillor of the Union of Italian Jewish Communities and Chair of the Jewish Community in Livorno (Leghorn).

## C. Bicameral Bodies: Parliamentary Commission for Children and Adolescents

The Parliamentary Commission for Children and Adolescents was set up by law 23 December 1997, No. 451, although its name and responsibilities were modified by law 3 August 2009, No. 112.

> Essentially, the Commission is entrusted with a supervisory and policymaking role related to the enforcement of international obligations and domestic law on children's rights. It may also present to the two Houses of Parliament observations and proposals concerning the effects and limitations of current legislation, and the possible need to amend it to ensure compliance with international law concerning the rights of the child.
>
> The Commission is composed of 20 Senators and 20 Representatives appointed, respectively, by the Chair of the Italian Senate and the Chair of the Italian Chamber of Deputies, proportionately to the total number of members in the various parliamentary groups. The Commission then elects its Chair, two Vice Chairs and two Secretaries. In 2016 the Commission was composed as follows: *Chair*: Michela Vittoria Brambilla; *Vice Chairs*: Rosetta Enza Blundo, Sandra Zampa; *Secretaries*: Maria Antezza; *Members from the Chamber of Deputies*: Maurizio Baradello, Eleonora Bechis, Annagrazia Calabria, Vittoria D'Incecco, Gabriella Giammanco, Maria Tindara Gullo, Vanna Iori, Roberta Lombardi, Loredana Lupo, Simona Malpezzi (until 17 November 2016), Gaetano Nastri, Marisa Nicchi, Giovanna Petrenga, Francesco Prina (from 17 November 2016), Giuseppe Romanini, Emanuele Scagliusi, Maria Valentina Vezzali, Giorgio Zanin; *Members from the Senate*: Donatella Albano, Lorenzo Battista, Ornella Bertorotta, Valeria Cardinali, Nunzia Catalfo, Stefano Collina, Elena Ferrara, Rosanna Filippin, Antonio Gentile, Pietro Langella, Donella Mattesini, Venera Padua, Antonio Razzi, Maria Rizzotti, Mariarosaria Rossi, Annalisa Silvestro, Erika Stefani, Mara Valdinosi.

In 2016, the Commission carried out two fact-finding surveys.

*Fact-finding survey on children in care.* This survey was launched in March 2015, and aims to look in-depth at critical issues associated with current legislation concerning children in care, with a view to improving it. More specifically, the Commission aims to carry out a census on the number and types of accommodation structures in Italy – and to examine their adequacy – the number of children passing through them and the length of their stays, considering not only Italian children but also, and especially, unaccompanied foreign minors. In the ambit of the survey, the following hearings were held.

- 12 January: Alessandra Maggi, Chair of the Istituto degli Innocenti (a child protection group – *TN*), and Arianna Saulini, Save the Children's head of monitoring and advocacy and coordinator of the CRC Italia group (a network promoting the rights of children and adolescents – *TN*);

- 19 January: Lara Sgobbi and Alessandra Pavani, head of child protection and head of research and advocacy, respectively, at the "L'Albero della Vita – Onlus" foundation (an NGO promoting children's wellbeing – *TN*), Carlo Menozzi and Cristiano Bondavalli, director of socio-educational services and coordination instructor, respectively, of the public agency for social services "Reggio Emilia – Città delle persone";
- 26 January: Fabio Gerosa, director of the non-profit Diocesan Council for Activities in Support of Children and Families, Genoa, and Matteo Zappa, head of the children's division of Caritas Ambrosiana in Milan;
- 2 February: Catia Pichierri and Paolo Cioni, head of the legal and legislative office and member of the Scientific Committee, respectively, of the Associazione Rete Sociale a.p.s. (non-profit supporting families struggling with delinquency – *TN*), Dora Artiaco, Vice Chair of the Italian coordinating body for services against the ill-treatment and abuse of children;
- 9 February: Daniele Biondo and Tommaso Romani, Chair and child psychologist, respectively, at the non-profit Centro Alfredo Rampi, Marzia Masiello, head of the institutional relations office of the association Amici dei Bambini (*Friends of Children*);
- 16 February: Maria Carsana, Chair of the Association for the Protection of Children and Persons who are Victims of Violence and Francesco Morcavallo, former judge at the Juvenile Court in Bologna;
- 23 February: Cosimo Maria Ferri, Undersecretary of State for Justice;
- 1 March: Amalia Settineri, Public prosecutor at the Juvenile Court in Palermo;
- 15 March: Domenico Manzione, Undersecretary of State for the Interior;
- 5 April: Gabriele Bartolucci, Vice Chair of the Associazione Genitori Sottratti (a non-profit promoting the principle of double-parenthood for divorced/separated families – *TN*) and Walter Correnti, Chair of the association Un Genitore per Amico (*a Parent as a Friend* – an organisation for separated parents who wish to retain a connection with their child – *TN*);
- 12 April: Beatrice Lorenzin, Minister of Health;
- 19 April: Liviana Marelli, General Manager of "La Grande Casa" Social Cooperative (a non-profit promoting rights and social integration – *TN*), Vittorio Vezzetti, Chair of the national association "Figli per sempre" (*Children Forever*);
- 27 April: Carla Lettere, board member of the Unione nazionale Camere Minorili (a lawyers' association – *TN*), and Massimiliano Porcelli, Chair of the "Utopia 2000 onlus" non-profit Social Cooperative;
- 3 May: Antonella Massaro, activities coordinator at the Civiltà cittadina association (a non-profit protecting citizens', consumers' and users' rights and interests – *TN*);

- 10 May: Gianmario Gazzi and Annunziata Bartolomei, Chair and Vice Chair, respectively, of the National Council of Social Workers;
- 17 May: Monya Ferritti, Chair of the Coordinating body of the network of foster family and adoptive family associations, and Annamaria Columbu, representative of the association coordinating body Ubi Minor (a service and information point for people working with children and adolescents – *TN*);
- 24 May: Riccardo Ripoli, Chair of the Amici della Zizzi association (a non-profit supporting children – *TN*);
- 8 June: Elena Cianflone, Chair of the Italian Union of Adoptive Families;
- 28 June: Filomena Albano, antitrust authority for children and adolescents;
- 5 July: Antonio Maria La Scala, Chair of the Associazione Penelope Italia (a non-profit for the families and friends of people who have disappeared – *TN*), Vincenzo Spavone, Chair of the Association of Parents Separated from their Children, Fabio Nestola and Giacomo Rotoli, national councillor and inter-association coordinator, respectively, of the Association of National members for the Protection of Children, and Matteo Villanova, Director of the Osservatorio laboratorio tutela rispetto emozionale età evolutiva;
- 12 July: Matteo Biffoni, mayor of Prato and ANCI delegate on integration policy and immigration, and Antonio Naddeo, Director of the Secretarial Office of the Unified Conference as well as Head of Department for regional affairs, autonomous provinces and sport at the Ministry for Regional Affairs and Autonomous Provinces;
- 14 July: Andrea Carletti, Mayor of the Municipality of Bibiano with social proxy, Federica Aghinolfi, head of integrated social services, and Maria Stella D'Andrea, forensic doctor and criminologist at the Reggio Emilia public health authority.

*Fact-finding survey on the protection of children's psycho-physical health*. In the ambit of the survey, which was launched in June 2016, the following hearings were held.

- 19 July: Marco Pandolfi, staff physician in the paediatric ward and Director of the adolescent medicine unit at the Fatebenefratelli Sacco Hospital Group, Milan;
- 20 September: Fulvio Giardina and Tancredi Di Iullo, Chair and Member, respectively, of the National Council of Psychologists;
- 27 September: Arianna Saulini, Save the Children's head of monitoring and advocacy and coordinator of the CRC Italia group, Maria Edoarda Trillò, representative of the Cultural Association of Paediatricians, Brunella Greco, representative of Save the Children Italy's Youth and New Media Unit and member of the CRC group, Antonella Costantino, Chair of the Italian Society of neuropsychiatry of children and adolescents and member of the CRC group, and Silvia Taviani representative of the CRC group's coordinating body;

- 4 October: Nicola Portinaro, scientific director of the Ariel Foundation Childhood neuromotor disability centre and Augusto Eugeni, Vice Chair of the National Association for the Promotion and Protection of the Rights of Persons with Disabilities;
- 11 October: Maura Massimino, Director of the Paediatrics Unit at the IRCCS Foundation of the National Tumour Institute in Milan and Carlo Alfredo Clerici, researcher at the Department of Oncology and haemo-oncology at the University of Milan;
- 18 October: Maurizio Mascarin, head of the Department of radiotherapeutic oncology, and Elisa Coassin, resident doctor in oncology radiation therapy at the Aviano Oncological Referral Centre;
- 25 October: Paola Puccini, Chair and scientific director of the Vygotsky Study Centre, and Nunzio Bonaccorso, Chair of the non-profit Italian Association of Support for the Disabled in Milan;
- 8 November: Angelo Ricci, Chair of the non-profit Italian Federation of parents' associations for Paediatric Haematology and Oncology and Marcello Orzalesi, scientific coordinator of the non-profit Fondazione Maruzza Lefebvre (a children's palliative care foundation – *TN*).

Furthermore, in June 2016 the concluding document of the fact-finding survey on child prostitution was adopted.

## D. Parliamentary Initiatives Concerning Human Rights

Presented below is a brief overview of the main human rights legislation produced by the Italian Parliament in 2014, subdivided into bills and guidelines and watchdog initiatives (motions, interpellations, questions for an oral or written answer, resolutions, agenda proposals). The proposer or first signer, the code (the letter 'C' indicating that the initiative was presented in the Chamber of Deputies and the letter 'S' that it was presented in the Senate), the title, the date of presentation and the most recent update are listed for each initiative.

In 2016, Parliament adopted 243 human rights initiatives overall, including 26 bills, 30 motions, 14 interpellations, 29 questions for an oral answer, 56 questions for a written answer, 31 questions submitted to Commissions, 12 Assembly resolutions, 10 Commission resolutions, and 35 Assembly agenda proposals.

## Bills

The 26 bills presented concerned the following issues: the right to vote (including granting foreigners the right to vote and to stand for election) (9); bioethics (3); the right to a private and family life (including civil unions (2)); the rights of refugees and asylum seekers (2); the rights of persons with disabilities (2); ratifying international instruments (1); freedom of opinion and expression (1); procedural safeguards (1); the right to work (1); civil rights (1); children's rights (1); the right to privacy (1); women's rights (1).

| Date | Initiative | Latest update |
|---|---|---|
| 03/02/2016 | Beatrice BRIGNONE (SI-SEL-POS) and others – *C.3581*<br>Amending the civil code in relation to informed consent, an indication of wishes regarding healthcare treatment and living wills, as well as establishing an electronic database for this purpose | 12/02/2016 withdrawn |
| 05/02/2016 | Andrea GIORGIS (PD) – *C.3591*<br>Amending the consolidated text as per legislative decree 18 August 2000, No. 267, relating to the right of foreigners residing in Italy to vote in and to stand for municipal, provincial and district elections | 03/03/2016 assigned (examination not yet begun) |
| 05/02/2016 | Roberta AGOSTINI (Art. 1-MDP) and others – *C.3590*<br>Establishing a National Day of Women's Suffrage | 09/03/2016 assigned (examination not yet begun) |
| 17/02/2016 | Mirella LIUZZI (M5S) – *C.3617*<br>Amending the code on personal data protection as per legislative decree 30 June 2003, No. 196, on unwanted sales communications | 02/11/2016 assigned (examination not yet begun) |
| 25/02/2016 | Monica CIRINNA' (PD) *C.3634*<br>Governing civil unions between persons of the same sex and cohabitation | 11/05/2016 definitively approved. Law |
| 02/03/2016 | Marcello GUALDANI (AP (Ncd-CpE)) and others – *S. 2264*<br>Provisions to recognise the age of majority as being sixteen years old | 02/03/2016 still to be assigned |
| 22/03/2016 | Enrico BUEMI (Aut(SVP-UV-PATT-UPT)-PSI) – *S. 2305*<br>New first book of the Civil Code containing norms on the rights of the individual | 22/03/2016 still to be assigned |
| 22/03/2016 | Paola TAVERNA (M5S) – *S. 2294*<br>Provisions concerning the right to work of persons with disabilities | 17/05/2016 assigned (examination not yet begun) |

| Date | Initiative | Latest update |
|---|---|---|
| 04/04/2016 | Arturo SCOTTO (Art. 1-MDP) and others – *C.3717*<br>Introduction of article 1 of decree-law 30 December 1989, No. 416, converted, with amendments, to law 28 February 1990, No. 39, relating to identifying persons entitled to the right to asylum and recognising this right to female victims of violence | 20/04/2016 assigned (examination not yet begun) |
| 04/04/2016 | Arturo SCOTTO (Art. 1-MDP) and others – *C.3716*<br>Amending article 2 of the consolidated act on provisions governing immigration and regulations on the condition of foreigners pursuant to legislative decree 25 July 1998, No. 286, on foreigners' right to vote in and stand for local elections and referenda | 20/04/2016 assigned (examination not yet begun) |
| 04/04/2016 | Arturo SCOTTO (Art. 1-MDP) and others – *C.3712*<br>Amending articles 48 and 51 of the Constitution relating to granting foreigners the right to vote and to stand for election | 18/04/2016 assigned (examination not yet begun) |
| 05/04/2016 | Gianni FARINA (PD) – *C.3721*<br>Amendments to law 27 December 2001, No. 459, relating to exercising the right to vote on the part of Italian citizens resident abroad | 26/04/2016 assigned (examination not yet begun) |
| 07/04/2016 | Guglielmo VACCARO (Mixed) and others – *C.3729*<br>Amending article 1 of legislative decree 12 April 1996, No. 197, relating to electoral rights in municipal and district elections for citizens from European Union Member States residing in Italy | 07/04/2016 still to be assigned |
| 02/05/2016 | Alessandra BENCINI (Mixed) and others – *S. 2357*<br>Empowering the Government to amend the consolidated text as per Decree of the President of the Republic 30 March 1957, No. 361, seeking to permit early voting for students and persons who, because of study, are not present in their registered place of residence | 26/07/2016 assigned (examination not yet begun) |
| 20/06/2016 | Paola TAVERNA (M5S) – *S. 998-B*<br>Provisions relating to compulsory neonatal diagnostic investigations to prevent and treat hereditary metabolic illnesses | 04/08/2016 definitively approved. Law |
| 21/06/2016 | Gregorio FONTANA (FI-PdL) – *C.3915*<br>Repealing regulations on issuing residence permits for humanitarian reasons and empowering the Government to revise international protection rules | 23/01/2017 assigned (examination not yet begun) |
| 24/06/2016 | Eleonora BECHIS (Mixed) and others – *C.3930*<br>Amending article 44 of law 4 May 1983, No. 184, concerning adoption in special cases in the ambit of civil unions | 18/07/2016 assigned (examination not yet begun) |

| Date | Initiative | Latest update |
|---|---|---|
| 30/06/2016 | Ferdinando AIELLO (PD) and others – *C.3957*<br>Introducing criminal code article 649-bis, relating to aggravating circumstances for certain crimes committed for the purpose of restricting freedom of opinion | 03/08/2016 assigned (examination not yet begun) |
| 08/07/2016 | Silvia GIORDANO (M5S) – *C.3970*<br>Provisions relating to informed consent, instructions for future treatment and living wills | 16/03/2017 under assembly examination |
| 12/09/2016 | Silvana AMATI (PD) – *S. 2517*<br>Empowering the Government in relation to the ways in which Italian citizens may exercise their right to vote when located in a Municipality other than that of their residence for reasons of study | 04/10/2016 assigned (examination not yet begun) |
| 15/09/2016 | Emanuele LODOLINI (PD) – *C.4034*<br>Empowering the Government to regulate Italian citizens who are located in a municipality other than that of their residence for reasons of study exercising their right to vote | 05/10/2016 assigned (examination not yet begun) |
| 29/09/2016 | Popular Initiative – *C.4064*<br>Charter of Universal Working Rights. The new statute for all workers | 09/03/2017 currently under examination by the Commission |
| 03/10/2016 | Maria Edera SPADONI (M5S) – *C.4067*<br>Ratifying and implementing Protocol XII of the Convention for the Protection of Human Rights and Fundamental Freedoms, done at Rome on 4 November 2000 | 14/10/2016 assigned (examination not yet begun) |
| 09/11/2016 | Ciro FALANGA (ALA-SCCLP) and others – *S. 2590*<br>Amending article 274 of the code of criminal proceedings relating to personal supervision measures | 09/11/2016 still to be assigned |
| 15/12/2016 | Giovanni MAURO (GAL) and Others – *S. 2624*<br>Amending law 27 December 2001, No. 459, containing "Provisions for Italian citizens resident abroad to exercise their right to vote" | 31/01/2017 assigned (examination not yet begun) |
| 20/12/2016 | Giuseppe L'ABBATE (M5S) – *C.4179*<br>Provisions relating to the right to work of persons with disabilities | 03/03/2017 assigned (examination not yet begun) |

Source: *openparlamento* (search criteria: "human rights", "rights of the person").

## Motions

Of the 30 motions presented, 12 were in relation to the protection of human rights in an international level (with particular reference to North Korea, Western Sahara, Pakistan, Syria, Iraq and Yemen); 7 to bioethics (with particular reference to surrogate pregnancy); 4 to the rights of children (with particular reference to early marriage); 2 to the right to a private and family life (including civil unions); 2 to the rights of migrants, refugees and asylum seekers, and 1 to each of the following: religious freedom, the right to education, and the right to work.

| Date | Initiative | Latest update |
|---|---|---|
| 09/02/2016 | Donatella DURANTI (Art. 1-MDP) and others – *C.1/01147*<br>Whereas: on 20 November 1989, the United Nations General Assembly approved the Convention on the Rights of the Child… | 09/02/2016 presented |
| 09/02/2016 | Massimo PARISI (SC-ALA CLP-MAIE) and others – *C.1/01144*<br>Whereas: following the earthquake on 6 January 2016 in North Korea, the regime in Pyongyang confirmed that a test was carried out… | 11/02/2016 accepted |
| 09/02/2016 | Anna FINOCCHIARO (PD) – *S. 1/00516*<br>Whereas: surrogate pregnancy, otherwise known as "gestation for others" (GFO) presupposes… | 09/02/2016 presented |
| 10/02/2016 | Fabio RAMPELLI (FdI) and others – *C.1/01149*<br>Whereas: the Commission of Enquiry into human rights in North Korea, established by the UN in May 2013… | 11/02/2016 not accepted |
| 10/02/2016 | Gianluca PINI (Lega) – *C.1/01150*<br>Whereas: expressing concern for what has come to light regarding the treatment of human rights in North Korea | 11/02/2016 accepted |
| 07/03/2016 | Maria Rosaria CARFAGNA (FI-PdL) – *C.1/01187*<br>Whereas: the term surrogate pregnancy, rent-a-womb or gestation for others (GPA) is used to mean… | 04/05/2016 concluded |
| 04/04/2016 | Erasmo PALAZZOTTO (SI-SEL-POS) – *C.1/01210*<br>Whereas: on 28 April 2015, the United Nations Security Council extended the mandate of the United Nations mission for the referendum in Western Sahara… | 04/04/2016 presented |
| 05/04/2016 | Deborah BERGAMINI (FI-PdL) – *C.1/01216*<br>Whereas: religious freedom is one of the fundamental, inalienable human rights… | 05/04/2016 presented |

| Date | Initiative | Latest update |
|---|---|---|
| 13/04/2016 | Maria Edera SPADONI (M5S) – *C.1/01223*<br>Whereas: law 19 February 2004, No. 40, uses the expression "medically-assisted procreation" (MAP)… | 04/05/2016<br>approved |
| 18/04/2016 | Lorenzo DELLAI (DS-CD) and others – *C.1/01225*<br>Whereas: on the topic of civil unions… | 04/05/2016<br>rejected |
| 18/04/2016 | Marco RONDINI (Lega) – *C.1/01226*<br>Whereas: coinciding with the discussion on recognising same-sex marriage… | 04/05/2016<br>rejected |
| 18/04/2016 | Valentina VEZZALI (SC-ALA CLP-MAIE) and others – *C.1/01227*<br>Whereas: "gestation for others" (gfo) or surrogate pregnancy is a practice through which… | 04/05/2016<br>rejected |
| 19/04/2016 | Fabio RAMPELLI (FdI) and others – *C.1/01228*<br>Whereas: in recent years, we have seen an increase what is known as reproductive tourism | 04/05/2016<br>rejected |
| 26/04/2016 | Rocco PALESE (Mixed) and others – *C.1/01233*<br>Whereas: the expression "rent-a-womb", surrogate pregnancy or gestation for others is used to mean… | 04/05/2016<br>rejected |
| 04/05/2016 | Ettore ROSATO (PD) – *C.1/01248*<br>Whereas: surrogate pregnancy (according to the terminology used by article 12 (6) of law No. 40, 2014)… | 04/05/2016<br>approved |
| 24/05/2016 | Giuseppe ROMANINI (PD) – *C.1/01288*<br>Whereas: on 19 June 2009 Ms Asia Bibi, a Catholic Pakistani, mother of five, was arrested… | 24/05/2016<br>presented |
| 25/05/2016 | Pia LOCATELLI (Mixed) – *C.1/01291*<br>Whereas: in 2014, when Daesh took over the border area between Syria and Iraq, some 600,000 Yazidi… | 27/09/2016<br>accepted |
| 26/07/2016 | Stefano LUCIDI (M5S) – *S. 1/00610*<br>Whereas to the best of the promoters' knowledge: since March 2015 the Kingdom of Saudi Arabia, supported by 8 other Arab countries… | 26/07/2016<br>presented |
| 04/08/2016 | Loredana DE PETRIS (Mixed) – *S. 1/00617*<br>Whereas: the current geopolitical climate is in constant flux and instability reigns supreme… | 04/08/2016<br>presented |
| 04/10/2016 | Valeria FEDELI (PD) and others – *S. 1/00637*<br>Whereas: early marriage is still widespread globally in various political and cultural contexts, violating the rights of young girls… | 13/10/2016<br>accepted |

| Date | Initiative | Latest update |
|---|---|---|
| 04/10/2016 | Andrea MAESTRI (SI-SEL-POS) and others – *C.1/01377*<br>Whereas: the most recent data available describes the reception system for migrants to Italy as permanently run under emergency management strategies… | 04/10/2016<br>not accepted |
| 12/10/2016 | Daniela DONNO (M5S) – *S. 1/00649*<br>Whereas: according to the recent dossier "Indifesa" (*Defenceless*) by "Terre des hommes" on the global situation for young girls, of whom 15 million are married each year before… | 13/10/2016<br>accepted |
| 12/10/2016 | Lucio BARANI (ALA-SCCLP) and others – *S. 1/00650*<br>Whereas: […] early marriage is still a dramatically widespread global phenomenon… | 13/10/2016<br>concluded |
| 18/10/2016 | Laura BIGNAMI (Mixed) and others – *S. 1/00659*<br>Whereas: right to education is listed in the Universal Declaration of Human Rights… | 18/10/2016<br>presented |
| 25/10/2016 | Alessia PETRAGLIA (Mixed) – *S. 1/00667*<br>Whereas: migration, a structural phenomenon which is one of the greatest challenges of our time… | 25/10/2016<br>concluded |
| 03/11/2016 | Maurizio Enzo LUPI (AP (Ncd-CpE)) and others – *C.1/01419*<br>Whereas: Syria has been in a living hell of civil war for over 5 years… | 08/11/2016<br>accepted |
| 03/11/2016 | Pierpaolo VARGIU (CI) – *C.1/01420*<br>Whereas: the current situation in Syria is a serious destabilising factor for global peace… | 08/11/2016<br>accepted |
| 08/11/2016 | Lucio BARANI (ALA-SCCLP) and others – *S. 1/00682*<br>Whereas: it is well-known that, over at least the past 6 years, legislators have used a number of interventions to suspend and extend the suspension of collective bargaining… | 08/11/2016<br>accepted |
| 08/11/2016 | Milena SANTERINI (DS-CD) and others – *C.1/01425*<br>Whereas: Since 2011 Syria has been torn apart by a devastating civil war… | 08/11/2016<br>accepted |
| 08/11/2016 | Renato BRUNETTA (FI-PdL) – *C.1/01429*<br>Whereas: the so-called Arab Springs, across the Middle East and North Africa, since late 2010 have in Syria turned into a civil war… | 08/11/2016<br>accepted |

Source: *openparlamento* (search criteria: "human rights", "rights of the person").

### Interpellations

Of the 14 interpellations presented, 4 related to the protection of human rights on an international level; 4 to international cooperation to combat the criminal organisations which control drug trafficking; 2 to the rights of migrants, refugees and asylum seekers; and 1 to each of the following: religious freedom, the right to health, prison conditions, and human rights in the fight against terrorism.

| Date | Initiative | Latest update |
|---|---|---|
| 12/02/2016 | Eleonora BECHIS (Mixed) and others – *C.2/01271*<br>Last week's so-called cabinet reshuffle confirmed that there will be no Undersecretary to the Prime Minister's Office delegated responsibility for narcotic drugs… | 16/02/2016<br>concluded |
| 16/02/2016 | Eleonora BECHIS (Mixed) and others – *C.2/01278*<br>Last week's so-called cabinet reshuffle confirmed that there will be no Undersecretary to the Prime Minister's Office delegated responsibility for narcotic drugs… | 02/03/2016<br>concluded |
| 23/02/2016 | Luigi MANCONI (PD) – *S. 2/00357*<br>Whereas: The United Nations General Assembly in New York will hold a special session on narcotic drugs from 19 to 21 April 2016… | 23/02/2016<br>presented |
| 25/02/2016 | Andrea MAESTRI (SI-SEL-POS) and others – *C.2/01289*<br>On 7 February 2016, the Senate's extraordinary commission for the protection and promotion of human rights presented its report on Centres for Identification and Expulsion (CIEs)… | 25/02/2016<br>presented |
| 01/03/2016 | Massimiliano FEDRIGA (Lega) – *C.2/01296*<br>The recent, incredible, ruling from the European Court of Human Rights in Strasbourg condemned the Italian Republic for "abusing State secrecy" in relation to alleged "extraordinary rendition"… | 04/03/2016<br>concluded |
| 02/03/2016 | Eleonora BECHIS (Mixed) and others – *C.2/01298*<br>Last week's so-called cabinet reshuffle confirmed that there will be no Undersecretary to the Prime Minister's Office delegated responsibility for narcotic drugs… | 11/03/2016<br>concluded |
| 06/04/2016 | Gianfranco CHIARELLI (Mixed) and Others – *C.2/01334*<br>It is known, in part due to the various repeated rulings against our Country from the European Commission of Human Rights (see, among many, the well-known Torreggiani ruling)… | 06/04/2016<br>presented |

| Date | Initiative | Latest update |
|---|---|---|
| 10/05/2016 | Alessandro PAGANO (Lega) and Others – *C.2/01366*<br>As early as late November 2015 Romanian press publicised the incredible events surrounding Mr Marius and Mrs Ruth Bodnariu, Romanian and Norwegian respectively… | 13/05/2016<br>concluded |
| 24/06/2016 | Andrea MAESTRI (SI-SEL-POS) and others – *C.2/01403*<br>Malek Adly, an Egyptian lawyer and human rights activist working on the case of Giulio Regeni, among others, was arrested on 6 May 2016 and is still being held in detention… | 24/06/2016<br>presented |
| 27/06/2016 | Corradino MINEO (Mixed) and others – *S. 2/00397*<br>Whereas: Malek Adly is a 35-year-old Egyptian lawyer and activist in… | 27/06/2016<br>presented |
| 02/08/2016 | Adriano ZACCAGNINI (Art. 1-MDP) and others – *C.2/01448*<br>The maternity ward at the hospital of Vipiteno is due to be closed by 31 October 2016… | 23/09/2016<br>concluded |
| 28/09/2016 | Arturo SCOTTO (Art. 1-MDP) and others – *C.2/01481*<br>Ethiopia is a federal State divided along ethnic lines which has been governed since 1999 by an electoral coalition, the Ethiopian People's Revolutionary Democratic Front… | 28/09/2016<br>presented |
| 04/10/2016 | Lia QUARTAPELLE PROCOPIO (PD) – *C.2/01488*<br>On 3 October 2013, a few miles from the port of Lampedusa, hundreds of migrants… | 13/10/2016<br>concluded |
| 11/10/2016 | Giulio MARCON (SI-SEL-POS) – *C.2/01499*<br>The Minister of Defence, Roberta Pinotto, visited Saudi Arabia in recent days for some high-level meetings… | 21/10/2016<br>appending of new signatures |

Source: *openparlamento* (search criteria: "human rights", "rights of the person").

## Questions for an Oral Answer

Of the 29 questions for an oral answer presented, 10 related to the protection of human rights on an international level (with particular reference to Egypt, Turkey, Ukraine, Pakistan, Burundi, Tibet, Yemen and Israel); 6 to the impact of Italian arms sales on human rights; 4 to torture, inhuman or degrading treatment; 2 to the rights of migrants, refugees and asylum seekers; 2 to bioethics; and one to each of the following themes: prison conditions and prisoners' rights; the right to health; freedom of expression; the right to work; the duration of trials.

| Date | Initiative | Latest update |
|---|---|---|
| 11/02/2016 | Ornella BERTOROTTA (M5S) – *S. 3/02574*<br>Whereas: it appears that the Friulian researcher Giulio Regeni... | 11/02/2016<br>assigned to a commission |
| 23/02/2016 | Erasmo PALAZZOTTO (SI-SEL-POS) – *C.3/02046*<br>A number of reports and dossiers compiled by humanitarian organisations show ongoing, prolific and serious human rights violations in Egypt... | 24/02/2016<br>concluded |
| 24/02/2016 | Enzo LATTUCA (PD) – *C.3/02052*<br>Article 19 of the 1948 Universal Declaration of Human Rights states: "Everyone has the right to freedom of opinion and expression... | 24/02/2016<br>presented |
| 25/02/2016 | Luis Alberto ORELLANA (Aut(SVP-UV-PATT-UPT)-PSI) and others – *S. 3/02622*<br>Whereas: "Hacking Team" is an information technology company... | 25/02/2016<br>presented |
| 01/03/2016 | Gian Luigi GIGLI (DS-CD) and others – *C.3/02069*<br>Surrogate pregnancy requires a woman to... | 02/03/2016<br>concluded |
| 02/03/2016 | Roberto COTTI (M5S) – *S. 3/02631*<br>Whereas: Saudi Arabia sparked a conflict in Yemen... | 02/03/2016<br>assigned to a commission |
| 04/03/2016 | Adriana GALGANO (CI) – *C.3/02080*<br>"Hacking Team" is an information technology company based in Milan selling offensive intrusion and surveillance services to governments, police bodies and secret services... | 02/02/2017<br>Followed up |
| 17/03/2016 | Alessandra BENCINI (Mixed) and others – *S. 3/02693*<br>Whereas on 23 July 2015, Judgement No. 178 of 2015 was deposited in which the Constitutional Court found, on 24 June of that year, that suspending collective bargaining was unconstitutional (from the day following the publication of the ruling itself in the Official Gazette and in the terms stated in the reasoning) ... | 17/03/2016<br>presented |

| Date | Initiative | Latest update |
|---|---|---|
| 23/03/2016 | Paolo BENI (PD) – *C.3/02135*<br>The Cairo Institute for Human Rights Studies is one of the main independent organisations for human rights accredited at the United Nations… | 23/03/2016<br>presented |
| 30/03/2016 | Arturo SCOTTO (Art. 1-MDP) and others – *C.3/02141*<br>3 April 2016 will mark two months since the death of Giulio Regeni… | 31/03/2016<br>concluded |
| 28/04/2016 | Daniela DONNO (M5S) – *S. 3/02811*<br>Whereas: 57 years on from the national uprising in Lhasa… | 28/04/2016<br>assigned to a commission |
| 03/05/2016 | Renato BRUNETTA (FI-PdL) – *C.3/02233*<br>Following "clear violations of Ukraine's sovereignty and territorial integrity caused by acts of aggression from the Russian armed forces"… | 04/05/2016<br>concluded |
| 19/05/2016 | Vincenzo SANTANGELO (M5S) – *S. 3/02869*<br>Whereas: on the evening of 5 May 2016, the satirical television show "Le Iene" broadcast a report on Italy supplying Saudi Arabia with weapons used in the war in Yemen… | 19/05/2016<br>presented |
| 20/05/2016 | Donatella DURANTI (Art. 1-MDP) and others – *C.3/02271*<br>On 20 December 2014, the Italian Minister of Defence Roberta Pinotti and the Minister of Defence of the Arab Republic of Egypt, Gen. Sedki Sobhi, signed a joint declaration… | 20/06/2016<br>concluded |
| 28/06/2016 | Paolo BENI (PD) – *C.3/02351*<br>On 8 June 2016 in the tent camp between San Ferdinando and Rosarno, a foreign farm labourer was murdered… | 29/06/2016<br>concluded |
| 30/06/2016 | Adriana GALGANO (CI) – *C.3/02359*<br>According to press reports, on 13 June 2016 the Directorate General for international trade policy (the authority for exporting dual-use goods)… | 02/02/2017<br>Followed up |
| 19/07/2016 | Erasmo PALAZZOTTO (SI-SEL-POS) – *C.3/02400*<br>On the night between 15 and 16 July 2016 there was an attempted – failed – coup in Turkey… | 20/07/2016<br>concluded |
| 19/07/2016 | Paola BINETTI (Mixed) and others – *C.3/02408*<br>As of 6 July 2016, Italy no longer faces charges relating to the thorny issue of conscientious objections from the Council of Europe… | 20/07/2016<br>concluded |

| Date | Initiative | Latest update |
|---|---|---|
| 28/07/2016 | Adele GAMBARO (ALA-SCCLP) and others – *S. 3/03065*<br>Whereas: According to the press across the globe, the numbers involved in the wave of oppression which is engulfing Turkey… | 28/07/2016 presented |
| 29/07/2016 | Adriano ZACCAGNINI (Art. 1-MDP) and others – *C.3/02432*<br>The maternity ward at the hospital in Vipiteno is scheduled to be closed… | 02/08/2016 concluded |
| 03/08/2016 | Gianni MELILLA (Art. 1-MDP) and others – *C.3/02455*<br>The Antigone association has presented its interim report on prisons in Italy, which shows some worrying data… | 03/08/2016 presented |
| 12/09/2016 | Pia LOCATELLI (Mixed) – *C.3/02465*<br>A dramatic political crisis has been ongoing in Burundi for over a year… | 13/09/2016 concluded |
| 20/09/2016 | Aniello FORMISANO (Art. 1-MDP) and others – *C.3/02495*<br>Despite a slight drop vis-a-vis recent years, court backlogs remain unacceptable… | 21/09/2016 concluded |
| 27/09/2016 | Ornella BERTOROTTA (M5S) – *S. 3/03160*<br>Whereas: "La Repubblica" newspaper, in an article from 2 September 2016 entitled "Italian business woman arrested in Libya for attempted fraud", we learn… | 27/09/2016 assigned to a commission |
| 12/10/2016 | Alessandro PAGANO (Lega) and Others – *C.3/02551*<br>According to a note circulated by the Fides Association, the "Pakistan Electronic Media Regulatory Authority" (a Government body in Pakistan) has declared 11 Christian television channels illegal… | 12/10/2016 presented |
| 13/10/2016 | Roberto COTTI (M5S) – *S. 3/03222*<br>Whereas: on 4 October 2016, the "Nova" and "Il Velino" press agencies reported a meeting held in Riyadh… | 13/10/2016 presented |
| 19/10/2016 | Gianni MELILLA (Art. 1-MDP) and others – *C.3/02570*<br>On 16 October 2000, the body of Radio Radicale journalist Antonio Russo was found some 20 kilometres from Tbilisi… | 19/10/2016 presented |

| Date | Initiative | Latest update |
|---|---|---|
| 25/10/2016 | Erasmo PALAZZOTTO (SI-SEL-POS) – *C.3/02581* On 18 October 2016, with the abstention of Italy, the executive committee of UNESCO approved a resolution focusing on the restrictions imposed by the State of Israel… | 26/10/2016 concluded |
| 26/10/2016 | Erasmo PALAZZOTTO (SI-SEL-POS) – *C.3/02589* On 21 October 2016, over 100 migrants, many of whom had valid papers… | 26/10/2016 presented |

Source: *openparlamento* (search criteria: "human rights", "rights of the person").

### Questions for a Written Answer

Of the 56 questions for a written answer, 20 related to the protection of human rights at the international level (with particular reference to Israel, Yemen, Turkey, Tanzania, Ukraine, Egypt, Pakistan, Iran, Eritrea, Burundi, Western Sahara and Honduras); 17 to the rights of migrants, refugees and asylum seekers; 4 to disarmament and the arms trade; 4 to the right to health; 3 to the rights of the Roma and Sinti minorities; 2 to children's rights; and 1 to each of the following: prison conditions and prisoners' rights; women's rights; combatting homophobia and transphobia; torture; the right to water; forced labour and modern forms of slavery.

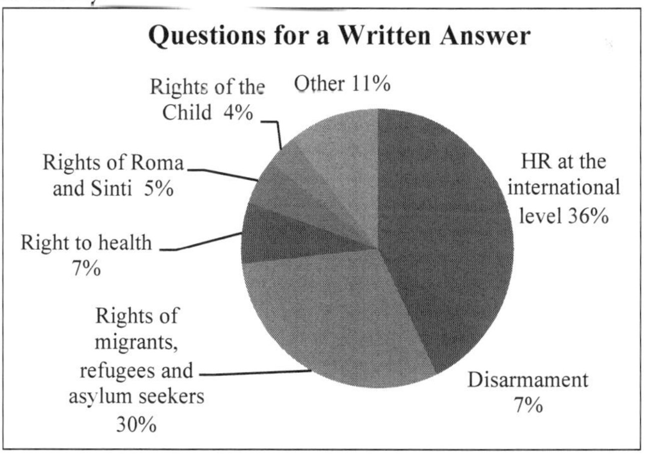


Source: *openparlamento* (search criteria: "human rights", "rights of the person").

## Questions submitted to Commissions

Of the 31 questions submitted to Commissions, 12 related to the protection of human rights at the international level (with particular reference to Israel, Yemen, Turkey, Egypt, Saudi Arabia, Somalia, Burundi, North Korea and Iraq); 9 to disarmament and the arms trade; 3 to the rights of migrants, refugees and asylum seekers; 2 to torture; 2 to the rights of persons with disabilities; and 1 to each of the following themes: prison conditions and prisoners' rights; the right to health; and the rights of the child.

| Date | Initiative | Latest update |
|---|---|---|
| 21/01/2016 | Donatella DURANTI (Art. 1-MDP) and others – *C.5/07476*<br>Some press reports said that on 16 January 2016 a further additional load of bombs… | 17/03/2016 change of minister responsible |
| 29/01/2016 | Donatella DURANTI (Art. 1-MDP) and others – *C.5/07582*<br>As part of the "EUTM Somalia" mission, Italy – in the form of military personnel – is present on Somali territory… | 30/06/2016 concluded |
| 05/02/2016 | Carlo SIBILIA (M5S) – *C.5/07688*<br>Giulio Regeni, the Italian student who vanished on the night of 25 January in Cairo, was found dead… | 09/02/2016 concluded |
| 08/02/2016 | Mariano RABINO (SC-ALA CLP-MAIE) e altri – *C.5/07701*<br>Our Country has been shaken by the recent barbaric killing of Giulio Regeni, the 28-year-old Italian student found dead on 4 February… | 09/02/2016 concluded |
| 17/02/2016 | Giulia DI VITA (M5S) – *C.5/07826*<br>Italy still has many facilities which host persons with disabilities… | 18/02/2016 concluded |
| 24/02/2016 | Andrea MAESTRI (SI-SEL-POS) and others – *C.5/07907*<br>Speaking on the TV show Agorà on Rai3 on 5 February 2016, the Minister for the Interior repeated the proposal he had made the day before at the Security Forum in Naples of lowering the age at which a minor can be legally incriminated, currently 18, to the age of 16… | 24/02/2016 change of commission to respond |
| 14/03/2016 | Giancarlo GIORDANO (SI-SEL-POS) – *C.5/08100*<br>In the previous question on 4 February 2016, which was also on the issue of hosting migrants in Irpinia… | 14/03/2016 change of commission to respond |

| Date | Initiative | Latest update |
|---|---|---|
| 30/03/2016 | Luca FRUSONE (M5S) – *C.5/08257*<br>A number of press sources including the agency Ansa at 18.57 on 23 March 2016 report that the Italian and Saudi governments have signed a technical agreement… | 30/03/2016 change of commission to respond |
| 08/04/2016 | Davide TRIPIEDI (M5S) – *C.5/08365*<br>On 24 March 2016 Mr Luigi Scudieri used a petition on the website change.org, which was taken up on a number of information sites, to decry his patient situation… | 08/04/2016 change of commission to respond |
| 18/04/2016 | Giulia DI VITA (M5S) – *C.5/08402*<br>Article 33 of the United Nations Convention on the Rights of Persons with Disabilities sets out some obligations which contracting parties must adhere to when implementing it… | 12/10/2016 concluded |
| 18/04/2016 | Adriana GALGANO (CI) – *C.5/08404*<br>"Hacking Team" is an information technology company based in Milan selling offensive intrusion and surveillance services to governments, police bodies and secret services… | 20/04/2016 concluded |
| 19/04/2016 | Adriana GALGANO (CI) – *C.5/08423*<br>"Hacking Team" is an information technology company based in Milan selling offensive intrusion and surveillance services to governments, police bodies and secret services… | 20/04/2016 concluded |
| 8/04/2016 | Maria Edera SPADONI (M5S) – *C.5/08539*<br>On 26 April 2016 Amnesty International condemned the arrest of at least 238 people, including local and foreign activists and journalists, in many Egyptian towns… | 30/06/2016 concluded |
| 12/05/2016 | Manlio DI STEFANO (M5S) – *C.5/08675*<br>The press has informed us that the Turkish Parliament's Constitutional Affairs Commission… | 12/05/2016 change of commission to respond |
| 25/05/2016 | Michele NICOLETTI (PD) – *C.5/08784*<br>According to press reports, after taking part in a camp organised in Perugia by Italian Soccer Management, nineteen-year-old North Korean Song-Hyok Choe… | 24/08/2016 change of Minister responsible |
| 26/05/2016 | Giovanni SANGA (PD) – *C.5/08799*<br>Ali Mohammed al-Nimr was sentenced to decapitation in Saudi Arabia… | 14/07/2016 concluded |
| 08/06/2016 | Giovanni SANGA (PD) – *C.5/08834*<br>We have learned from press reports that nineteen Kurdish girls have been publicly burned alive by Daesh jihadists in Mosul in northern Iraq… | 22/03/2017 concluded |

| Date | Initiative | Latest update |
|---|---|---|
| 21/06/2016 | Manlio DI STEFANO (M5S) – *C.5/08939*<br>According to various news sources, the United Nations General Secretary Ban Ki-moon explained his decision to remove the coalition led by Saudi Arabia… | 30/06/2016<br>concluded |
| 21/06/2016 | Luca FRUSONE (M5S) – *C.5/08942*<br>On 16 June 2016, a contract worth 4 billion euro was signed in Rome in the presence of the Italian Minister of Defence Roberta Pinotti and the Qatari Minister of Defence… | 13/10/2016<br>concluded |
| 21/06/2016 | Donatella DURANTI (Art. 1-MDP) and others – *C.5/08944*<br>On 20 December 2014, the Italian Minister of Defence Roberta Pinotti, and the Minister of Defence of the Arab Republic of Egypt, Gen. Sedki Sobhi, signed a joint declaration… | 22/06/2016<br>concluded |
| 05/07/2016 | Stefano QUARANTA (Art. 1-MDP) and others – *C.5/09077*<br>For around a year, Ventimiglia has been at the centre of the migrant issue… | 06/07/2016<br>concluded |
| 06/07/2016 | Michele MOGNATO (Art. 1-MDP) and others – *C.5/09095*<br>The External Offices for Execution of Penal Sentences (UEPE) are a crucial part of Italy's penitentiary system… | 06/07/2016<br>change of commission to respond |
| 13/07/2016 | Diego DE LORENZIS (M5S) – *C.5/09141*<br>"La Stampa" newspaper on the 28th of June 2016 published an article entitled "Italy to export surveillance software to Egypt…" | 20/07/2016<br>initiative amended |
| 19/07/2016 | Manlio DI STEFANO (M5S) – *C.5/09195*<br>After an Israeli settler killed 29 Palestinian citizens and injured a further 60 in the city of Hebron… | 19/07/2016<br>change of commission to respond |
| 19/07/2016 | Pia LOCATELLI (Mixed) – *C.5/09201*<br>A dramatic political crisis has been ongoing in Burundi for over a year… | 09/09/2016<br>concluded |
| 19/07/2016 | Manlio DI STEFANO (M5S) – *C.5/09203*<br>The tragic events of the night of 15 July 2016 in Turkey, i.e. the failed coup by a section of the Turkish armed forces… | 21/07/2016<br>concluded |
| 20/07/2016 | Tatiana BASILIO (M5S) – *C.5/09232*<br>The deplorable attempted coup d'état in Turkey and subsequent wave of arrests – many of which unjustifiable… | 21/07/2016<br>concluded |

| Date | Initiative | Latest update |
|---|---|---|
| 26/07/2016 | Gianluca RIZZO (M5S) – *C.5/09262*<br>The press reports that a vessel from Tunisia heading toward Europe sank on Saturday 2 July 2016 off the shore of Sabratha… | 06/10/2016 change of minister responsible |
| 03/10/2016 | Erasmo PALAZZOTTO (SI-SEL-POS) – *C.5/09660*<br>On 17 September 2016, the Cairo Criminal Court ruled to freeze the funds and assets of 5 prominent Egyptian human rights activists… | 03/11/2016 concluded |
| 14/11/2016 | Maria Edera SPADONI (M5S) – *C.5/10009*<br>On 26 October 2016 during Assembly question time No. 3–02584 the Minister being questioned by Di Stefano said in relation to actually authorising the transit and export of arms from Italy to Saudi Arabia… | 01/02/2017 concluded |
| 19/12/2016 | Mauro PILI (Mixed) and others – *C.5/10141*<br>The Obama administration has decided to suspend sending "aerobombs" and "precision ammunition" to Riyadh… | 19/12/2016 amended by commission being questioned |

Source: *openparlamento* (search criteria: "human rights", "rights of the person").

## Assembly Resolutions

| Date | Initiative | Latest update |
|---|---|---|
| 20/01/2016 | Daniele FARINA (SI-SEL-POS) – *C.6/00195*<br>Having heard the Minister of Justice's statements on justice administration… | 20/01/2016 accepted |
| 16/03/2016 | Arturo SCOTTO (Art. 1-MDP) and others – *C.6/00216*<br>Whereas: on 17 and 18 March 2016, the European Council will discuss further measures to tackle the refugee and migrant crisis… | 16/03/2016 not accepted |
| 16/03/2016 | Marco BALDASSARRE (Mixed) and others – *C.6/00218*<br>To maintain the mechanism for verifying reception standards for refugees in Turkey… | 16/03/2016 concluded |
| 16/03/2016 | Sergio BATTELLI (M5S) – *C.6/00221*<br>Having heard the Prime Minister's comments on the European Council's ordinary meeting on 17 and 18 March 2016… | 16/03/2016 not accepted |
| 16/03/2016 | Edmondo CIRIELLI (FdI) and others – *C.6/00222*<br>To work for the request for respect of democracy to be included in all negotiations with Turkey… | 16/03/2016 concluded |

| Date | Initiative | Latest update |
|---|---|---|
| 16/03/2016 | Roberto CALDEROLI (Lega) – *S. 6/00166*<br>Given that at the last meeting of the European Council the Prime Minister asked that as a condition for Italy supporting an agreement on rules for migrants, the question of respect for fundamental freedoms be raised… | 16/03/2016<br>accepted |
| 16/03/2016 | Peppe DE CRISTOFARO (Mixed) – *S. 6/00171*<br>Having heard the Prime Minister's comments on the European Council meeting on 17 and 18 March 2016… | 16/03/2016<br>not accepted |
| 27/06/2016 | Stefano LUCIDI (M5S) – *S. 6/00196*<br>On the occasion of the European Council meeting to be held in Brussels on 28 and 29 June next; whereas: at the meeting between Heads of State and Government, the issue of migratory flows will be discussed, as it has been for the past three years… | 27/06/2016<br>not accepted |
| 27/06/2016 | Arturo SCOTTO (Art. 1-MDP) and others – *C.6/00252*<br>Having heard the Prime Minister's comments on the European Council meeting of 28 and 29 June 2016… | 27/06/2016<br>not accepted |
| 27/06/2016 | Sergio BATTELLI (M5S) – *C.6/00253*<br>Having heard the Prime Minister's comments on the European Council meeting of 28 and 29 June 2016… | 27/06/2016<br>not accepted |
| 12/10/2016 | Loredana DE PETRIS (Mixed) – *S. 6/00203*<br>Whereas: in May 2016, the European Commission presented a package of proposals to reform the common European asylum system… | 12/10/2016<br>presented |
| 12/10/2016 | Arturo SCOTTO (Art. 1-MDP) and others – *C.6/00266*<br>Whereas: the European Council will focus on migration issues, discussing the most recent developments and progress made in relation to its overall approach… | 12/10/2016<br>not accepted |

Source: *openparlamento* (search criteria: "human rights", "rights of the person").

## Commission Resolutions

| Date | Initiative | Latest update |
|---|---|---|
| 11/02/2016 | Maria Edera SPADONI (M5S) – *C.7/00916*<br>Whereas: from the 2015 Amnesty International report "Generation Jail: Egypt's youth go from protest to prison"… | 11/02/2016<br>presented |
| 18/03/2016 | Erasmo PALAZZOTTO (SI-SEL-POS) – *C.7/00950*<br>Whereas: since 26 March 2016 war has been ongoing in Yemen between coalition forces led by Saudi Arabia… | 18/03/2016<br>presented |

| Date | Initiative | Latest update |
|---|---|---|
| 11/04/2016 | Beatrice BRIGNONE (SI-SEL-POS) and others – *C.7/00967*<br>Whereas: from 19 to 21 April 2016 a special session of the United Nations General Assembly will be held in New York on narcotic drugs… | 11/04/2016 presented |
| 04/05/2016 | Sandra ZAMPA (PD) – *C.7/00988*<br>Whereas: on 16 and 17 April 2015, the international conference of G7 and G20 parliamentarians "She matters. Empowering women and girls to lead self-determined, healthy and productive lives" was held in Berlin at the German Ministry of Economic Cooperation and Development… | 26/05/2016 accepted |
| 20/05/2016 | Manlio DI STEFANO (M5S) – *C.7/01002*<br>Whereas: on 9 May 2011 with Council Decision 2011/273/CFSP, without any cover from the United Nations Security Council, the European Union put in place restrictive measures against Syria… | 20/05/2016 presented |
| 25/05/2016 | Maria Edera SPADONI (M5S) – *C.7/01010*<br>Whereas: some thirty Syrian refugee children between the ages of 8 and 12 suffered sexual abuse… | 25/05/2016 presented |
| 05/07/2016 | Maria Edera SPADONI (M5S) – *C.7/01043*<br>Whereas: pursuant to article 1 (6) of law No. 185 of 1990 (new regulations on the control of import, export and transit of armament material)… | 07/10/2016 initiative amended |
| 15/07/2016 | Marietta TIDEI (PD) – *C.7/01051*<br>Whereas: protecting fundamental human rights is one of the main regulatory innovations of Western legal culture… | 31/01/2017 accepted |
| 06/10/2016 | Sandra ZAMPA (PD) – *C.7/01112*<br>Whereas: on the night between Friday 15 and Saturday 16 July 2016, an attempted coup d'état took place in Turkey… | 19/10/2016 appending of new signatures |
| 20/12/2016 | Fabrizio CICCHITTO (AP (Ncd-CpE)) and others – *C.7/01156*<br>Whereas: recalling in its entirety motion No. 1–01419, approved by the Chamber of Deputies on 8 November 2016 on "European and international initiatives relating to the situation in Syria… | 20/12/2016 presented |

Source: *openparlamento* (search criteria: "human rights", "rights of the person").

**Assembly Agenda Points**

Of the 35 agenda points presented to the Assembly, 7 related to the protection of human rights at the international level; 6 to private and family life; 5 to disarmament and the arms trade; 4 to the rights of children; 3 to the rights of migrants, refugees and asylum seekers; 2 to the right to health; 2 to the rights of persons with disabilities; and 1 to each of the following themes: women's rights; ratifying international instruments; torture; bioethics; procedural guarantees; freedom of religion.

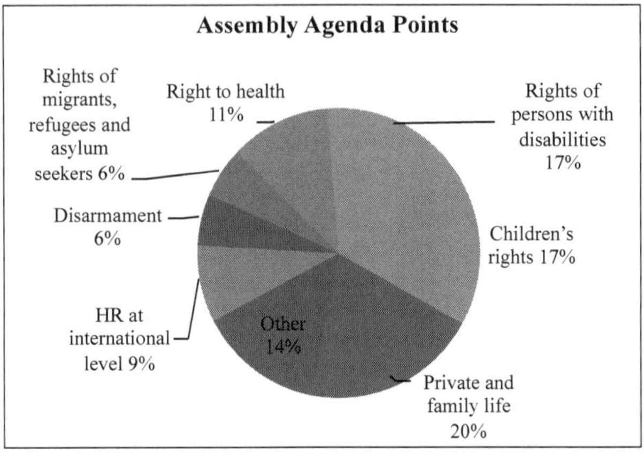


Source: *openparlamento* (search criteria: "human rights", "rights of the person").

## II. Prime Minister's Office (Presidency)

The organisation of the Prime Minister's Office is regulated by the decree of the Prime Minister of 1 October 2012. The Prime Minister's Office has a number of departments and offices (the so-called general structures), which the Prime Minister draws on for guideline and coordination functions regarding specific political and institutional fields. Of particular importance for human rights is the Department for Equal Opportunities.

A number of committees and commissions with specific tasks of economic and social relevance operate within the ambit of the Prime Minister's Office. These include the Commission for International Adoptions and the National Committee on Bioethics.

## A. Department for Equal Opportunities: UNAR and Observatory for the Fight against Paedophilia and Child Pornography

The Department for Equal Opportunities, established under the auspices of the Prime Minister's Office, plans and coordinates legislative, administrative and research initiatives in all areas pertaining to equal opportunities policies. In May 2016 duties relating to equal opportunities, which had previously been held by Giovanna Martelli MP, were entrusted to Minister Maria Elena Boschi.

> The Department was instituted by the d.p.c.m. of 28 October 1997, No. 405, subsequently amended by various decrees (the most recent being M.D. 4 December 2012). It comprises three offices: the Office of General Affairs, International Affairs and Social Measures; the Office for Measures to Promote Equality and Equal Opportunities; and the National Anti-Racial Discrimination Office (UNAR).
>
> UNAR was established by lgs.d. 9 July 2003, No. 215, in compliance with the European Community directive 2000/43/CE. Its mission is to guarantee observance of the principle of equal treatment of individuals, to monitor the efficacy of current instruments against discrimination, and to help to stamp out forms of discrimination based on race or ethnic origin, while analysing their diversified impact on gender, and their connection with other forms of racism of a cultural and religious nature.

In October 2016, the new edition of the Statistical Dossier on Immigration was published, edited by the IDOS/Immigration Study and Research Centre in collaboration with the UNAR. According to the dossier, at the end of 2015 there was almost no change in the number of foreign nationals residing in Italy compared with the previous year: 5,026,153 residents, an increase of barely 12,000 individuals. However, in municipal registry offices, 250,000 foreign nationals arriving from abroad were recorded (the same figure as the previous year). That there is no corresponding increase in foreign residents is attributable to the fact that in the same period, fully 178,000 foreigners became Italian citizens, bringing the total number of Italians of foreign origin to approximately 1,150,000. Furthermore, between January and 30 August 2016, 107,089 people reached Italy by boat.

Finally, in February 2016 the Council of Ministers adopted the first National Action Plan against Human Trafficking and Serious Exploitation as per the provisions of 9 of lgs.d. 4 March 2014, No. 24 (implementing Directive 2011/36/EU on preventing and combating trafficking in human beings and protecting its victims). The Plan aims to set out multiannual strategies for acting to prevent and combat the trafficking and serious exploitation of human beings, along with awareness-raising, social prevention, getting victims to come forward and helping with their social integration. The Plan will facilitate the rolling out of the new unified programme of bringing out victims, supporting and overseeing their social integration, as well as the relative procedures for implementation and financing. Adopting this Plan meets the systematic need to reorganise and streamline Government actions, mainly to promote a comprehensive coordinated approach based on synergies between the various central, territorial and local administrations involved and their respective available resources. Furthermore, ensuring cooperation between the standard benchmark institutional and private social sector – which must be enhanced to build the Italian strategy – is fundamental, with a view to maintaining and strengthening integrated public and private networks operating in their area, focusing on what is known as "multi-agency working". Lastly, the transnational nature of human trafficking requires the Government to adopt partnership and collaboration instruments with the other countries concerned, both for the purpose of crime prevention and for investigative and legal cooperation, as well as to promote exchange of good practice and working tools, especially as regards countries of origin.

In addition to the three offices mentioned above, the following collegial bodies also have their secretariat within the Department for Equal Opportunities: the Inter-Ministerial Commission for support to victims of trafficking, violence and severe exploitation (as per Presidential Decree 14 May 2007, No. 102); the Committee for prevention and combating female genital mutilation; the Committee to Evaluate the Legitimacy to Act on Behalf of People with Disabilities; the Committee for equal opportunities for men and women; the Observatory for the Fight against Paedophilia and Child Pornography.

The Observatory for the Fight against Paedophilia and Child Pornography was established in accordance with l. 3 August 1998, No. 269, as amended by l. 6 February 2006, No. 38, with the task of acquiring and monitoring data and information relating to activities carried out by all Government bodies to prevent and stamp out the sexual abuse and exploitation of minors. A further significant task of the Observatory is to prepare the National Plan for preventing and combating sexual abuse and exploitation of minors.

## B. Commission for International Adoptions

Article 6 of the Hague Convention on the Protection of Minors and Cooperation in Respect of Intercountry Adoption, which was adopted on 29 May 1993 and came into force on 1 May 1995, requires State

Parties to establish a central authority to ensure that adoptions of foreign children adhere to the principles established by the Convention itself. To comply with this requirement, via law 31 December 1998, No. 476, Italy instituted the Commission for International Adoptions, which operates through the Prime Minister's Office. The Commission is Italy's central authority for the implementation of the Hague Convention.

The Commission comprises a Chair, nominated by the Prime Minister (in 2016, Silvia Della Monica, Counsellor to the Court of Cassation), and the following members: three representatives from the Prime Minister's office; one from the Ministry of Foreign Affairs; one from the Ministry of Education; one from the Ministry for Labour and Social Policy; one from the Ministry of the Interior; two from the Ministry of Justice; one from the Ministry of Health; one from the Ministry of the Economy; four from the Unified Conference between State and Region; three from family associations; and experts.

Since 2013, the Commission has stopped publishing updated data about the situation of international adoptions in Italy.

## C. National Committee on Bioethics

The National Committee on Bioethics performs an advisory role vis-à-vis the Government, Parliament and other institutions, with a view to providing guidelines on legislative and administrative instruments designed to define the criteria to use in medical and biological practice in order to protect human rights. It also has a role in informing the public and in raising awareness with regard to ethical problems arising in connection with progress in scientific research and in technological applications in the life sciences and in healthcare.

The Committee was established by the d.p.c.m. of 28 March 1990. It is made up of the following bodies: Chair (Lorenzo d'Avack, Professor in the Philosophy of Law); Vice Chairs (Riccardo Di Segni, Chief Rabbi of Rome; Laura Palazzani, Professor in the Philosophy of Law); Office of the President (made up of the Chair and the Vice Chairs); Assembly.

One of the tasks of the Committee is to produce studies and make recommendations that can also be used for legislative purposes. The Committee's documents offer in-depth focus and reflection on ethical and legal issues that arise as knowledge in the field of the life sciences advances. According to their nature and purpose, the documents are classified as: opinions (approved in the Committee's assembly on the basis of inquiries conducted by working groups); motions (urgent documents approved with a two-thirds majority of those present in the assembly); responses (documents in which the Committee makes recommendations on issues about which its opinion has been sought by other bodies or by physical persons).

The following opinions and motions were approved in 2016:

*Opinions*:

- Information and communications technology and big data: bioethical profiles (25 November 2016);
- Managing incidental findings in genome investigation with new technology platforms (17 March 2016);
- Ongoing deep palliative sedation prior to death (29 January 2016).

*Motions*:

- Paid surrogate motherhood (18 March 2016).

## III. Ministry of Foreign Affairs and International Cooperation

The Ministry of Foreign Affairs has a number of directorate-generals and offices that deal specifically with human rights, disarmament and cooperation. Since March 2016, responsibility for issues dealt with in the United Nations ambit have been entrusted to Undersecretary Vincenzo Amendola.

Particularly worthy of note is Office II – Human rights advocacy and international humanitarian law, Council of Europe, which falls within the directorate-general for Political Affairs and Security. Other offices in the same directorate are: Office I – The United Nations system and the institutional reform process, peacekeeping operations and preventive diplomacy; Office V – Disarmament, arms control and nuclear, biological and chemical non proliferation, Office of the national authority for the banning of chemical weapons; Office VI – Organisation for Security and Cooperation in Europe. The theme of human rights also relates across the board to the directorate-general for Global Affairs (Office IV – Energy, environmental protection and sustainable global development policies), the directorate-general for the European Union (Office III – European space of freedom, security and justice, the free movement of people and migratory flows towards the European Union) and the directorate-general for Development Cooperation (Office I – Development of cooperation policies within the European Union; Office II – Multilateral development cooperation; Office VI – Emergency and humanitarian aid; Office VIII – Planning and monitoring of the cooperation budget; gender issues, the rights of children and people with disabilities).

## A. Inter-Ministerial Committee for Human Rights (CIDU)

The Inter-Ministerial Committee for Human Rights (CIDU) was established by decree of the Minister of Foreign Affairs on 15 February 1978, No. 519; its composition was updated by d.c.p.m. on 11 May 2007. Over 2012–2013 the CIDU was involved in a restructuring process: initially phased out as a result of the spending review, it was re-established on 5 September 2013. It maintained its functional competences because it was regarded as indispensable, both for its advice and its strategic guidance regarding the promotion and protection of human rights, and in ensuring correct compliance with the obligations that Italy assumed following the signature and ratification of conventions and international agreements in this field.

CIDU is chaired by a functionary of the diplomatic service appointed by the Minister of Foreign Affairs: in September 2016 Fabrizio Petri succeeded to Gian Ludovico De Martino. Committee members include representatives of the Prime Minister's Office, of various Ministries and of many different institutions (such as the Association of Italian Municipalities (ANCI); the Conference of Presidents of the Regions and Autonomous Provinces; the Union of Italian Provinces (UPI); the National Commission for UNESCO; the Italian Committee for UNICEF; the Italian Society for International Organisation (SIOI); as well as three eminent personalities in the field of human rights.

CIDU has the following tasks: to promote measures necessary for ensuring full compliance with international obligations assumed by Italy; to facilitate the implementation of international conventions in Italy; to draft the reports Italy is required to submit to the pertinent international organisations; to maintain and develop appropriate relations with civil society organisations engaged in promoting and protecting human rights.

As well as its usual collaboration activities with United Nations and Council of Europe bodies relating to presenting periodic reports and to visits from these organisations (see this *Yearbook*, Part III), in 2016 the CIDU presented two national action plans.

- *Third National Action Plan 2016–2019 on women, peace and security, in implementation of United Nations Security Council Resolution 1325(2000).* The plan was drawn up by the National Inter-Ministerial and participatory Working Group on women, peace and security, coordinated by the CIDU. A number of meetings were held during 2016 with the participation of civil society organisations, the world of academia, other institutional actors, and representatives from the culture and communications sectors. The Plan seeks to ensure that a gender perspective is considered in all policy areas supporting the concept of peace, and that this consideration is adopted in all practical measures which aim to promote and protect peace. More specifically, the plan has two aims: to reduce the impact of conflict on women and girls by promoting their effective and transformative involvement in processes for the prevention, mitigation and resolution of conflict and in decision-making processes at all levels; and to raise awareness, educate and strengthen existing structures, with reference to the *Women, Peace and Security Agenda* and issues linked to it. The Plan is therefore based around 7 specific aims: 1) to strengthen the role women play in peace processes and in all decision-making processes; 2) to continue to promote the gender aspect in peace operations; 3) to continue to ensure specific training on various cross-cutting considerations of Security Council resolution 1325, especially for personnel who take part in peace operations; 4) to further enhance the presence of women in national armed forces and police forces, expanding the role they play in decision-making processes in relation to peace missions; 5) to protect the human rights of women and girls in conflict and post-conflict areas; 6) to grow synergies with civil society to implement resolution 1325; 7) to ensure strategic communication and result-oriented advocacy.

- *National Action Plan on business and human rights 2016–2021*. A specific working group coordinated by the CIDU was set up to draft this plan. A number of Ministers and institutions were involved in this, and experts from the sector and representatives from the world of business, trade unions and non-governmental organisations were consulted widely, before being open for public consultation on-line from 27 July to 10 September 2016. The Plan is structured around 6 main application lines: 1) promoting human rights due diligence procedures which aim to identify, prevent and mitigate potential risks, with a particular focus on SMEs; 2) combating illegal recruitment (particularly in the agricultural and construction sectors) and other forms of exploitation, forced labour, child labour, slavery and undocumented work, with a particular focus on migrants and victims of human trafficking; 3) promoting fundamental labour rights when internationalising business, with particular reference to worldwide production processes; 4) strengthening the role Italy plays in human rights-based international development cooperation; 5) combating discrimination and inequality and promoting equal opportunities; 6) promoting environmental protection and sustainability.

## B. Italian National Commission for UNESCO

The Commission was established by inter-ministerial decree on 11 February 1959, at the Ministry of Foreign Affairs, two years after Italy entered the Organisation, and pursuant to article 7 of the UNESCO Constitution.

Its composition has been regulated and updated by a series of successive decrees, the most recent one dating back to 24 May 2007. Members of the Commission include representatives from Parliament, the Prime Minister's

Office, various Ministries, public and private agencies, local authorities and civil society.

The Commission's mission is to promote the implementation of UNESCO programmes in Italy; to spread the ideals of the Organisation, especially among the younger generations; to disseminate information on its principles, goals and activities, thus stimulating action by institutions, civil society and the world of culture, education and science. The Commission also advises the Government regarding its dealings with UNESCO.

From April 2016 the President, nominated by the Ministry of Foreign Affairs, is Franco Bernabè, while the post of Secretary General is held by Enrico Vicenti. The National Commission receives funding for institutional activities and its functioning through chapter 2471/10 of the budget forecast of the Ministry of Foreign Affairs.

In 2016, this funding was around 11,000 euros which covers no more than the basic functioning of the Commission, making it extremely difficult to perform its public activities.

Despite these shortages, in 2016 the National Commission carried out many activities (seminars, conferences, meetings in schools, competitions, exhibitions, workshops, shows) in various Italian towns, especially on the various UN International Days, including International Mother Language Day (21 February), World Poetry Day (21 March), World Book and Copyright Day (23 April) and the International Jazz Day (30 April).

## IV. Ministry of Labour and Social Policies

A number of the departments and offices belonging to the Ministry of Labour and Social Policies deal specifically with human rights.

The following are particularly worthy of note:

- Directorate-general for employment service policies. Functions: guidance, promotion and coordination of employment services in order to sustain employment policies; initiatives to combat irregular labour; guidance, coordination and initiatives to facilitate entry and reentry to the labour market of persons with disabilities; promotion of female employment; promotion of equal opportunities for entry into the labour market; support for the activities of parity advisors.
- Directorate-general for inclusion and social policies. Functions: promoting policies to combat poverty, social exclusion and severe marginalisation; promoting and monitoring policies for children and adolescents, and the protection of minors; coordination policies for the social inclusion, protection and promotion of the rights and opportunities of persons with disabilities; managing the National Fund for Social Policies, the National Fund for the

Non-self-sufficient, the National Fund for Childhood and Adolescence and other funds for financing social policies and monitoring transferred resources; study, research and investigations concerning social policies; participation in all the pertinent internationally significant activities, and managing relations with the European Union, the Council of Europe, the International Labour Organisation, the United Nations and the Organisation for Economic Cooperation and Development.

- Directorate-general for the third sector and social groups. Functions: promoting and supporting the activities carried out by third sector subjects, especially initiatives relating to social promotion and voluntary associations, in order to facilitate the growth of an active society welfare to support policies of social inclusion and integration.
- Directorate-general for immigration and integration policies. Functions: programming migratory flows, and managing and monitoring entry quotas of foreign workers as well as bilateral cooperation agreements with countries of origin; coordinating policies for social and job integration of foreign immigrants and initiatives designed to prevent and combat discrimination, xenophobia and racism; developing international cooperation for activities to prevent and study social and employment emergencies, and for initiatives regarding work-related migratory flows.

In 2012 the Directorate-general for immigration and integration policies took over the functions of the Committee for Foreign Minors, which was abolished in accordance with the decree on the so-called spending review (article 12, para. 20 of l.d. 95/2012, converted into law, with amendments, in l. 135/2012). The Directorate-general is consequently now responsible for monitoring the presence, and modes thereof, of foreign minors temporarily present on Italian territory, whether they be unaccompanied minors present on Italian soil or admitted minors.

As regards unaccompanied minors, the Directorate-general may adopt two kinds of measures: the first is "no repatriation", which amounts to activating the procedures for integrating the person into Italy; the second is "assisted repatriation", designed to reunite the child with his or her family in their Country of origin. As regards the first option, responsibility for managing and monitoring the measures is placed in the hands of local authorities. The most frequent choice made for unaccompanied minors in Italy is to place them in residential care facilities for children.

As regards admitted minors, the Directorate-general makes decisions, following due appraisal and according to predetermined criteria, at the request of organisations, associations or Italian families, regarding the temporary admission of children into the framework of humanitarian programmes. The Committee then makes decisions on temporary fostering and repatriation. It keeps a register of minors already admitted into the framework of humanitarian programmes and predefines criteria for assessing requests for the admission of temporarily admitted minors.

During 2016, 17,373 unaccompanied foreign minors were registered with the Committee as of 31 December 2016, a 45.7% increase compared with 31 December 2015. The great majority of these (93.3% of the total) were again boys. The main countries of origin are Egypt (15.9%), Gambia, (13.3%), Albania (9.3%), Nigeria (8.3%) and Eritrea (7.7%): taken together, these five are the countries of origin of over half (54.5%) of all unaccompanied foreign minors in Italy. The region with the highest number of minors (40.9% of the total) in its reception centres is still Sicily, in line with a trend which has consolidated over many years, followed by: Calabria (8.2%), Emilia Romagna (6.2%), Lombardy (6.1%), Lazio (5.3%) and Apulia (5.1%).

## A. National Observatory for Children and Adolescents

The Observatory performs a role of coordination among central administrations, local and regional bodies, associations, professional groups and non-governmental organisations dedicated to children's issues.

It was instituted by law 23 December 1997, No. 451, and is currently regulated by decree of the President of the Republic (d.p.r.), No. 103, 14 May 2007, which assigns it joint chairmanship by the Ministry of Labour and Social Policies and the Undersecretary of State to the Prime Minister's Office mandated with family policies. It is made up of representatives from national and local public administrations, associations and professional orders, voluntary and third sector organisations as well as experts in the field of children's rights.

Presidential decree 103/2007 assigns to the Observatory the task of preparing three documents about the condition of childhood and adolescence in Italy:

- The *National Plan of Action and of Measures to safeguard the rights and development of children and adolescents*. Drawn up every two years, the Plan contains the fundamental strategic guidelines and concrete commitments that the Government intends to pursue in order to develop a satisfactory policy for children and adolescents in Italy. On 10 August 2016, the Council of Ministers approved the 4th National Action Plan 2016/2017. The Plan is based around four broad areas of intervention: action lines to combat child and family poverty; early years socio-educational services and the quality of the school system; strategies and interventions for social and educational integration; support with parenting, integrated services and reception system.
- The *Report on the condition of children and adolescents in Italy*, which aims to provide an updated picture of the aspects and phenomena characterising the condition of children and adolescents in Italy, and of the system of social services and measures for promoting and protecting the rights of children

and adolescents. The latest report published by the Observatory refers to the two-year period 2010–2011.

- The *Periodic Report of the Government to the UN Committee on the Rights of the Child* regarding the application of the 1989 International Convention on the Rights of the Child, pursuant to article 44 of the Convention. The latest report (combining the 3rd and 4th reports) was sent by Italy in January 2009, and discussed in October 2011 (see *2012 Yearbook*, p. 114).

In carrying out its functions, the National Observatory makes use of the National Centre of Documentation and Analysis for Children and Adolescents, which performs documentation, analysis, research, monitoring and training tasks.

More specifically, the National Centre of Documentation deals with:

- collecting and disseminating regional, national, European and international norms and regulations, as well as statistical data and scientific studies;
- creating an annually updated map, based on information provided by regional authorities, of public, private and non-governmental services, including social and health care services, and of financial resources dedicated to children at the national, regional and local level;
- analysing the situation of childhood and adolescence in Italy, including the conditions of foreign minors;
- preparing an outline, based on National Observatory directives, of the biennial report on the condition of children in Italy, and of the Government report to the United Nations Committee on the Rights of the Child on the domestic implementation of the Convention on the Rights of the Child;
- formulating proposals, also at the request of local authorities, for the creation of pilot projects designed to improve children's living conditions as well as to assist mothers during the prenatal period.

## B. National Observatory Monitoring the Conditions of Persons with Disabilities

The Observatory is an advisory body offering technical and scientific support in defining national policies regarding disabilities.

It was instituted by law 3 March 2009, No. 18, at the Ministry of Labour, Health and Social Policies. It is chaired by the Ministry of Labour and includes a maximum number of 40 members, who are appointed by ministerial decree and represent central administrations involved in defining and implementing disability-related policies; regional and local authorities; social security institutions; the National Statistics Institute; trade unions; and most representative associations and organisations of persons with disabilities, joined by a maximum number of five experts of proven experience in the field of disabilities.

The Observatory's tasks include the following: to promote the implementation of the United Nations Convention on the Rights of Persons with Disabilities and to prepare, together with CIDU, the national report for the monitoring procedure established by that Convention; to prepare a biennial plan of action on disability implementing national and international laws; to promote and develop statistic-based studies and research that may contribute to defining priorities and needs.

The Observatory carried out the following activities in 2016.

- *Preparation of Italy's first periodic report to the United Nations Committee on the Rights of Persons with Disabilities* (see Part II, National Bodies with Jurisdiction over Human Rights, V, G). The Observatory contributed to drawing up the report containing Italy's responses to the list of 34 issues the United Nations produced on the implementation of the Convention on the Rights of Persons with Disabilities. The drafting of the report coordinated by CIDU and the Ministry of Labour and Social Policies, with the involvement of the administrations and bodies which make up the Observatory. Although the federations and associations representing persons with disabilities which are members of the Observatory had already drawn up their own "shadow report" and sent this to the United Nations Committee, Italy's draft response was shared with all Observatory members, including the organisations representing persons with disabilities, before the text was finalised.
- *Two-year action plan for promoting the rights and for the integration of persons with disabilities*, adopted by presidential decree on 4 October 2013 (see *2014 Yearbook*, p. 109). The Observatory working groups monitored the level of implementation of the Programme and drew up the input necessary to define the proposal for the second two-year action plan which is currently being drafted and which was discussed at the national conference in Florence on 16 and 17 September 2016.
- *Promoting the collection of statistical data which shows the conditions of persons with disabilities, including references to the different territorial situations.* To this end, the "Reporting and statistics" working group was formed, specifically mandated to set up the statistical indicator system to monitor the conditions of persons with disabilities, aiming to contribute to the process of enhancing the quality of policies.
- *Writing the Report on the implementation of disability policies* (pursuant to art. 41 (8) of l. 5 February 1992, No. 104). This Report is the main point of reference used to align Italian law with the United Nations Convention on the Rights of Persons with Disabilities, and aims to provide the key quantitative and qualitative information on the implementation status of disability policies in Italy in the years 2009–2014 at the national and regional level. The survey was launched in 2015 and is currently being completed.

- *Carrying out studies and research*. In 2016, the Observatory examined the following themes: judicially-appointed guardians: regional implementation models and planning an IT system based on the use of this institution; personalised planning and health budget; persons with disability and ageing: guidelines for services; "Farming for health": social agriculture as an opportunity for social inclusion for persons with disabilities; intellectual disabilities and psychiatric comorbidity: indications for organising services and treatment.

## V. Ministry of Justice

Within the Ministry of Justice there are various departments and bureaus specifically involved with human rights. The most relevant are:

- Office II (Directorate-general for litigation and human rights – Department of legal affairs): it is actively involved in examining cases pending before the European Court of Human Rights and in procedures relating to compliance with international obligations, and to the amendment of domestic law in accordance with the provisions of international instruments;
- Directorate-general for the enforcement of judgments – Department of juvenile justice: the office deals with promoting and protecting the rights of unaccompanied foreign minors and of persons at risk of social exclusion.

## VI. Judicial Authorities

The judiciary, that is to say the various organs of justice – ordinary, administrative and auditing – constituting judicial power, is the fundamental guarantee of rights and legality in a State that respects the principles of democracy, the division of powers and the rule of law. The Italian courts – the Constitutional Court, which delivers judgments regarding the constitutionality of laws, the Supreme Court, which is the court of last resort, the penal and civil tribunals and trial courts, and those concerned with administrative, audit and military matters – deal in a contentious manner with cases which often affect human rights in the most various ways and according to the most disparate perspectives. Access to a judge to obtain a ruling on a right that a plaintiff claims has been breached is a fundamental human right, linked to which are the many other procedural rights that distinguish the fair trial.

Besides ruling on individual cases, the justice system contributes to building and to the evolution of applicable law, through its own case-law. In recent years, and in relation to the theme of fundamental rights in particular, Italian rulings have been strongly influenced by that of international courts, especially the European Court of Human Rights and the Court of Justice of the European Union. The interaction between national judicial organs and international courts with jurisdiction over human rights stresses the universal nature of the latter. The dialogue with international courts and with those of other countries called upon to apply the same standards regarding individual human rights does not just concern the supreme courts of a State, but all judges, who can draw on rulings made in foreign or international courts to improve existing guarantees regarding fundamental rights, fully respecting the Constitution and the law.

Part IV of this *Yearbook* is specifically devoted to a summary presentation of cases in the Italian courts on which rulings were delivered in 2016 (with particular reference to those made by the Constitutional and the Supreme Court), and of case law elaborated by the European Court of Human Rights or the Court of Justice of the European Union which directly concerns Italy, either because the Italian State was the "defendant" or because the intervention of the European judge regarded pleas presented by Italian citizens or related to Italian legal norms.

## VII. Independent Authorities

There are ten independent authorities in Italy: the Communications Regulatory Authority (AGCOM); the Data Protection Authority; the Committee Guaranteeing the Implementation of the Law on Strikes Affecting Essential Public Services; the Authority Protecting Free Competition and the Market (Antitrust Authority); the Italian Companies and Stock Exchange Commission (CONSOB); the Institute for Vigilance on Private Insurance and Insurances of Collective Interest (ISVAP); the Regulatory Authority for Electricity and Gas; the Authority for Vigilance on Contracts for Public Works, Services and Supplies; the National Ombudsperson for Children and Adolescents; the National Ombudsperson for the Rights of Persons in Prison or Deprived of Liberty.

The five authorities that relate more pertinently to human rights are described below.

### *A. Communications Regulatory Authority (AGCOM)*

AGCOM was set up by law 31 July 1997, No. 249. It has a dual mandate: to ensure correct competition among market actors and to guarantee the fundamental freedoms of citizens in the area of communications, particularly as regards the protection of minors.

The composition of the Authority is disciplined by decree 6 December 2011, No. 201 (the so-called Save Italy decree), and its conversion into law (22 December 2011, No. 214). In 2016 the Authority was made up as follows: Chair: Angelo Marcello Cardani; members of the Services and Products Commission: Antonio Martusciello and Francesco Posteraro; members of the Commission for Infrastructure and Networks: Maurizio Dècina Antonio Nicita and Antonio Preto (prematurely passed away in November 2016). The Council consists of the Chair and all the Commissioners.

As detailed in the 2016 annual report of its activities and work programmes (reference period: May 2015 – April 2016), the Authority focused in particular on supervisory activities relating to the protection of personal data, to private lives and to minors. In particular, action taken to protect the rights of minors led to a number of disciplinary proceedings, 78% of which led to a sanction. However, in recent years the number of sanctions has fallen in absolute terms, in part due to a greater level of clarity (to which the Authority has contributed) on the classification criteria of seriously harmful programmes and technical features of filtering and parental oversights, meaning that the focus of watchdog activities could shift to specific higher-risk programmes and genres.

### B. Data Protection Authority

The Data Protection Authority was instituted by l. 31 December 1996, No. 675, later substituted by lgs.d. 30 June 2003, No. 196 (Personal data protection code), with the aim to ensure protection of the fundamental rights and freedoms and respect for the dignity of persons, in the processing of personal data.

The Data Protection Authority is a collegial body made up of four members elected by Parliament, who remain in office for a seven-year non-renewable mandate. The current body is made up of Antonello Soro (Chair), Augusta Iannini (Vice Chair), Giovanna Bianchi Clerici and Licia Califano.

During 2016, the Authority issued 770 *provisions* to protect the fundamental rights of individuals with regard to the processing and circulation of personal data, with particular reference to the following issues (among others): the right to be forgotten; freedom of the press; the right to education, work, health and scientific research; the rights of minors; the handling of sensitive data; and internet and social media.

## C. Commission Guaranteeing the Implementation of the Law on Strikes Affecting Essential Public Services

The Commission was instituted by law 12 June 1990, No. 146, modified by law 11 April 2000, No. 83. It comprises nine members designated by the Chairs of the Chamber of Deputies and the Senate among experts in matters of constitutional law, labour law and industrial relations, and appointed by decree of the President of the Republic. From June 2016, the members of the Commission are: Giuseppe Santoro Passarelli (Chair), Lauralba Bellardi, Alessandro Bellavista, Domenico Carrieri, Orsola Razzolini.

Some of the Commission's main tasks are:

- assessing the capacity of essential services to guarantee protection of both the right to strike and the enjoyment of constitutionally guaranteed human rights;
- requesting that those calling the strike delay the date of abstention from work if the Commission intends to attempt conciliation, or if it finds that the abstention violates legal and/or contractual obligations for strikes in essential public services;
- pointing out to those calling the strike any violations of norms concerning advance notice or any other requirements relative to the phase preceding collective abstention;
- notifying the appropriate authority which can order strikers back to work of situations where the strike or collective abstention could give rise to an imminent, probable risk of infringing constitutionally protected human rights;
- taking note of behaviour by administrations or enterprises which provide essential public services in clear violation of the law;
- assessing behaviour of both parties and if any non-compliance or violation of legal or contractual obligations relative to essential services emerges, inflicting penalties pursuant to art. 4 of law 146/1990 as amended by art. 3 of law 83/2000, ordering the employer to apply the disciplinary actions.

The second annual report on activity carried out in 2015 was submitted in July 2016. According to data in the report, the overall number of strikes (national, local, sectoral etc.) called in essential public services was 2,261, an increase of around 10% vis-à-vis the previous year. And so, despite a decline in the number of strikes in the industrial sector compared with the average of previous years, in essential pubic services, the numbers remain decidedly high. However, though many strikes were called, the number of strike actions which actually took place fell to around 1,400.

The majority of strike actions were called in full compliance with the law: indeed, the Commission only intervened with 324 preventative actions to highlight potential breaches of legislation, which led to adjustments in 99.69% of cases. The importance of the Commission's preventative actions explains the reduction in the number of assessment procedures opened (of which there were 9 in 2015). In particular, there is still a high level of tension in the following sectors: environmental hygiene (407 calls to strike), local public transport (337), cleaning and multi-service (242), regions and local autonomy (202), air transport (153) and rail transport (113).

## D. National Ombudsperson for Children and Adolescents

The National Ombudsperson for Children and Adolescents was established with law No. 112 of 12 July 2011. A monocratic organ, the holder of the post is appointed by the Presidents of the Chamber of Deputies and of the Senate, who choose a figure of unquestioned morality, independence and professional competence in the field of children's rights. The term of office is four years. From March 2016, the post of Ombudsperson is held by Filomena Albano.

The Ombudsperson has, amongst others, the following responsibilities:

- to promote the implementation of the UN Convention on the Rights of the Child, and of other pertinent international and European instruments, and to ensure appropriate forms of collaboration with all the national and international bodies and organisations engaged in promoting and protecting children and adolescents;
- to express opinions on legislative initiatives concerning the protection of the rights of children and adolescents, and the report that the Government presents periodically to the UN Committee on the Rights of the Child;
- to inform the Government, Regions and other local or territorial bodies involved, in relation to their respective responsibilities, of all appropriate measures to ensure full promotion and protection of the rights of children and adolescents;
- to inform judicial authorities and bodies concerned of problem cases or risks of minors' rights being infringed, as well as serious cases of neglect of minors, so that they can be taken into care by the appropriate authorities;
- to enhance knowledge of the rights of children and adolescents, organising, to this end, awareness-raising activities, studies and research.

Article 6 of law 112 also allows anyone to address the Ombudsperson to report violation of rights or the risk thereof. Finally, article 3 states that the Ombudsperson is to establish appropriate forms of cooperation with the regional Ombudspersons or similar figures. The National Conference for the Rights of Children and Adolescents was set up for this purpose; coordinated by the National Ombudsperson, it brings together all the other Ombudspersons, where these have been established (see in this Part, Sub-national Human Rights Structures, IV).

In April 2016, the Ombudsperson presented her fifth report to Parliament on the actions undertaken over the course of 2015 to benefit the approximately 10 million children and adolescents living in Italy (comprising about 17% of the population).

Over the years, the number of reports to the Ombudsperson have consistently risen: there were 45 in 2012, 193 in 2013, 506 in 2014 and 526 in 2015. Over half of these reports relate to family situations (conflicts which could not be managed within the family and criticisms of the work done by Institutions and professionals able to intervene), and to issues related to the media and the internet, and to conflict between individuals and school institutions.

In 2015, the Ombudsperson strengthened dialogue with the Government and Parliament at a national and international level. More specifically, two formal hearings were held at the Chamber of Deputies. On 15 July, the Authority was heard by the Constitutional Affairs Commission, the Prime Minister's Office and Ministry of the Interior in relation to citizenship. The Ombudsperson urged the Commission to quickly create a new legislative framework that considers the greater interests of the child and removes all sources of discrimination regarding foreign minors, including those born in Italy to foreign parents; which enhances citizenship training and education pathways promoting community interaction and inclusion, but which does not make high performance at school a prerequisite for access to citizenship for minors; which sets out clear, accessible procedures for citizenship applications, specific response periods, and a precise appeals procedure for refused citizenship applications for minors. On 20 October, the Authority voiced its concerns and set out some suggestions on the bill "Amendment to article 28 of the law 4 May 1983, No. 184, and other provisions relating to accessing information of the origins of a child not recognised at birth" before the Justice Commission. The Ombudsperson believes that the bill as approved at first reading did not strike the correct balance between the adoptee's right to access his or her origins, and the right to be forgotten of the woman who gave birth to the child.

The Ombudsperson also continued to ensure its participation at observatories and inter-institutional tables held by various bodies, including: the National Observatory for Childhood and Adolescence, the Observatory for the Integration of Foreign Pupils and for Inter-Culture, the Standing Observatory on the Exercise of Jurisdiction (hosted at the National Lawyers' council), the Inter-Institutional Table on Support Procedures and the Protection of Children and their Families (promoted by the National Council of Social Workers) and the Scientific Committee for LGBT Issues (hosted by the Prime Minister's Office).

On an international level, the Ombudsperson contributed to the definition of the new Council of Europe Strategy for the Rights of the Child 2016–2021

As regards the central issue of training operators, during 2015, the collaboration launched by the Memorandum of Understanding with the Public Security Department of the Ministry of the Interior continued. Accordingly, further training sessions were held for police force staff, focusing mainly on illustrating the United Nations Convention on the Rights of the Child, the functions and activities of the National Ombudsperson for Children and Adolescents and the contents of the guide for police forces written by the Technical Inter-Institutional Group set up under the above protocol. During 2015, ten meetings were held in different Police and Military Police training schools, with an estimated total audience of around 1,500 people.

One especially sensitive issue which the Ombudsperson has often been involved in relates to the relationship between minors and the media. As well as activities included in the Safer Internet project (a strategic project supported by the European Commission and coordinated by the Ministry of Education, Universities and Research), the Ombudsperson has continued its dialogue with the main bodies responsible for communications and by taking part in public debates on the issue. It also continued to promote the contents of the Milan Charter, which the Ombudsperson signed in 2014, as well as its collaboration with the IAP, Italy's advertising standards authority.

In this area, twenty-one complaints from the public were received between October 2014 and October 2015 which the Ombudsperson forwarded to the IAP to be assessed in line with agreements. In one case, advertisement was blocked; in three cases, the Institute used moral suasion, after which the advertising companies resolved the issues highlighted; however, in fourteen cases no violations of the Self-Regulatory Code were identified, and those cases were dismissed; three were dismissed following a decision not to proceed, as they did not fall within the Institute's remit.

Furthermore, with a view to improving awareness of the world of children and adolescents, the Ombudsperson launched a collaboration with the national statistics body Istat; as part of this, in 2015 the sample survey "Aspects of Daily Life" investigated in detail some aspects of the everyday life of children and adolescents. This allowed 11–17-year-olds to be asked questions for the first time seeking to estimate the number of victims of bullying. According to the survey, in 2014 slightly more than 50% of 11–17-year-olds had been subjected to an incident of offensive, disrespectful and/or violent behaviour at the hands of other young people in the previous 12 months. 19.8% were frequent victims of "typical" bullying, meaning that they experienced it several times a month. Some 9.1% experienced bullying on a weekly basis.

Finally, in 2015 the Ombudsperson launched the European and national project "*Io sono qui*" (I am here), aiming to create an initiative that would meet the need to promote legality while at the same time combating truancy and dropout rates, through a range of actions promoting direct participation pathways for minors, creating a "bridge" between them and the institutions responsible for realizing their rights.

## E. National Ombudsperson for the Rights of Persons in Prison or Deprived of Liberty

This Ombudsperson was established by article 7 of l.d. 23 December 2013, No. 146, converted with amendments by l. 21 February 2014, No. 10. It is collegial, and consists of the Chair and two members chosen from independent people who are competent in areas relating to the protection of human rights. Members are nominated, following a decision of the Council of Ministers, by a Decree of the President of the Republic, having heard the competent parliamentary commissions, with a five-year mandate which may not be extended.

In 2016, the National Ombudsperson for the Rights of Persons in Prison or Deprived of Liberty was Mauro Palma; the other members were Daniela De Robert and Emilia Rossi.

> The Ombudsperson is tasked with ensuring that custody of persons in prison and persons subject to other types of limitations on personal freedom is carried out in accordance with the rules and principles set out in the Constitution, in international conventions on human rights, and the laws of the land. To this end, it has the faculty to visit penitentiary institutions and other structures used to host persons subject to measures restricting their personal freedom without requiring authorisation.
>
> The Ombudsperson has been identified as an independent national monitoring mechanism required under the Optional Protocol to the Convention against Torture (OPCAT), which Italy ratified in 2012.
>
> The National Ombudsperson is also tasked with coordinating the network of local ombudspersons, promoting their solidity as an institution through the recognition of sufficient guarantees of independence and autonomy vis-à-vis the local government which appointed them.
>
> Finally, the Ombudsperson monitors procedures relating to forced repatriations pursuant to the system provided for in article 8, paragraph 6, of EU Directive No. 115 of 2008.

At the end of its first year of operation, the National Ombudsperson has identified a number of critical issues in the Italian system, with particular reference to the following aspects.

*Freedom and Imprisonment*

- Despite a general background of keeping prisoner numbers down, a slight tendency towards increased "presences" has emerged, a sign that the use of alternative measures is slowing. Furthermore, the population is not distributed evenly, and there are some cases of extreme overcrowding.
- While there was a considerable focus on numbers, less attention was paid to the quality of prison life: penal institutions are still too closed, offer limited activities and few reintegration projects.
- Taking over responsibility for prisoners with mental health issues is going slowly: there are few "structures for protecting mental health" which are fully operational. The number of suicides and attempted suicides in 2016 – often linked to mental distress – is a particular cause of concern.
- The so-called "reserved areas", dispensing special, even harsher conditions under the special regime 41-bis (of the law on the Italian penitentiary system – *NdT*), have some characteristics of unacceptable prison conditions and expose Italy to potential criticism from international monitoring bodies.

*Migration*

- The so-called hotspots are in a legal limbo: they are not covered by any legislation, and foreign citizens stay there deprived of their freedom despite the absence of any judicial measures.
- It is often the most vulnerable, such as unaccompanied foreign minors, who have protracted stays in hotspots while waiting for a host centre for them to be identified.
- There is no monitoring of what happens following the return of repatriated foreign citizens: in this respect, the National Ombudsperson intends to establish handover procedures with the network of national prevention mechanisms in third countries.

*Security and Freedom*

- Lack of security rooms: of the 2,143 security rooms run by the State and Military Police forces, 749 are partly or entirely unusable. The remaining 1,395 fall well short of the number needed, particularly considering that in 2016, 29,121 persons were detained or arrested. There is a risk, often identified during visits, of a return to the "revolving door" phenomenon.

## VIII. Non-Governmental Organisations

In Italy, numerous non-governmental organisations are active in promoting and protecting human rights. Some of them, organised in networks at national and international levels, have gained consultative status with international organisations and actively participate in their programmes.

As of 31 December 2016, 101 Italian non-governmental organisations held consultative status with the United Nations Economic and Social Council, eight of which have general status; 76 have special status and 17 have roster status. There are 158 non-governmental organisations with headquarters or representative offices in Italy enjoying participatory status with the Council of Europe dealing specifically with human rights.

In addition, some of the most important international nongovernmental organisations have local branches in Italy. These include Amnesty International, the International Federation on Human Rights, Save the Children, Médecins sans Frontières and Action Aid. The Italian associations Nessuno tocchi Caino (Hands off Cain) and Non c'è pace senza giustizia (No Peace without Justice) also have high profiles internationally.

Non-governmental organisations play an important role in monitoring the level of compliance with and protection of human rights in Italy. In 2016, the following monitoring reports, which are of particular interest, were published.

- Working group for the Convention on the Rights of the Child (CRC Group): *9th Monitoring Report on the Implementation of the Convention on the Rights of the Child in Italy.* The Report states that there are 2,293,778 adolescents aged between 14 and 17 in Italy, 186,450 of whom are foreign. Over 50% have experienced bullying and/or cyber-bullying; 7,000 of them are in care; they go to school, but many of them stop studying when compulsory education ends, particularly pupils who have a disability. Levels of early school leaving in Italy are among the highest in Europe: 15% of young people between the ages of 18 and 24 only finished middle school. In 2015, 8.4% of adolescents between the ages of 14 and 17 participated in a cultural or recreational organisation or similar, while 9.7% volunteered. Given this data, policy regarding young people is in limbo, as they straddle polices targeted at children and those for young adults. Many laws are at a stand-still in Parliament, including a reform to the system of protection and reception for unaccompanied foreign minors, as well as the acquisition of citizenship for minors of foreign origin. Consequently, the CRC Group has made 143 recommendations to representatives of local and national institutions, seeking to improve policies for children and adolescents nationwide.

- Antigone Association – XII National Report on detention conditions – *Galere d'Italia* (Italian Prisons). The data contained in the report show that in the year up to 31 March 2016, there were 1,331 more people registered in prisons in Italy. Prisons are currently at 108% capacity, and 3,950 people do not have a regular bed. On the other hand, imprisonment rates in Italy are in line with the European average, with around 90 detainees per 100,000 inhabitants. The number of people in prison before any sentence becomes final is particularly high, representing 34.6% of all prisoners (the European average is 20.4%).

  There are fewer foreign detainees than there were in 2009 in percentage terms, currently making up 33.45% of the prison population compared with a European average of around 21%. As a percentage, there are more foreign citizens in pre-trial detention than there are Italians; the use of probation is also increasing, and the data show that alternative measures to detention and electronic bracelets lead to recidivism rates of almost zero. Furthermore, the results of the Antigone Observatory's visits to psychiatric divisions, were presented, as were some cases followed by the Association's ombudsperson relating to deaths and alleged instances of violence.

  Lastly, the report highlights that the States General of the Execution of Criminal Sentences, requested by the Minister of Justice Andrea Orlando, were an important and innovative opportunity to democratically participate in institutional decisions relating to the execution of criminal sentences. The States General were a time to reflect and take an in-depth look at criminal sentences, taking place over about a year, during which 18 round tables made up of experts in the prison system and a range of other disciplines, who debated and produced observations and proposals relating to the execution of sentences. Antigone played an active role in these events via some of its members. The final outcome now must now be crossed with the parliamentary discussion on the Government bill reforming the prison system, which has been approved by the Lower Chamber and is currently pending in the Senate.
- *A Buon Diritto* Association: Article 3: report on the status of rights in Italy. The Report analyses the state of implementation of fundamental human rights and guarantees which protect minorities in Italy. In particular, the report considers a wide range of rights and guarantees related to ability to fully exercise fundamental personal rights: personal freedom, freedom of movement, religious freedom, freedom from discrimination of any kind, the rights of persons with disabilities, rights, gender identity and sexual orientation, minority rights, the rights of migrants, refugees and asylum seekers, justice and guarantees, freedom of expression and information, sensitive data, confidentiality and the right to be forgotten, protection of minors, education and social mobility, women's rights, the right to health, the protection of jobs and income and environmental protection.
- *Istituto di Ricerche Internazionali Archivio Disarmo* (Institute for International Research Disarmament Archive): *Light Weapons, Heavy Wars. 2016 Report.* The aim of this report is to monitor the development of Italy's regulatory framework and export of weapons for "civil use". According to the data in

the Report, over the last 15 years there has been an increase in exports of weapons for civil use from Italy, with a low of 320 million euro in 2006 and a peak of 553 million euro in 2010, from which point it has settled at values between 400 and 500 million euro. Data for 2015 (around 520 million euro) show a slight increase compared with the years immediately prior to 2015. Italy has confirmed its position as the second-biggest global exporter of light weapons, after the United States; the Country now sells light weapons across the globe, often paying no heed to the conditions of human rights and the spread of violence. The three main destinations for Italian exports are North America, the Middle East and North Africa, areas which already receive most exports of larger weapons systems and areas which, for different reasons and to differing degrees, are affected by armed violence. Current national and international legislation on the trade of common weapons is therefore patently ineffective at limiting the spread of these weapons in the most sensitive areas.

- *Sbilanciamoci!* Campaign: 2017 Report – How to use public spending for rights, peace, and the environment. This report begins with an analysis of public spending in Italy and contains 115 detailed proposals drawn up by the 47 organisations making up *Sbilanciamoci!* to generate savings or increased revenue on the one hand, and cuts to spending in the wrong areas and increased allocations in the right areas on the other, in seven key areas: revenue and finance, work and income, culture and knowledge, environment and sustainable development, welfare and rights, cooperation, peace and disarmament, and the alternative economy.
- ANCI, Caritas Italiana, Cittalia, Fondazione Migrantes, SPRAR Headquarters (in collaboration with the UNHCR): *Report on international protection in Italy 2016*. Beginning with an analysis of the role played by the State, local bodies and the third sector in matters of asylum and the reception of beneficiaries of international protection, the Report aims to set out how integrated reception is developing in Italy over the years, and on how the phenomenon of migration affects an increasingly vast number of vulnerable groups such as foreign minors, stateless persons and victims of trafficking whose conditions often overlap with those of refugees. The report contains four chapters, dedicated to: international protection in Italy in 2015; the phenomenon of those seeking international protection in Italy; forced migration in the world; and immigration and mental health in Italy in 2016.

## IX. Human Rights Teaching and Research in Italian Universities

The Italian academic world has shown growing interest in research and education in the area of human rights. This issue is now included in teaching programmes across a number of disciplines and in the curricula of various degree courses at undergraduate and post-graduate levels, as well as in interdisciplinary research programmes. The following pages offer an overview of the universities and research centres which are specifically involved with human rights issues, including the teaching of three- and five-year degrees, Masters and PhD courses which were available in 2016 or which opened for registration during that year, on the subject. In the interests of precision, the list comprises only the courses and structures which include the phrase "human rights" or equivalent expressions (rights of man, rights of the person, fundamental rights) in their full title. The picture thus obtained offers reasonably reliable evidence as to how widespread and penetrating issues regarding the multifaceted aspects of the rights of the person have become in Italian academia.

### University Institutions and Research Centres

| University | Name | Founding year |
|---|---|---|
| University of Padova | University Human Rights Centre | 1982 |
| University of Salento | Inter-University Centre on Bioethics and Human Rights | 1992 |
| 41 European universities in partnership | European Inter-University Centre for Human Rights and Democratisation (EIUC) | 2002 |
| University of Naples | Centre for Studies on Human Rights in the era of globalisation and conflicts | 2003 |
| University of Ca' Foscari, Venice | Human Rights Research Centre (CESTUDIR) | 2003 |
| University of Salerno | Department of Individual Rights and Comparison | 2011 |

Source: elaboration by the *2017 Yearbook* research and editorial committee.

### Bachelor's Degree Courses

| University | Name | Scientific Area |
|---|---|---|
| University of Padova | Political Science, International Relations, Human Rights | L-36: Political science and International Relations |

Source: elaboration by the *2017 Yearbook* research and editorial committee.

**Master's Degree Courses**

| University | Name | Scientific Area |
|---|---|---|
| University of Bergamo | Human Rights and the Ethics of International Cooperation | LM-81: Cooperation development sciences |
| University of Bologna | International Cooperation, Protection of Human Rights and Ethno-cultural Heritage | LM-81: Cooperation development sciences |
| | International cooperation, development and human rights | LM-81: Cooperation development sciences |
| University of Padova | Human rights and multi-level governance | LM-52: International Relations |

Source: elaboration by the *2017 Yearbook* research and editorial committee.

## Teachings

In 2016, a total of 96 human rights teachings were run in 36 universities. Over 60% of these were delivered via degree courses in the field of political and social science (59 teachings), while slightly under one-third related to the area of law (30 teachings); 4 teachings to the area of history, philosophy, pedagogy and psychology, and a further three to economics and statistics.

As in the years between 2010 and 2015, in 2016 the University with the greatest number of human rights teachings was Padova (17 teachings), followed by Bologna (8), Bari (7) and the University of Milan (6 teachings). Of the 96 teachings available, 15 are taught in English (8 of which are at the University of Padova) and 2 at the University of Milan, as well as one at each of the following universities: Palermo, Roma Tre, Rome "La Sapienza", Salerno and Trento.

| University | Area | Degree Course | Teaching | Lecturer/ Professor |
|---|---|---|---|---|
| Aldo Moro University of Bari | Law | BA in Science of Law Services | International Protection of Human Rights – the Protection of Human Rights in the European Convention on Human Rights | Andrea Cannone |
| | | 5-Year Degree in Law | International Protection of Human Rights | Andrea Cannone |
| | | MA in Designing Social Inclusion Policy | Citizenship and Human Rights | Giuseppe Campesi |
| | Political and social science | BA in Political Science, International Relations and European Studies | International Protection of Human Rights | Egeria Nalin |
| | | MA in International Relations | Theory of Human Rights | Ivan Pupolizio |
| | | | Legal Philosophy, Human Rights and Religion in the Middle and Far East | Gianfranco Longo |
| | History, philosophy, pedagogy and psychology | MA in Philosophy | History of the Philosophy of Human Rights | Francesca Recchia and Romana Luciani |
| University of Bergamo | History, philosophy, pedagogy and psychology | MA in Pedagogy | Pedagogy of Marginalisation and Human Rights | Ivo Lizzola |
| | Law | MA in Human Rights and the Ethics of International Cooperation | International Cooperation and Human Rights | Paolo Scevi |

| University | Area | Degree Course | Teaching | Lecturer/ Professor |
|---|---|---|---|---|
| University of Bologna | Political and Social Science | MA in Local and Global Development | Human Rights, Constitutions and Institutions | Raffaella Gherardi |
| | | MA in International Relations and Diplomatic Affairs | International Protection of Human Rights (Seminar) | Marco Balboni |
| | | MA in International Cooperation, Protection of Human Rights and Ethno-Cultural Heritage | International Human Rights Law and European Law on Cooperation | Elisa Baroncini |
| | | | Human Rights and History of International Law | Gustavo Gozzi |
| | | | Human Rights and the Rights of Minors | Annalisa Furia |
| | | | Public Law and Protection of Fundamental Rights | Caterina Drigo |
| | | | Philosophy of Human Rights | Silvia Vida |
| | Law | 5-Year Degree in Law | Fundamental Rights | Luca Mezzetti |
| University of Cagliari | Political and Social Science | MA in International Relations | History of Political Thought of Human Rights | Federica Falchi |
| University of Camerino | Economics and Statistics | BA in Social Sciences for Non-profit Organisations and International Cooperation | International Protection of Human Rights | Agostina Latino |
| | Law | BA in Social Sciences for Non-profit Organisations and International Cooperation | History of Human Rights | Maria Pia Paternò |
| University of Ferrara | Law | 5-Year Degree in Law | Human rights and humanitarian law in armed conflicts | Francesco Salerno |

| University | Area | Degree Course | Teaching | Lecturer/ Professor |
|---|---|---|---|---|
| University of Florence | Law | BA in Science of Law Services | Legal systems and protection of rights | Beatrice Gambineri |
| | | | Welfare state and rights | Emilio Santoro, Marta Picchi, Antonio Gorgoni |
| | | MA in International Relations and European Studies | Constitutional Courts and Multi-Level Protection of Fundamental Rights | Ginevra Cerrina Feroni |
| University of Genova | Law | 5-Year Degree in Law | Rights to Freedom and Social Rights | Astride Canepa |
| University of Acquila | Economics and Statistics | BA in Economics | Theory of Interpretation and Fundamental Rights | Francesca Caroccia |
| University of Macerata | Political and Social Science | BA in Political Science and International Relations | Philosophy of Human Rights | Natascia Mattucci |
| | | MA in Theories, Cultures and Techniques for Social Work | Social and Citizenship-related Rights | Angela Cossiri |
| | Law | MA in International Politics | Human Rights and Differences | Ines Corti |
| University of Messina | Politics and social science | MA in International Relations and Development Aid | International organisations and human rights | Carmela Panella |
| Sacro Cuore (Sacred Heart) Catholic University Milan | Politics and social science | BA in Politics and International Relations | International protection of Human rights | Marinella Fumagalli Meraviglia |
| | Law | 5-Year Degree in Law | Human Rights | Pasquale De Sena |

| University | Area | Degree Course | Teaching | Lecturer/ Professor |
|---|---|---|---|---|
| University of Milan | Politics and Social Science | BA in International Studies and European Institutions | International Protection of Human Rights | Ilaria Viarengo |
| | | BA in Administration and Management | Theory of Equality and Rights | Beatrice Magni |
| | | MA in Politics and Government | Theories of Fundamental Rights | Alessandra Facchi |
| | | MA in International Cooperation and Trans-National Social Processes | Anthropology of Human rights | Nicola Riva |
| | Law | 5-Year Degree in Law | EU law on business and human rights | Angelica Bonfanti |
| | | | International refugee and human rights law | José Henrique Fischel De Andrade |
| University of Milan-Bicocca | Politics and social science | MA in Sociology | Rights and European citizenship | Marina Calloni |
| | | MA in Planning and Managing Social Policy and Social Services | Cooperation and human rights protection | Gabriella Citroni |
| | Law | 5-Year Degree in Law | European constitutional law (fundamental rights) | Stefania Ninatti |
| | | | International protection of human rights | Gabriella Citroni |
| University of Modena and Reggio Emilia | Law | 5-Year Degree in Law | Theory and practice of human rights | Thomas Casadei |
| University of Molise | Politics and social science | BA in Media Studies | Human rights and globalisation | Lorenzo Scillitani |
| Federico II University of Naples | Economics and Statistics | MA in Economics and Business Law | International Protection of Human Rights | Rossella De Rosa |

| University | Area | Degree Course | Teaching | Lecturer/ Professor |
|---|---|---|---|---|
| Second University of Naples | Political and Social Science | BA in Politics | Protection of Rights in Multi-Cultural States: Western and Asian Models | Domenico Amirante |
| | | MA in International Relations and Organisations | Human rights | Pasquale Femia |
| | Law | 5-Year Degree in Law | International Protection of Human Rights | Andrea Saccucci |
| University of Padova | Politics and Social Science | BA in Politics, International Relations and Human Rights | Human Rights | Elena Pariotti |
| | | | European Sports Law and Policy | Jacopo Tognon |
| | | | Public Policy and Human Rights | Paola Degani |
| | | | General Sociology and Human Rights Sociology | Giuseppe Giordan |
| | | | Economic Development and Human Rights | Mario Pomini |
| | | | International Protection of Human Rights | Paolo De Stefani |
| | | MA in European Studies | Fundamental Rights and European Citizenship | Costanza Margiotta Broglio Massucci |
| | | Master's Degree in Human Rights and Multi-Level Governance | European Union Law of Human Rights | Paolo Piva |

| University | Area | Degree Course | Teaching | Lecturer/ Professor |
|---|---|---|---|---|
| | | | Human Rights and International Justice | Costanza Margiotta Broglio Massucci |
| | | | International Law of Human Rights | Paolo De Stefani |
| | | | Women's Human Rights | Paola Degani |
| | | | Culture, Society and Human Rights | Andrea Maria Maccarini |
| | | | Economic Globalization and Human Rights | Roberto Antonietti |
| | | | Human Rights Governance | Leonce Maria Bekemans, Angela Melchiorre |
| | | | Religions and Human Rights | Giuseppe Giordan |
| | Law | 5-Year Degree in Law | Human Rights and Public Ethics | Umberto Vincenti |
| | History, Philosophy, Pedagogy and Psychology | BA in Primary Education | Pedagogy of childhood, adolescence and rights of the child | Mirca Benetton |
| University of Palermo | Political and Social Science | BA in Cooperation and Development | Human rights: theory and policies | Serena Marcenò |
| University of Pavia | Law | 5-Year Degree in Law | Constitutional Law and Fundamental Rights | Francesco Rigano |
| University of Perugia | Politics and Social Science | MA in International Relations | Human Rights, Crime and International Humanitarian Law | Amina Maneggia |
| | Law | 5-Year Degree in Law | Public Law of Islamic Countries | Maurizio Oliviero |

| University | Area | Degree Course | Teaching | Lecturer/ Professor |
|---|---|---|---|---|
| University of Pisa | Political and Social Science | BA in Sciences for Peace: international cooperation and conflict transformation | Legal and political theories and human rights | Vittorio Benedetti |
| | | | Technology, development aid and peace | Fabio Fineschi |
| | Law | 5-Year Degree in Law | Multilevel protection of human rights | Elena Malfatti |
| Guido Carli Free International University of Social Studies – LUISS | Law | 5-Year Degree in Law | International protection of human rights | Pietro Pustorino |
| Roma Tre University | Politics and social science | BA in Political Science for Cooperation and Development | International organisation and protection of human rights | Carlo Focarelli |
| | | MA in International Relations | Theory of human rights | Francesco Maiolo |
| La Sapienza University of Rome | Politics and social science | MA in Development and International Cooperation Sciences | Human rights and bioethics | Luca Marini |
| | | | European Union Law and Human Rights | Alessandra Mignolli |
| | | MA in International Relations | International Human Rights Law | Luigino Manca |
| University of Salento | Politics and social science | BA in International Relations | Human rights | Attilio Pisanò |
| University of Salerno | Law | 5-Year Degree in Law | Human rights | Stefano Pietropaoli |
| | | | Human rights and Biolaw | Anna Malomo |
| | | | International Human Rights Law | Stefania Negri |
| University of Siena | Politics and social science | MA in International Studies | International protection of human rights | Alessandra Viviani |

| University | Area | Degree Course | Teaching | Lecturer/ Professor |
|---|---|---|---|---|
| University of Teramo | Law | 5-Year Degree in Law | Human rights | Mario Sirimarco |
| University of Turin | Politics and social science | MA in Sociology | Theories of human rights | Valentina Pazé |
| | | MA in International Studies | Human rights and immigration | Alessandra Algostino |
| | | | History of human rights | Franco Motta |
| | | MA in Social Policy and Social Services | Citizenship, social rights, justice | Franco Prina |
| | | | Vulnerable People and the Protection of Rights | Maurizio Riverditi |
| University of Trento | Politics and social science | BA in International Studies | International Relations and Human Rights | Alessia Donà |
| | | MA in European and International Studies | Human Rights and Natural Resources under International Law | Marco Pertile |
| University of Udine | Law | 5-Year Degree in Law | Theory of Human Rights | Giovanni Turco |
| Carlo Bo University of Urbino | Law | 5-Year Degree in Law | Human Rights | Maria Paola Mittica |
| Ca' Foscari University of Venice | History, philosophy, pedagogy and psychology | MA in Cultural Anthropology, Ethnology, Anthropological Linguistics | Human Rights and Citizenship Policies | Lauso Zagato |
| University of Verona | Politics and social science | MA in Social Services in challenging environments | Social and Citizenship-related Rights. | Marco Peruzzi |
| | | | Protection of Fundamental Rights | Stefano Catalano |

Source: elaboration by the *2017 Yearbook* research and editorial committee based on data from the prospectuses of each university.

## Doctoral programmes (Academic years 2015–2016 and 2016–2017)

| University | Name | Area of scientific discipline |
|---|---|---|
| University of Camerino, School of Advanced Studies | Doctorate in Law, Politics and Social Science – Curriculum on Fundamental rights in the global society | M-STO/02; M-STO/04; M-DEA/01; M-FIL/03; M-FIL/06; IUS/04; IUS/08; IUS/09; IUS/13 – IUS/21 SECS-P/01; SECS P/02; SECS-P/04; SPS/01; SPS/02; SPS/04; SPS/06; SPS/07; SPS/11; SPS/12 |
| University of Florence | Theory and history of law – Theory and history of human rights | IUS/18, IUS/19, IUS/20 |
| University of Padova, Western Sydney University (Australia), Zagreb University (Croatia), Panteion University of Athens (Greece) | Joint Ph.D Degree in Human Rights, Society, and Multi-level Governance | IUS/13: IUS/20; IUS/21; SPS/04; SPS/08; SECS-P/01 |
| University of Palermo | International Doctorate in Human rights: evolution, protection and limits | IUS/01, IUS/09, IUS/12, IUS/20, SPS/02, IUS/13, IUS/19, IUS/10, SPS/09, SECS-P/01, IUS/08 |
| Amedeo Avogadro University of Eastern Piedmont | Local autonomies, public services and citizenship rights | Amedeo Avogadro University of Eastern Piedmont |
| Sant'Anna School of Advanced Studies of Pisa | Politics, human rights and sustainability | SPS/01, SPS/06, IUS/13, IUS/03, IUS/14, SPS/04, SECS-P/02, SECS-P/06, SECS-P/08 |
| La Sapienza University of Rome | International order and human rights | IUS/13, IUS/14, IUS/08, IUS/07, IUS/01 |
| University of Salerno | Comparazione e diritti della persona | IUS/01, IUS/02, IUS/07, IUS/13, IUS/14, IUS/16, IUS/17 |

Source: elaboration by the *2017 Yearbook* research and editorial committee.

## Master's degree programmes – postgraduate

| University | Name | Level |
|---|---|---|
| University of Bologna | Human rights, migration and development | I |
| European Inter-University Centre for Human Rights and Democratisation (EIUC, 41 università europee partner) | European Master's degree in human rights and democratisation E.MA – Master europeo in diritti umani e democratizzazione | I |
| Sant'Anna School of Advanced Studies of Pisa | Human rights and conflict management | I |
| University of Siena | European Joint Master of Human Rights and Genocide Studies | I |
| Università degli studi di Bari – Aldo Moro | Etica della pace, educazione ai diritti umani e inclusione | I |
| La Sapienza University of Rome | "Maria Rita Saulle" International protection of human rights | II |
| Roma Tre University | Peace studies: international cooperation, human rights and policies of the European Union | II |
| Italian Society for International Organisation (SIOI) | International relations and international protection of human rights | - |

Source: elaboration by the *2017 Yearbook* research and editorial committee.

# Sub-national Human Rights Structures

## I. Peace Human rights Offices in Municipalities, Provinces and Regions

At the sub-national level, especially by virtue of the inclusion of the "peace human rights norm" in thousands of Municipal, Provincial and Regional Statutes, and of the adoption of dedicated regional laws on this topic (see Part I, Italian Law, III), Italy has a number of consultancies, offices, departments, bureaux and centres for human rights, peace, equal opportunity, development cooperation, fair trade and international solidarity. Statistical data on the spread of these structures were given in the *2011 Yearbook* (pp. 133–134), and specific examples were presented in the ensuing editions.

During 2016, some municipal human rights structures were involved in a European research project entitled ADPOLIS (Anti-discrimination policies successfully implemented). The project seeks to analyse factors which made some policies against racial or ethnic discrimination implemented in various European towns successful, and to set out, based on the experience of the towns chosen, a series of model policies which may be implemented by any other municipal administration working on these issues. The ADPOLIS project is coordinated by the European Training Centre for Human Rights and Democracy at Graz University, with the participation of researchers from different European centres including the Human Rights Centre at the University of Padova, UNESCO, and the European Coalition of Cities against Racism (ECCAR).

## II. Ombudspersons in the Italian Regions and Provinces

In 2016 there were 15 incumbent Ombudspersons (or Human Rights Authority which also fulfil the duties of an Ombudsperson), of a total of 19 Regions and Autonomous Provinces (17+2) whose respective Statues or specific regional laws included provisions for such an institution: Abruzzo, Basilicata, Campania, Emilia-Romagna, Lazio, Liguria, Lombardy, Marche, Piedmont, Sardinia, Tuscany, Valle d'Aosta and Veneto (Ombudsperson for Human Rights, see this Part, Region of Veneto, VI), as well as the Autonomous Provinces of Bolzano and Trent. The post is currently vacant in Umbria (where a document for the establishment of a "Digital Ombudsman" was recently presented), while no Ombudsperson has ever been appointed in Calabria and Apulia. No legislative provision is made for the role by the Regions of Sicily and Trentino-Alto Adige (where, however, the Region has delegated full responsibility in their respective territories to the Ombudspersons of the Autonomous Provinces), while in Friuli-Venezia Giulia and Molise, the laws establishing this institution were abrogated in 2008 (r.l. 14 August 2008, No. 9) and 2013 (r.l. 20 December 2013, No. 25) respectively.

At European and international levels, the European Ombudsman Institute (EOI) Executive Committee in 2016 comprises: Lucia Franchini, Ombudsperson for the Region of Tuscany, Vittorio Gasparrini, Office of the Ombudsperson of the Region of Tuscany, Gabriele Morandell, Ombudsperson of the Autonomous Province of Bolzano, and Antonia Fiordelisi, Ombudsperson of the Region of Basilicata. Several regional and provincial ombudspersons are also members of the EOI (Abruzzo, Basilicata, Emilia-Romagna, Marche, Lombardy, Piedmont, Valle d'Aosta, Veneto, Bolzano, Trent, Rome, Milan and Massa Carrara).

The Ombudspersons of the autonomous Province of Bolzano and the Regions of Basilicata, Lombardy, Tuscany and Valle d'Aosta are members of the International Ombudsman Institute (IOI). The Ombudsman of Tuscany is also one of the representative of the European region in the IOI Executive Board.

## III. National Coordinating Body of Ombudspersons

The National Coordinating Body of Regional and Autonomous Provinces Ombudspersons is an associative body working to harmonise and enhance the institutional role of the Ombudsperson in Italy, and to guarantee every citizen, regardless of where he or she resides, protection in dealing with the public administration at all levels, whether State, regional or local.

The Coordinating Body is made up of the incumbent Ombudspersons in the Regions and the Autonomous Provinces. It operates through the office of the Ombudsperson collectively elected from time to time and its Headquarters are in Rome, at the Network of the Presidents of the Legislative Assemblies of the Regions and the Autonomous Provinces, where it usually meets. Between March 2013 and December 2016, the position of National Coordinator was held by Lucia Franchini, Ombudsperson for the Region of Tuscany. On 14 February 2017, the Coordinating Body elected the Ombudsperson of the Region of Abruzzo, Fabrizio di Carlo, as its new President.

The Coordinating Body met periodically during 2016. One of the main topics discussed during these meetings was the possibility of proposing an amendment to bill 1908 (Establishing a National Ombudsperson for Human Rights), presented by Senators Manconi and Mazzoni and currently being discussed in the Senate (in the "institutional affairs" commission). The amendment in question seeks to give greater prominence to regional ombudspersons and to transition from a "National Human Rights Ombudsperson" to having a true National Ombudsperson who acts as a link between ombudspersons across the Country and a new "Human Rights Commission" made up of at least 6–7 people, including representatives from civil society (associations and intellectuals), sectoral experts (children and prisoners) and the National Ombudsperson. Other issues discussed by the Coordinating Body concerned, among other things, the follow-up to the meeting between the Coordinator and the President of the Inter-ministerial Human Rights Commission CIDU of 16 December 2015 at the Ministry for Foreign Affairs; the Coordinating Body's proposals to consult the European Mediator on lobbying transparency; the new regulation from the National Authority for Electricity, Gas and the Water System; the role played by Ombudspersons in the health sector. At the time of writing this *2017 Yearbook*, the Coordinating Body's third periodic report on Ombudspersons in Italy had not yet been presented to Parliament.

In 2016, the Coordinating Body signed a Protocol for the protection of human rights, to overcome inequalities and to promote equal opportunities, with the National Conference of Presidents of Regional and Autonomous Provinces' Equal Opportunities Bodies. The aim of this Protocol is to promote a mutual exchange of useful information for carrying out their respective institutional functions, and to work together on the designing and implementation of joint information, training and consultancy meetings on the protection of human rights and on the role of equal opportunities and ombudspersons in the non-judicial protection of persons; to host public events to promote and raise awareness of the means of protection and promotion of rights, and the role Equal Opportunities Bodies and Ombudspersons can play in this context, to coordinate for hearings at the Parliamentary Commissions for legislative proposals and to make the Ombudspersons skills in investigating complaints and non-judicial conflict resolutions available to Equal Opportunities Bodies where necessary.

## IV. Network of Ombudspersons for Children and Adolescents

As of today, 18 Italian Regions and the Autonomous Provinces of Trent and Bolzano have approved legislation introducing a Ombudsperson for Children and Adolescents at a regional level. Ombudspersons have actually been nominated in 15 Regions (Apulia, Basilicata, Calabria, Campania, Emilia-Romagna, Friuli-Venezia Giulia, Lazio, Liguria, Lombardy, Marche, Tuscany, Umbria, Veneto) and in the Autonomous Provinces of Trent and Bolzano. Some of these are exclusively charged with ensuring rights for children and adolescents (Apulia, Basilicata, Calabria, Campania, Emilia-Romagna, Lazio, Lombardy, Tuscany, Umbria and the Autonomous Province of Bolzano), whereas others have additional competence in areas such as those dealt with by Ombudspersons and/or ensuring rights for persons whose personal freedom is restricted (Liguria, Marche, Friuli-Venezia Giulia, Veneto and the Autonomous Province of Trent).

The approval of l. 12 July 2011, No. 112 established the figure of Ombudsperson for Children and Adolescents at the national level (see this Part, National bodies with Jurisdiction over Human Rights, X) and formally defined and established the National Network for the Protection of the Rights of Children and Adolescents, made up of the Regional Ombudspersons for Children (or equivalent). The Network is charged with creating common lines of action to protect the rights of children and adolescents for regional and national Ombudspersons, to be promoted and supported at the international level. It is also charged with identifying ways of ensuring a constant exchange of data and information on the condition of minors living in Italy. The Network has drawn up a set of internal regulations governing its functioning.

The Network is chaired by the National Authority, and meets in Rome at least twice annually to discuss issues of common interest. The specific issues the Network discussed in 2016 were as follows: the system of protection for unaccompanied foreign minors; the selection, training and appointment of guardians for minors; the need to strengthen ombudspersons and their roles; whether the regional Ombudspersons and the national Ombudsperson should receive, from the Regions and from Parliament and the Government respectively, the texts of proposed legislation concerning the rights of minors, so that they can be in a position to express an opinion on their areas of expertise; the need for dialogue with the competent institutions to obtain data on the number of children affected by ADHD and ASD; the need to increase awareness of the new provisions of l. 173/2015 on the right to affective continuity for children in care and monitoring how these provisions are initially applied nationwide.

## V. National Coordinating Body of Local Authorities for Peace and Human Rights

Founded in 1986, the National Coordinating Body of Local Authorities for Peace and Human Rights brings together over 600 municipalities, provinces and regions involved in promoting peace, human rights, solidarity and international cooperation in Italy. In 2016, the Coordinating Body celebrated its 30th anniversary. Thousands of marches, events, meetings, conferences, conventions, courses, debates, gatherings, programmes, projects, missions and journeys took place; 30 years spent cultivating the idea that (1) peace is everyone's responsibility, (2) all institutions and people are responsible for contributing to building and defending peace, and (3) peace, like human rights, starts in towns and is built bottom-up. The Coordinating Body is chaired by Andrea Ferrari and directed by Flavio Lotti.

In celebration of its thirty years of intense political, institutional and cultural activity following in the footsteps of Giorgio La Pira, the Coordinating Body dedicated 2016 to promoting peace and human rights education, and to strengthening the commitment of citizens and institutions to peace. These joint efforts culminated in the organisation of a further Perugia-Assisi March for peace and fraternity, which was held on 9 October 2016. Over 100,000 young people, children, students, teachers, schools, groups, associations, local authorities and Regional governments from across the Country took part, in doing so contributing to the creation of a positive, peaceful and joyful atmosphere.

The March, accompanied by the slogan "*Ora tocca a te!*" ("Now it's up to you!"), was headed by 277 Mayors and representatives of local authorities and Regions which support the Coordinating Body. They were joined by 119 schools, 87 national associations and 354 local associations. A total of 837 organisations from 480 towns in 96 provinces took part. Thousands of students and teachers joined in the Perugia-Assisi event with readings, poems, placards, banners, music and dancing.

In preparation for the March and to denounce the violence and indifference surrounding many recent tragedies, the Coordinating Body and the Peace Roundtable organised an extraordinary PerugiAssisi event on 10 September 2016; this was a different march, held at night for the first time, following the path travelled by Aldo Capitini. This unprecedented gesture was a further stimulus for many people to be a part of it.

The Coordinating Body began the year's events in Senigallia (Ancona), with a training and research course entitles "Global Threats/Glocal Education", held on 8 and 9 January, 20 years after the founding of the Peace Roundtable. Over 250 teachers, school directors, local administrators and social workers from a hundred towns across Italy met to create new educational policies and teaching itineraries for responsible citizenship education.

Additionally, on 15 and 16 April, the Coordinating Body, along with the Franciscans of Assisi, the National Network of Schools for Peace and Human Rights and the Peace Roundtable, organised the 15th national Meeting of schools for peace, entitled "Peace, fraternity and dialogue. In the footsteps of Francis" in Assisi. 5,500 students, teachers, local administrators, journalists, academics, secular and religious spokespeople from a number of associations and experts from nineteen Regions across Italy took part in the Meeting.

Throughout the year, the Coordinating Body developed the programme "From the Great War to the Great Peace," launched in 2014 along with the Friuli Venezia Giulia Autonomous Region, the Regional Education Department and the Regional Coordinating Body of Local Authorities for Peace and Human rights. As part of this programme, the Coordinating Body held the teacher training and research programme "*La pace si insegna e si impara*" ("Peace can be taught and learnt"). A number of meetings were held between January and December: on 25 January the "Peace can be taught and learnt" meeting launching the programme was held in Udine; on 20 February in Zugliano (Udine), a seminar on "Understanding and explaining modern wars"; on 14 and 15 March in Udine, the training and research course "Teaching peace, today"; on 19 April in Monfalcone (Gorizia), the seminar "Is my school a place of peace?"; on 12 May in Pordenone, the seminar "The School and Municipality for a community of peace"; on 26 May in Udine, the final event of the regional project "An Atlas for peace"; on 31 May in Udine, "Peacebuilder" seminar, closing the programme; on 5 September in Udine, seminar "For young people. With young people"; on 24 October in Gorizia, meeting/conversation "Different perspectives on the Great War"; 22 November in Gorizia, a sung history lesson "One, none, six hundred thousand"; on 12 December in Udine, the first meeting of the Regional Working Group of teachers for education for peace and glocal citizenship.

Just before the start of the 2016–2017 school year, the Coordinating Body and the Peace Roundtable promoted the National Programme for education for peace and glocal citizenship "*Proteggiamo la nostra casa*" ("Let's protect our home"). The programme aims to prepare young people to face the big challenges of today by reflecting on the proposals in Pope Francis's Encyclical "Laudato Sì" and in the 2030 Agenda for Sustainable

Development promoted by the United Nations. The Programme will close on 5 and 6 May 2017 in Rome, with the national Meeting of Schools for peace "*Proteggiamo la nostra casa*".

## VI. Archives and Other Regional Projects for the Promotion of a Culture of Peace and Human Rights

Besides the "Pace Diritti Umani – Peace Human Rights" Archive of the Region of Veneto, established by r.l. 18/1988 and managed by the Human Rights Centre of the University of Padova (see this Part, Region of Veneto, IV), there are other more recent archives and similar projects set up by Italian Regions and Autonomous Provinces to foster the promotion and dissemination of a culture of human rights and peace.

The "Peace and Human Rights" project in the Region of Emilia-Romagna was set up by the Regional Council in collaboration with the Department for Social Policies, Immigration, Youth Projects and International Cooperation and the Regional Governments Management Control and Statistics Systems Department. This project, managed by the Europe Direct Centre of the Legislative Assembly of Emilia-Romagna, follows the principles laid out in r.l. 24 June 2002, No. 12 (Regional interventions for cooperation with developing countries and countries in transition, international solidarity and the promotion of a culture of peace), aims to support activities described in the law. Their website is at http:// www.paceediritti.it/.

During 2016 the Regional Service for European Policy and International Relations – International Cooperation, which has been associated with the project since 2013, continued to expand the website with news and information on projects in the Region's provinces, as well as on peace and international cooperation negotiation tables and publications of interest on the issues on which the project focuses and promoting access to the multimedia contents of "Diritti si Nasce – Conoscere i tuoi diritti è un dovere" ("Born with rights – knowing your rights is a duty"), a teaching kit on the themes of European citizenship and rights created by the Europe Direct Centre for teachers in the Region. Among the activities for 2016, the "Peace and Human Rights" Project launched two competitions: the Competition for the graduation prize "Communicating Europe Today" and "La Befana dell'Europa 2017" for preschool and elementary school pupils. Lastly, the Project promoted a number of initiatives to raise popular awareness of issues linked to the European Union, with a particular focus on the aims of the European Year of Citizens.

The "Forum Trentino per la pace e i diritti umani" (Trentino for Peace and Human Rights Forum), a standing body, was established in 1991 at the behest of the Provincial Council of Trent with p.l. 10 June 1991, No. 11 (Promotion and dissemination of the culture of peace). Its website is at http://www.forumpace.it/.

The theme for the year approved by the Forum assembly on 19 February 2016 was "Overcoming war, practices of hope and non-violent choices". In the ambit of this year-long path, the Forum focused its attention on possible alternatives to armed conflict and on the choices to be made, even on a day-to-day basis, to prevent conflict arising.

## Region of Veneto

The Region of Veneto has been operating organically for the promotion of human rights, the culture of peace and international cooperation, ever since 1988, the year when the first regional law on such issues was adopted in Italy (regional law 30 March 1988, No. 18). In 1999, regional law 18/1988 was replaced by the current r.l. 16 December 1999, No. 55, on "Regional measures for the promotion of human rights, a culture of pace, development cooperation and solidarity". With r.l. 24 December 2013, No. 37, the Region established the post of Regional Ombudsperson for the Rights of the Person which integrates the functions of the Ombudsperson, of the Ombudsperson for Children and Adolescents (both created in 1988), as well as those of promotion and protection of the rights of persons deprived of their liberty.

In the context of the Regional Government, issues concerning human rights pertain to the Councillor on Social Services, a post currently held by Manuela Lanzarin. Measures and activities concerning international relations and development cooperation are overseen directly by the Regional Governor, Luca Zaia.

In virtue of r.l. 55/1999, the Committee on Human Rights and the Culture of Peace (articles 12–13) and the Committee on Development Cooperation (articles 14–15) operate to fulfil their mandate of formulating three-year programmes and annual plans of implementation according to their respective areas of competence and intervention. In addition, the law promotes and supports the Regional Archive "Pace Diritti Umani – Peace Human Rights" (article 2), the Venice for Peace Research Foundation (article 17) (both established with r.l. 18/1988), the activities of the European Commission for Democracy through Law (Venice Commission) of the Council of Europe (article 19) and initiatives of decentralised cooperation promoted by the Ministry of Foreign Affairs and by the European Union (article 7). The regional infrastructure for peace and human rights is completed by the Commission for the Realisation of Equal Opportunities between Men and Women and the Regional Observatory for Immigration. Moreover, by way of r.l. 28 December 1998, No. 33, the Region promotes and supports financially the European Masters degree Programme in Human Rights and Democratisation (E.MA), located in Venice. With the adoption of r.l. 22 January 2010, No. 6, the Region has recognised the social and cultural value of fair trade, proclaiming its support for the organisations which operate in this sector. Finally, regional law 23 April 2013, No. 5 established a Regional

Coordination Table for Preventing and Combating the Violence against Women within the Regional Government.

## I. Department for International Relations, Communications and Sistar

Among other things, the Department is responsible for the implementation of r.l. 55/1999. During 2016, the Director managing this structure was Diego Vecchiato.

The Department oversees a series of international activities undertaken by the Region, including: the management of international relations; the signature of memoranda of understanding with national and foreign institutions; the participation in international bodies and initiatives; international solidarity; and all activities in the sectors of human rights, the culture of peace, the promotion of equal opportunities and the protection of linguistic minorities. The Department also hosts the Veneto Regional Committee for UNICEF.

In the specific area of promotion of human rights, the Department provides technical support to the Committee for human rights and the culture of peace; it oversees the organisation of events, takes part in the activities of the Council of Europe Venice Commission and fulfils the obligations deriving from the Regions promotion and financial support of the European Masters Programme in Human Rights and Democratisation (E.MA).

During 2016, the Region allocated 30,000 euro to fund 50 educational vouchers managed by 30 non-profit bodies in primary and secondary schools in the region, with a value of 600 euro each. The vouchers were introduced in 2014 to create opportunities for schools and associations in the region to meet and compare ideas on human rights issues.

## II. Committee for Human Rights and the Culture of Peace

Established pursuant to art. 12 of r.l. 55/1999, the Committee is charged with contributing to drawing up the three-year programmes and annual plans regarding initiatives promoted by the Region of Veneto on human rights and a culture of peace (art. 13). The Committee comprises representatives from local authorities, civil society, academia, the business world and social partners.

With Regional Council Decision No. 1859 of 25 November 2016, the Council adopted its new three-year programme for the period 2016–2018.

> The general aims of the programme include: confirming and consolidating the Region of Veneto's role as a reference point at an intra-regional level (by strengthening coordination networks which are already active in the region; stimulating information, promotion and sharing of best practices implemented by local actors in relation to human rights and culture pf peace; enhancing the educational and training aspects of the culture of human rights, while at the same time improving accessibility to and usability of human rights issues to all citizens and at all ages, as part of a holistic human rights education); consolidate the Region's role as a reference point in policies to promote human rights and the culture of peace at an extra-regional level, in particular by incentivising and supporting the candidature for financing of projects designed in the region as part of programmes to promote human rights and the culture of peace launched by the Italian Government, the European Union, or other international bodies; to give exposure to and support positive, innovative actions piloted in Veneto which implement a development model combining respect for human rights in a perspective of social, economic and environmental sustainability, and making them accessible outside of the region; by participating in national and inter-regional coordination tables on the promotion of human rights and a culture of peace. The main issues on which the Region wishes to focus during the next three years are: intercultural and inter-religious dialogue; giving value to diversity as a foundation for promoting peaceful coexistence, social cohesion, and to promote an inclusive society, with particular focus on the most vulnerable individuals and groups such as minors, the elderly, persons with disabilities, and the unemployed; active citizenship; the culture of non-discrimination and equal opportunities for all; the culture of peace and non-violent conflict resolution; corporate social responsibility for businesses and local authorities; and the rights of children and adolescents.

As part of this programme, the regional Council adopted its *2016 Annual Plan* to implement regional interventions to promote human rights and the culture of peace, with a total budget of 55,000 euro, in line with the previous year. This financing, in addition to assuring cover for the costs associated with the "Peace Human Rights" Archive, as per the provisions of r.l. 55/1999, also allowed the Region to grant 50 educational vouchers to promote human rights training in schools in Veneto (see this Part, 3.1). This aside, it was not possible to launch direct regional activities focused on human rights, or interventions financed by tender. Among the obligations provided for by r.l. 55/1999, the 2016 action plan confirms the Region's plans to award the Regional Prize "Veneto for peace and solidarity among peoples", and membership of the "Venice for Peace Research" Foundation. No financial allocation has been made for either of these initiatives.

## III. Committee for Development Cooperation

The Committee for Development Cooperation was established pursuant to art. 14 of r.l. 55/1999. The Committee is charged with contributing to the drafting of the three-year programmes and annual plans for decentralised development cooperation and international solidarity activities. The Committee comprises representatives from local administrations, civil society, academia, the business world and social partners.

With Regional Council Decision No. 1837 of 25 November 2016, the Council adopted its new three-year Programme on decentralised cooperation operations for development and international solidarity for the years 2016–2018. The regional programme will focus in particular on the following topics: promoting human and sustainable development, with actions seeking to use local resources to create self-development projects; protecting, safeguarding and enhancing the value of territories, their natural resources and environmental heritage, while at the same time improving settlement conditions in urban areas and promoting types of transition towards the "green economy"; strengthening the role of women with a view to social and economic promotion; protecting children, with actions seeking to ensure access to primary education, improving hygiene, health and dietary conditions, social inclusion and assistance to children and adolescents who have been victims of violence and in situations of social deprivation; strengthening democratic institutions and local administrations by giving support to decentralisation processes, supporting economic and institutional reforms and promoting forms of civil society participation and developing the fabric of the local economy; supporting the active role of migrants in co-development initiatives by strengthening relations with local institutions in countries which are beneficiaries of decentralised cooperation and promoting partnerships with migrant associations active in the region; greater integration and inter-relation between development cooperation activities and regional sectors involved in internationalisation activities, by promoting and fostering circularity which can benefit both the countries receiving aid and the home region. The priority geographical areas for intervention, in line with the Ministry of Foreign Affairs and International Cooperation "Three-year Planning Document 2015–2017", are Sub-Saharan Africa, the Mediterranean, and the Middle East.

As part of this three-year plan, the Council has adopted the Action Plan for the year 2016, for which 400,000 euro from the 2016 regional budget has been set aside for decentralised cooperation development interventions promoted by private bodies and groups. No direct regional activities are planned.

## IV. Regional Archive "Pace Diritti Umani – Peace Human Rights"

The Regional Archive was created pursuant to r.l. 18/1988 and reconfirmed by the subsequent r.l. 55/1999. The Archive is managed by the Human Rights Centre of the University of Padova, as laid down in art. 2 of the aforementioned law, which reads: "1. The Region promotes and supports: [ ] c) the Archive established by regional law 30 March 1988, No. 18, in cooperation with the Centre of Studies and Training on the Rights of Man and of Peoples of the University of Padova, according to a special agreement [...]". It is one of the main instruments through which the Region of Veneto promotes the culture of human rights, peace, development cooperation and solidarity in Italy and abroad.

The Archive works to collect, elaborate and publish documents, thematic databases and informational resources on topics regarding regional law 55/99, particularly through the regular updating of the portal "Archivio Pace Diritti Umani" (http://unipd-centrodirittiumani.it/en/), available in Italian and in English, and the distribution of knowledge on human rights through multi-media tools and social networks. In addition, it oversees publication of books, teaching aids, in-depth studies and multi-media, and offers technical and scientific support to the actors most closely involved in the promotion and practice of the culture of peace, especially as concerns initiatives promoted by teachers, education staff and schools. In 2016 the Archive published and distributed 18 editions of the "peace human rights" newsletter in Italian and in English to a long and qualified mailing list.

During 2016, the archive updated the databases available on its website, notably the Italian translation of the database of international legal instruments on human rights, humanitarian, criminal and refugee law; the University of Padova Human Rights Centre publications from 1982 to the present; and the associations and NGOs active in the field of human rights and development cooperation in Veneto. In addition to its usual activities of updating, providing in-depth studies and information, the Archive published several books and a number of editions *Human Rights Academic Voice*, in-depth articles by university professors on current issues involving human rights. The Archive also contributed to the publication and promotion of the 2016 edition of the *Italian Yearbook of Human Rights* in Italian and in English, and the institutional presentation of this publication at the Ministry of Foreign Affairs and International Cooperation.

Also during 2016, the Archive helped organise a series of events at the University of Padova, in collaboration with national and international organisations and experts, particularly as concerns the documentation and media side. Particularly noteworthy are the following:

- the presentation of the book *Mamme dentro. Figli di donne recluse: testimonianza, riflessioni e proposte* (Mothers on the inside. Children of women in prison: first-hand accounts, reflections and proposals) by Carla Forcolin (4 April 2016);
- the international conference "Religions and Human Rights" (14–15 April);
- the poetry reading and conversation with Neal Hall, "The poet of human rights" (20 April);
- the cycle of seminars "Music and Human Rights" organised in collaboration with the organisation Musicians for Human Rights (April-June);
- the international conference "Looking beyond the 50th Anniversary of the Covenants. What Interdependence and Indivisibility of Human Rights?" (13–14 December);
- performance of "*Noi, Diritti Umani*" ("We, Human Rights"), based on Antonio Papisca's stage play of the same name, with the participation of human rights students from the University of Padova (13 December).

## V. Venice for Peace Research Foundation

As was the Regional Archive, the Foundation was established by r.l. 18/1988, and reconfirmed by r.l. 55/1999. The Foundation's main goal is to carry out research, partly in collaboration with national and international institutions, on matters of security, development and peace.

During 2016, the Foundation continued to work on the *Blind Spots* project, carried out in collaboration with University Ca' Foscari of Venice, which aims to highlight the overlaps and common reference points between different environments and experiences of poets – as victims, witnesses or inheritors of crimes – and recurring themes concerning human rights abuses. In 2016, the Foundation also supported the publication of the third volume in the series "*Sapere L'Europa, Sapere d'Europa*" ("Knowing Europe, Knowing about Europe"), entitled "*Citizens of Europe. Culture e Diritti*" ("Citizens of Europe. Cultures and Rights") (edited by Lauso Zagato and Marilena Vecco).

## VI. Human Rights Authority

2016 was the first real year that the Human Rights Authority was in operation in Veneto. This Institution was provided for by regional law 24 December 2013, No. 37 (Regional Human Rights Authority), but was only implemented as of 16 June 2016, the date on which the full powers of the first Authority, appointed a few months previously, entered into force.

Reconstructing the timeline of important dates in the history of this Authority is certainly not an end in itself; the value of doing so can be appreciated most fully if this reconstruction is read in conjunction with the associated abolition of the two authorities which existed and operated until this point and which protected rights, i.e. the Ombudsperson and Public Guardian for Children and Adolescents in the Veneto Region.

Assigning what were hitherto fundamentally the responsibilities of the Regional Ombudsperson and the Public Guardian for Children and Adolescents to the Authority, while at the same time assigning (for the first time to an Authority in Veneto) the activities of promoting, protecting and facilitating the fulfilment of the rights of persons subject to restrictions to their personal freedom, meant that in the second half of 2015 was spent structuring the organisation of the Authority's support office and setting in motion the operation of an Institution with complex, comprehensive responsibilities, while at the same time seeking to ensure that open cases and ongoing projects from the former ombudsperson bodies were continued.

A more substantial exercise of all the functions was therefore achieved in 2016; both through actions and initiatives on some aspects cross-cutting the three different areas where the Authority is responsible for guaranteeing rights (i.e. the rights of physical or legal persons against public administrations; the promotion, protection and facilitating of the pursuit of rights for minors; the promotion, protection and facilitating of the pursuit of rights for persons subject to restrictions on their personal freedom), and through activities which involved those three same positions individually.

Among the various initiatives implemented which are common to the three different positions, the following are of note:

– participating, as a member, in institutionalised working and discussion group coordinating meetings between rights Ombudspersons equally competent in the area; i.e.: the National Conference for the Ombudspersons for Children and Adolescents, provided for by the law establishing the Ombudsperson for Children and Adolescents (art. 3 (7), law 12 July 2011, No. 112) and chaired by the Authority itself, as well as the working meetings between the National Ombudsperson for the Rights of Persons in Prison or Deprived of Liberty and equivalent territorial Ombudspersons created by the Regions and Autonomous Provinces as provided for in the legislative provisions which established the National Ombudsperson for the Rights of Persons in Prison or Deprived of Liberty (art. 7 "National Ombudsperson for the Rights of Persons in Prison or Deprived of Liberty" of l.d. 23 December 2013, No. 146 (Urgent measures concerning the protection of the fundamental rights of prisoners and the controlled reduction of the prison population), converted with l. 21 February 2014, No. 10);

- participating, as a member, in coordinating meetings between the Ombudspersons of the Regions and Autonomous Provinces of Trent and Bolzano;
- participating, as a member, in coordinating meetings of regional Ombudspersons for the Rights of Persons in Prison or Deprived of Liberty, a free and spontaneous association between regional, provincial and municipal Ombudspersons with similar functions;
- promoting, pursuant to art. 7(1)(h) of the law establishing the body, coordination, discussion and working meetings with regional Ombudspersons for the Rights of Persons with Restricted or Limited Liberty, which are established in some municipalities in Veneto;
- participating as a member in observatories, inter-institutional round tables, and committees established at a regional level;
- promoting targeted meetings with representatives from other regional Institutions, with a view to deepening mutual acquaintance and promoting the establishment of collaborative relationships on issues of common interest;
- participating (including as a rapporteur) in meetings, seminars, and round tables; these events all seek to gain an in-depth understanding of and promote debate on questions the Authority is already acting upon or on new emerging issues;
- providing information and consultancy, facilitating and mediating on public administration office procedures and activities as well as those of public service managers in the regional context, at the request of public or private entities.

These are the activities that, for the most part, allowed the Authority to carry out its institutional duties by adopting a "proactive" and "open-minded" approach, i.e. adopting operating modes which allowed it to focus its efforts for a more effective protection of human rights, both on aspects which can be controlled or redirected in advance (proactive approach) and on listening to new and different experiences, procedures, and potential solutions to emerging issues ("open-minded" approach).

These approaches can also be seen in initiatives implemented by the Veneto Human Rights Authority, which affected the various areas of activity differently, such as:

- promoting and running training courses which aim to train people who are suitable and prepared to take on the protection of minors, including with specific reference to the possible protection of unaccompanied foreign minors and applicants for international protection;
- joining European, national and local projects which seek to explore possible means of more effectively implementing the rights of minors, while at the same time identifying best practice;

- hosting the meeting "*La garanzia dei legami affettivi: un diritto dei bambini. Affido e adozione alla luce delle modifiche della legge n. 184/1983*" ("Guaranteeing emotional ties: a right of children. Fostering and adoption in light of the amendments to law No. 184/1983"), organised to promote discussion on the meanings taken on by the new prospects for fostering as well as on the contents and objectives of the training, assessment and support to be guaranteed to new foster/adoptive families in the interests of the minors themselves;
- the active role played by the Veneto Human Rights Authority in terms of consideration and contents in compiling the *Guidelines for managing procedures for processing reports by Ombudspersons of the Regions and Autonomous Provinces of Trent and Bolzano*, a document subsequently approved by the National Conference for the Rights of Children and Adolescents in January 2017;
- promoting and hosting information seminars at the various penal institutes in Veneto to encourage a new and different prison culture between people in prisons and prison workers, that is genuinely respectful of the dignity and fundamental human rights of detainees and genuinely focused on reintegrating prisoners into society, bearing in mind the conclusions reached by the States General of the Execution of Criminal Sentences. This initiative was shared within the Veneto Regional Coordinating Body of Ombudspersons for the Rights of Prisoners and carried out with the collaboration and participation of the Regional Department of Penal Administration (Ministry of Justice), and Managers of the penal institutions which hosted the seminars, as well as the different local Ombudspersons for detainees which are involved each time;
- being willing to promote and/or share places and opportunities to exchange and create a network of information, knowledge, skills and proposals designed to create synergies and effective responses protecting human rights.

Alongside initiatives taking a proactive approach to the protection human rights, the traditional activities, seen as complementary to the former, were also performed: accepting and managing reports, applications, complaints, and requests for consultancy or guidance in the field of protecting the rights of physical and legal persons against public administrations and activities promoting, protecting and facilitating the pursuit of rights for minors and the rights of persons subject to restricted personal liberty.

Furthermore, given that the Regional Human Rights Authority is a new institution, and after finding that users had difficulty identifying the new Authority as replacing the former – now abolished – institutions, the Human Rights Authority, working with Veneto Regional Council, promoted the information campaign "*Parlami dei miei diritti*" ("Talk to me about my rights"), in order to help the general public, and the various public bodies involved, to get to know the new Authority and the services it offers. It was launched at a press conference held in June at the Veneto Regional Council, attended by the President of the Council.

For this same purpose, a new approach to communications was organised through websites. This was launched in 2016 and will be implemented more fully throughout 2017.

## VII. Regional Commission for Equal Opportunities between Men and Women

The Commission was established by r.l 30 December 1987, No. 62, and it is the regional consultative body on gender policies for the actual implementation of the principles of equality and equal opportunities enshrined in the Constitution and Regional Statute. Regional Council Decision No. 802 of 27 May 2016 assigned the Commission to the Human Capital and Culture Department – Labour Directorate. In the Region's official bulletin No. 83 of 28 August 2015, notice was given of the proposed candidacy and designation of new members of the Commission; this has since been reconstituted by Decision of the President of the Regional Council No. 88 of 26 July 2016. The Commission's new Chair is Elena Traverso.

> The main function of the Commission is to carry out investigations and research into the condition of women in Veneto, with particular reference to issues involving employment, labour and professional training, and to disseminate information on these areas. At the same time, the Commission respects its commitment to being present on the ground and to developing new synergies with all the actors and forces involved to promote and support the realisation of equal opportunities in the social, political and economic life of the population of Veneto. It may offer opinions on the current state of implementation of laws and on bills, as well as drawing up proposals of its own. The Veneto Equal Opportunities Commission carries out its mission in contact with other Commissions at the local, regional and national level and maintains a constant exchange with all womens organisations in the region.

Among the activities of the reconstituted Commission for the remaining months of 2016, the publication of research on "*Città intelligenti in ottica di genere*" (Smart Cities from a Gender Perspective) is highlighted; promoted by the Commission itself and carried out by the Local Area Network Association, it sought to establish guidelines for planning and making towns in the region more liveable, as well as for the services it proposes to offer to local administrators, with a particular focus on the needs of female residents.

## VIII. Regional Observatory on Immigration

The Observatory is a service within the Region of Veneto "Migratory Flows" organisational unit and is managed by Veneto Lavoro. Its establishment was included in the three-year plan 2007–2009 comprising measures and initiatives in the field of immigration, and was confirmed in subsequent three-year plans, pursuant to article. 3 of r.l. 9/1990 (Measures in the immigration sector).

> The Observatory is a technical-scientific instrument aiming to monitor, analyse and disseminate data and information on migratory flows and integration at the regional and national level. To this end, it: collaborates with the other regional observatories which are affected in various ways by the migration phenomenon; assures the proper functioning and constant input for databases, the monitoring of immigration dynamics, further study on various thematic aspects, housing conditions, the social and educational integration of minors, schooling and training; it ensures updated reconnaissance of specialised laws, proposing training sessions to facilitate acquaintance with these laws and their correct implementation.

In December 2016, the Observatory published its 13th "Annual report on foreign migration to Veneto". The report presents a systematic analysis of data and trends in migratory flows in relation to certain aspects crucial for Veneto and for Italy as a whole, such as demographic dynamics, employment and unemployment figures, and the presence of young foreigners in the regional school system.

In general terms, the statistical data presented in the report show that the number of foreign citizens, resident in Veneto as of 31 December 2015 was 497,291, constituting 9.9% of the total number of foreigners in Italy. This represents a significant fall of over 13,600 people compared to the figures for the previous year (511,558, representing 10.4% of the national total). Compared to the other Italian regions, Veneto has the fourth highest number of foreign residents (after Lombardy, Lazio and Emilia-Romagna). The total percentage of foreigners within the regional population is 10% (at the end of 2014, it was 10.4%), giving Veneto the sixth-highest percentage after Emilia-Romagna, Lombardy, Lazio, Umbria and Tuscany. The Provinces with the highest percentage of foreigners are Verona (11.6%), Treviso (10.7%), Padova (10.2%) and Vicenza (10.1%). The number of foreign nationals in municipal registers who have gained Italian citizenship has continued to grow strongly compared with previous years (14,592 in 2013; 20,331 in 2014), reaching a total of 25,8021, equivalent to 14.5% of the total citizenships granted on a national level (around 180,000). The main countries of origin of resident foreign citizens as of 31 December are Romania (23.5%), Morocco (10%), the

Republic of Moldova (7.5%), Albania (7.4%) and China (6.6%). As of 1 January 2016, the largest number of residence permits in Veneto were held by foreigners from Morocco (63,426), China (42,551), Albania (40,394) and the Republic of Moldova (37,886).

# Part III

## Italy in Dialogue with International Human Rights Institutions

# The United Nations System

## I. General Assembly

The General Assembly, which is the main deliberative body of the United Nations, comprises six Committees, each of which is made up of all 193 United Nations Member States. Human rights issues are handled mainly within the Third Committee (the Social, Humanitarian and Cultural Committee). The responsibilities of this Committee include issues such as torture and other cruel, inhuman and degrading treatment or punishment; the advancement of women; the rights of refugees and displaced persons; the promotion and protection of the rights of children; the rights of indigenous peoples; the elimination of racism, racial discrimination, xenophobia and related intolerance; the right of peoples to self-determination; and social development.

In December 2016, the 71st General Assembly adopted 50 human rights resolutions (of which 35 by consensus) which had been debated and approved by the Third Committee during October and November, on a wide range of issues, from the rights of migrants to the right to privacy in the digital age, from protection from discrimination based on sexual orientation and gender identity to country-specific situations. Of particular interest was the GA's December 19 2016 approval, as recommended by the Human Rights Council (July 1 2016) of the "Declaration on the right to peace", thus granting formal recognition of the "right to enjoy peace" as a fundamental right of every human being (131 votes in favour, 34 against and 19 abstentions). This act aims to provide further detail as to the content of the "entitlement to a social and international order in which the rights and fundamental freedoms set forth in this Declaration can be fully realized", as stated in art. 28 of the Universal Declaration of Human Rights.

In 2016 Italy's Permanent Representative to the United Nations in New York was Ambassador Sebastiano Cardi; the Deputy Permanent Representative was Ambassador Inigo Lambertini; Emilia Gatto was responsible for following the activities of the Third Committee. The chart below shows the most significant interventions by the Italian delegation and Government representatives in General Assembly meetings in 2016.

| Date | Event | Speaker |
|---|---|---|
| 11/01/2016 | Plenary of the GA marking the 70th anniversary of the first meeting of the United Nations General Assembly | H.E. Amb. Cardi (representing the countries in the Western Group) |
| 3/02/2016 | GA meeting on the question of Equitable Representation on and Increase in the Membership of the Security Council | H.E. Amb. Cardi (representing the "Uniting for Consensus" Group) |
| 16/02/2016 | 86th Plenary Meeting of the GA on "Culture of Peace: the Global Counter-Terrorism Strategy of the United Nations" | H.E. Amb. Cardi |
| 22/02/2016 | Meeting of the GA on the question of Equitable Representation on and Increase in the Membership of the Security Council | H.E. Amb. Cardi (representing the "Uniting for Consensus" Group) |
| 9/03/2016 | Meeting of the GA on the question of Equitable Representation on and Increase in the Membership of the Security Council | H.E. Amb. Cardi (representing the "Uniting for Consensus" Group) |
| 8/04/2016 | Informal meeting of the GA on "Humanitarian Response in Africa: the Urgency to Act" | H.E. Amb. Cardi |
| 18/04/2016 | Side Event of the GA Special Session "The World Drug Problem: Effective Drugs Policies without the Death Penalty" | H.E. Amb. Lambertini |
| 20/04/2016 | Special Session of the GA on The World Drug Problem | The Minister of Justice, hon. Andrea Orlando, at Roundtable 3 "Cross-cutting issues: drugs and human rights, youth, women, children and communities" |
| 20/04/2016 | Special Plenary Session of the GA on the World Drug Problem | The Minister of Justice, hon. Andrea Orlando |
| 20/04/2016 | Special Session of the GA on The World Drug Problem | The Minister of Justice, hon. Andrea Orlando at the Side Event "Drug Use and Women: Best Practices in the Design and Implementation of Programmes and Public Policies for Prevention and Treatment with a Gender Approach". |

| Date | Event | Speaker |
|---|---|---|
| 21/04/2016 | Special Session of the GA on The World Drug Problem | The Minister of Justice, hon. Andrea Orlando at Roundtable 4: "Cross-cutting issues: new challenges, threats and realities in preventing and addressing the world drug problem in compliance with relevant international law, including the three drug control conventions; strengthening the principle of common and shared responsibility and international cooperation" |
| 21/04/2016 | High-Level Debate on the Sustainable Development Objectives | Italian Prime Minister Matteo Renzi |
| 27/04/2016 | GA Meeting on the adoption of the resolution "Revision of the UN Peacebuilding Architecture" | H.E. Amb. Lambertini |
| 2/05/2016 | Meeting of the GA on the question of Equitable Representation on and Increase in the Membership of the Security Council | H.E. Amb. Cardi (representing the "Uniting for Consensus" Group) |
| 4/05/2016 | Informal meeting of the GA – Secretary-General's Report on Refugees and Migrants | H.E. Amb. Lambertini |
| 6/05/2016 | GA Meeting "High-Level Conversation on Religions for Peace" | H.E. Amb. Cardi |
| 9/06/2016 | Plenary Session of the GA High-Level meeting on HIV/AIDS | Deputy Minister for Foreign Affairs and International Cooperation, Mario Giro |
| 14/06/2016 | General Debate of the 9th Session of States Party to the Convention on the Rights of Persons with Disabilities | H.E. Amb. Cardi |
| 15/06/2016 | 9th Session of States Party to the Convention on the Rights of Persons with Disabilities | H.E. Amb. Cardi, at the Side Event "Mental health in the context of 2030 Agenda. Moving from global commitment to local action" |
| 22/06/2016 | Meeting of the GA on the question of Equitable Representation on and Increase in the Membership of the Security Council | H.E. Amb. Cardi (representing the "Uniting for Consensus" Group) |

| Date | Event | Speaker |
|---|---|---|
| 13/07/2016 | High-level thematic debate "UN@70 – Human Rights at the Centre of the Global Agenda" | H.E. Amb. Cardi |
| 27/07/2016 | Meeting of the GA on the question of Equitable Representation on and Increase in the Membership of the Security Council | H.E. Amb. Lambertini (representing the "Uniting for Consensus" Group) |
| 1/09/2016 | High-Level Forum on the Culture of Peace | H.E. Amb. Lambertini |
| 7/09/2016 | Plenary Meeting on Strengthening of the United Nations System – Sexual Exploitation and Abuse | H.E. Amb. Lambertini |
| 19/09/2016 | United Nations Summit on Refugees and Migrants | Minister for Foreign Affairs and International Cooperation, hon. Paolo Gentiloni |
| 20/09/2016 | Opening of the General Debate at the 71st Session of the GA | Italian Prime Minister, Matteo Renzi |
| 21/09/2016 | High-Level Event on "Moving Away from the Death Penalty: The Voices of Victims' Families" | Minister for Foreign Affairs and International Cooperation, hon. Paolo Gentiloni |
| 5/10/2016 | 71st GA, General Debate of the First Committee | H.E. Amb. Vinicio Mati, Permanent Representative of Italy to the Conference on Disarmament |
| 5/10/2016 | 71st GA Meeting of the Third Committee on Social Development | H.E. Amb. Lambertini |
| 6/10/2016 | 71st GA Meeting of the Third Committee on Crime Prevention and Criminal Justice | H.E. Amb. Lambertini |
| 10/10/2016 | 71st GA Meeting of the Third Committee on the Advancement of Women | H.E. Amb. Lambertini |
| 17/10/2016 | 71st GA Meeting of the First Committee on Nuclear Weapons | H.E. Amb. Vinicio Mati, Permanent Representative of Italy to the Conference on Disarmament |
| 17/10/2016 | 71st GA Meeting of the First Committee on Weapons of Mass Destruction | H.E. Amb. Vinicio Mati, Permanent Representative of Italy to the Conference on Disarmament |

| Date | Event | Speaker |
|---|---|---|
| 18/10/2016 | 71st GA Meeting of the First Committee on Outer Space | H.E. Amb. Vinicio Mati, Permanent Representative of Italy to the Conference on Disarmament |
| 20/10/2016 | Informal Meeting of the Plenary with the Secretary-General-Designate, Antonio Guterres | H.E. Amb. Cardi |
| 21/10/2016 | 71st GA Meeting of the First Committee on Conventional Weapons | Deputy Permanent Representative of Italy to the Conference on Disarmament, Palma D'Ambrosio |
| 24/10/2016 | 71st GA Meeting of the First Committee on Other Disarmament Measures | Deputy Permanent Representative of Italy to the Conference on Disarmament, Palma D'Ambrosio |
| 26/10/2016 | 71st GA Meeting of the Sixth Committee on the UN International Law Commission's Report | Director for International Legal Affairs, Min. Plen. Andrea Tiriticco |
| 27/10/2016 | 71st GA, Meeting on the International Court of Justice Report | Director for International Legal Affairs, Min. Plen. Andrea Tiriticco |
| 31/10/2016 | 71st GA Meeting on the Report of the International Criminal Court | H.E. Amb. Cardi |
| 7/11/2016 | Meeting of the GA on the question of Equitable Representation on and Increase in the Membership of the Security Council | H.E. Amb. Cardi (representing the "Uniting for Consensus" Group) |
| 17/11/2016 | 71st GA Meeting on the Situation in Afghanistan | H.E. Amb. Lambertini |
| 22/11/2016 | 71st GA, Third Committee | Min. Plen. Gatto, on the Draft Resolutions A/C.3/71/L.11/Rev.1 and A/C.3/71/L.12/Rev.1 "Crime Prevention and Criminal Justice" |

Source: Italy's permanent mission to the United Nations in New York.

## A. Resolutions on Human Rights – Italy's Voting Behaviour

As in the past, again in 2016 Italy's action in support of human rights prioritised the following thematic areas: promotion of the rule of law and strengthening of democracy; the fight against torture, xenophobia, racism and all forms of discrimination, with special attention to religious discrimination and intolerance; the rights and protection of children; the abolition of the death penalty; combating violence against women and female genital mutilation.

More specifically, Italy presented the resolution Strengthening the United Nations crime prevention and criminal justice programme, in particular its technical cooperation capacity (A/RES/71/209), adopted by consensus.

In addition, Italy sponsored 31 resolutions and was asked to pass an open vote on 15 resolutions (7 votes in favour, 4 against and 4 abstentions), the outcome of which is shown below.

| Subject | Resolution | Main Sponsor of the Resolution | Information regarding Italy | Outcome of the plenary vote |
|---|---|---|---|---|
| Social Development | A/RES/71/162 Implementation of the outcome of the World Summit for Social Development and of the twenty-fourth special session of the General Assembly | Thailand, China | Co-sponsor of the resolution | Adopted without a vote |
| | A/RES/71/164 Follow-up to the Second World Assembly on Ageing | Thailand, China | Co-sponsor of the resolution | Adopted without a vote |
| | A/RES/71/165 Inclusive development for persons with disabilities | Argentina *et al.* | Co-sponsor of the resolution | Adopted without a vote |
| | A/RES/71/166 Literacy for life: shaping future agendas | Mongolia | Co-sponsor of the resolution | Adopted without a vote |

| Subject | Resolution | Main Sponsor of the Resolution | Information regarding Italy | Outcome of the plenary vote |
|---|---|---|---|---|
| Advancement of Women | A/RES/71/167 Trafficking in women and girls | Argentina *et al.* | Co-sponsor of the resolution | Adopted without a vote |
| | A/RES/71/168 Intensifying global efforts for the elimination of female genital mutilation | Burkina Faso | Co-sponsor of the resolution | Adopted without a vote |
| | A/RES/71/169 Intensification of efforts to end obstetric fistula | Senegal | Co-sponsor of the resolution | Adopted without a vote |
| | A/RES/71/170 Intensification of efforts to prevent and eliminate all forms of violence against women and girls: domestic violence | Armenia *et al.* | Co-sponsor of the resolution | Adopted without a vote |
| Refugees, displaced persons and humanitarian issues | A/RES/71/172 Office of the United Nations High Commissioner for Refugees | Austria *et al.* | Co-sponsor of the resolution | Adopted without a vote |
| Report of the Human Rights Council | A/RES/71/174 Report of the Human Rights Council | Botswana | Abstained | 106 in favour, 2 against, 74 abstentions |
| Promotion and protection of the rights of children | A/RES/71/175 Child, early and forced marriage | Canada, Iceland, Mongolia, Netherlands, Peru, United Kingdom, Zambia | Co-sponsor of the resolution | Adopted without a vote |
| | A/RES/71/176 Protecting children from bullying | Armenia *et al.* | Co-sponsor of the resolution | Adopted without a vote |
| | A/RES/71/177 Rights of the child | Albania *et al.* | Co-sponsor of the resolution | Adopted without a vote |

| Subject | Resolution | Main Sponsor of the Resolution | Information regarding Italy | Outcome of the plenary vote |
|---|---|---|---|---|
| Rights of indigenous peoples | A/RES/71/178 Rights of indigenous peoples | Argentina *et al.* | Co-sponsor of the resolution | Adopted without a vote |
| Elimination of racism, racial discrimination, xenophobia and related intolerance | A/RES/71/179 Combating glorification of Nazism, neo-Nazism and other practices that contribute to fuelling contemporary forms of racism, racial discrimination, xenophobia and related intolerance | Russian Federation | Abstained | 136 in favour, 2 against, 49 abstentions |
| | A/RES/71/180 International Convention on the Elimination of All Forms of Racial Discrimination | Armenia *et al.* | Co-sponsor of the resolution | Adopted without a vote |
| | A/RES/71/181 A global call for concrete action for the total elimination of racism, racial discrimination, xenophobia and related intolerance and the comprehensive implementation of and follow-up to the Durban Declaration and Programme of Action | Thailand, China | Abstained | 133 in favour, 9 against, 45 abstentions |

| Subject | Resolution | Main Sponsor of the Resolution | Information regarding Italy | Outcome of the plenary vote |
|---|---|---|---|---|
| The right of peoples to self-determination | A/RES/71/182 Use of mercenaries as a means of violating human rights and impeding the exercise of the right of peoples to self determination | Algeria *et al.* | Voted against | 132 in favour, 53 against, 4 abstentions |
| | A/RES/71/184 The right of the Palestinian people to self-determination | Egypt | Co-sponsor of the resolution. Voted in favour | 177 in favour, 7 against, 4 abstentions |
| Implementation of human rights instruments | A/RES/71/185 Human rights treaty body system | Australia *et al.* | Co-sponsor of the resolution | Adopted without a vote |
| Human rights questions, including alternative approaches to improve the effective enjoyment of human rights and fundamental freedoms | A/RES/71/186 Human rights and extreme poverty | Peru | Co-sponsor of the resolution | Adopted without a vote |
| | A/RES/71/187 Moratorium on the use of the death penalty | Mongolia | Co-sponsor of the resolution Voted in favour | 117 in favour, 40 against, 31 abstentions |
| | A/RES/71/188 Human rights in the administration of justice | Armenia *et al.* | Co-sponsor of the resolution | Adopted without a vote |
| | A/RES/71/189 Declaration on the Right to Peace | Cuba | Abstained | 131 in favour, 34 against, 19 abstentions |
| | A/RES/71/190 Promotion of a democratic and equitable international order | Cuba | Voted against | 130 in favour, 53 against, 6 abstentions |
| | A/RES/71/191 The right to food | Cuba | Co-sponsor of the resolution | Adopted without a vote |

| Subject | Resolution | Main Sponsor of the Resolution | Information regarding Italy | Outcome of the plenary vote |
|---|---|---|---|---|
| | A/RES/71/192 The right to development | Cuba and China | Voted in favour | 146 in favour, 3 against, 39 abstentions |
| | A/RES/71/193 Human rights and unilateral coercive measures | Cuba and China | Voted against | 133 in favour, 54 against, no abstentions |
| | A/RES/71/196 Freedom of Religion or belief | Albania *et al.* | Co-sponsor of the resolution | Adopted without a vote |
| | A/RES/71/197 Globalization and its impact on the full enjoyment of all human rights | Egypt | Voted against | 135 in favour, 53 against, 1 abstention |
| | A/RES/71/198 Extrajudicial, summary or arbitrary executions | Albania *et al.* | Co-sponsor of the resolution Voted in favour | 125 in favour, 2 against, 56 abstentions |
| | A/RES/71/199 The right to privacy in the digital age | Albania *et al.* | Co-sponsor of the resolution | Adopted without a vote |
| | A/RES/71/200 The role of the Ombudsman, mediator and other national human rights institutions in the promotion and protection of human rights | Australia *et al.* | Co-sponsor of the resolution | Adopted without a vote |
| | A/RES/71/201 Missing persons | Azerbaijan | Co-sponsor of the resolution | Adopted without a vote |

| Subject | Resolution | Main Sponsor of the Resolution | Information regarding Italy | Outcome of the plenary vote |
|---|---|---|---|---|
| Human rights situations and reports by Special Rapporteurs and Representatives | A/RES/71/202 Situation of human rights in the Democratic People's Republic of Korea | Andorra *et al.* | Co-sponsor of the resolution | Adopted without a vote |
| | A/RES/71/203 Situation of human rights in the Syrian Arab Republic | Qatar | Co-sponsor of the resolution Voted in favour | 116 in favour, 16 against, 52 abstentions |
| | A/RES/71/204 Situation of human rights in the Islamic Republic of Iran | Canada | Co-sponsor of the resolution Voted in favour | 85 in favour, 35 against, 63 abstentions |
| | A/RES/71/205 Situation of human rights in the Autonomous Republic of Crimea and the city of Sevastopol (Ukraine) | Ukraine | Co-sponsor of the resolution Voted in favour | 70 in favour, 26 against, 77 abstentions |
| Crime prevention and criminal justice | A/RES/71/207 United Nations African Institute for the Prevention of Crime and the Treatment of Offenders | Uganda | Co-sponsor of the resolution | Adopted without a vote |
| | A/RES/71/208 Preventing and combating corrupt practices and the transfer of proceeds of corruption, facilitating asset recovery and returning such assets to legitimate owners, in particular to countries of origin, in accordance with the United Nations Convention against Corruption | Argentina, Botswana, Brazil, Colombia, Costa Rica, Mexico, Thailand | Co-sponsor of the resolution | Adopted without a vote |

Source: United Nations, General Assembly.

## II. Human Rights Council

The Human Rights Council is the subsidiary body of the General Assembly responsible for promoting worldwide respect of all human rights and fundamental freedoms for all, without distinction of any kind.

> Established in 2006 under resolution 60/251, the Council is an intergovernmental body made up of 47 United Nations Member States elected by the General Assembly for an initial period of three years, extendable for not more than two consecutive terms. It meets in Geneva, usually in three ordinary sessions per year, for an overall period of at least ten working weeks. Furthermore, although it is a body of Government representatives, the Council is open to the contributions of nongovernmental organisations which enjoy advisory status with the ECOSOC, which may participate in the meetings and submit written documents.
>
> The Council has established several different "mechanisms" for monitoring human rights (resolution A/HRC/RES/5/1 of June 2007), including: the Universal Periodic Review (UPR), the Special Procedures (which include mandates by Country and thematic mandates), the Advisory Committee and a Complaints Procedure.

In 2016, the Council held:

- three ordinary sessions: the 31st (29 February - 24 March); the 32nd (13 June - 1 July); and the 33rd (13–30 September);
- two special sessions: on the deteriorating human rights situation in Syria and the recent situation in Aleppo (25th session, 21 October); and on the human rights situation in South Sudan (26th session, 14 December);
- three UPR sessions: the 24th (18-29 January); the 25th (2-13 May); and the 26th (31 October - 11 November).

In 2016, Italy was represented on the Human Rights Council by H.E. Amb. Maurizio Enrico Serra, Permanent Representative of Italy to the International Organisations in Geneva, by the First Counsellors Cristina Carenza and Daniela d'Orlandi, and by Maja Bova, specialist at the Ministry of Foreign Affairs. Listed below are the main interventions by the Italian mission in 2016.

| Date | Event | Intervention |
|---|---|---|
| 2/03/2016 | 31st session of the Human Rights Council | Benedetto della Vedova, Under-secretary of State – Ministry of Foreign Affairs, at the high-level segment |
| 8/03/2016 | 31st session of the Human Rights Council | H.E. Amb. Serra, at the interactive dialogue with the Special Rapporteur on Torture |
| 13/06/2016 | 32nd session of the Human Rights Council | H.E. Amb. Serra, at the opening session |
| 16/06/2016 | 32nd session of the Human Rights Council | H.E. Amb. Serra, at the interactive dialogue on violence against women and gender discrimination |
| 17/06/2016 | 32nd session of the Human Rights Council | H.E. Amb. Serra, at the interactive dialogue on the right to education and on the right to peaceful association and assembly |
| 13/09/2016 | 33rd session of the Human Rights Council | H.E. Amb. Serra, at the opening session |
| 14/09/2016 | 33rd session of the Human Rights Council | H.E. Amb. Serra, at the High-level panel discussion five years after the adoption of the United Nations Declaration on Human Rights Education and Training |
| 15/09/2016 | 33rd session of the Human Rights Council | Maja Bova, at the dialogue on the human rights of older persons |
| 16/09/2016 | 33rd session of the Human Rights Council | H.E. Amb. Serra, at the general debate on the promotion and protection of all human rights, civil, political, economic, social and cultural rights, including the right to development |
| 20/09/2016 | 33rd session of the Human Rights Council | H.E. Amb. Serra, at the interactive dialogue with the Consultative Committee of the Human Rights Council |
| 21/09/2016 | 33rd session of the Human Rights Council | Maja Bova, at the Universal Periodic Review of Greece and Sudan |
| 22/09/2016 | 33rd session of the Human Rights Council | Maja Bova, at the panel discussion on youth and human rights |
| 26/09/2016 | 33rd session of the Human Rights Council | First Counsellor Cristina Carenza, at the Annual discussion on the integration of a gender perspective throughout the work of the Human Rights Council and that of its mechanisms |

| Date | Event | Intervention |
|---|---|---|
| 26/09/2016 | 33rd session of the Human Rights Council | First Counsellor Daniela d'Orlandi, at the interactive dialogue with the UN Working Group of Experts on People of African Descent |
| 27/09/2016 | 33rd session of the Human Rights Council | First Counsellor Daniela d'Orlandi, at the interactive dialogue on the human rights situation in Libya |
| 28/09/2016 | 33rd session of the Human Rights Council | First Counsellor Daniela d'Orlandi, at the interactive dialogue on the human rights situation in Somalia |
| 5/10/2016 | Social Forum | H.E. Amb. Serra, at the side event "Human Rights and SDGs: Monitoring and Mutual Reinforcement" |

Source: Italy's permanent mission to the United Nations in Geneva.

## A. Italy's Behaviour at the Human Rights Council in 2016

In 2016, Italy participated in the three ordinary sessions of the Human Rights Council as an Observer State (hence, without the right to vote).

Over the course of 2016, the Human Rights Council adopted 100 resolutions (+ 12 compared to 2015), distributed as follows: 37 resolutions during the 31st session; 33 during the 32nd session; and 30 during the 33rd session. Special mention is made of the fact that in the course of the 32nd session, the Council adopted the Declaration on the Right to Peace (A/HRC/RES/32/28), which was not sponsored by Italy, with 34 votes in favour, 9 against and 4 abstentions.

Of these resolutions, 69 were adopted with the consensus of all Member States, whereas a majority vote by Council members was necessary for the remaining 31, showing a slightly lower level of disagreement than in the previous year, when majority voting was required for 36% of the resolutions adopted.

The following paragraphs aim to analyse Italy's behaviour at the Human Rights Council in 2016, with a special focus on Italy's diplomatic efforts in the negotiation and presentation of resolutions.

On this issue, 65% of the resolutions adopted by the Council were negotiated with the direct participation (sponsoring) or with diplomatic support (co-sponsoring) from Italy. Indeed, of the 100 resolutions adopted, Italy sponsored 11 (as compared to the 12 of 2015) and co-sponsored 54 (39 in 2015). Three of the 11 resolutions sponsored by Italy are of a thematic nature and refer to the rights of children, to education and training on human rights and to youth and human rights. The remaining eight resolutions are on the human rights situations in Syria, The People's Democratic Republic of Korea, Myanmar, Burundi and Belarus.

The table below summarises the resolutions approved by the Council in 2016 and shows that, of the resolutions sponsored and co-sponsored by Italy, the Council adopted 77% by consensus and 23% by a majority vote.

**Human Rights Council – resolutions sponsored by Italy in 2016**

| Resolution | Other sponsors of the resolution | Outcome of the voting process |
|---|---|---|
| A/HRC/RES/31/7<br>Rights of the child: information and communications technologies and child sexual exploitation | Netherlands and Uruguay | Adopted without a vote |
| A/HRC/RES/31/17<br>The human rights situation in the Syrian Arab Republic | United Kingdom | 27 in favour, 6 against, 14 abstentions |
| A/HRC/RES/31/18<br>Situation of human rights in the Democratic People's Republic of Korea | Japan and Netherlands | Adopted without a vote |
| A/HRC/RES/31/21<br>Human rights education and training | Morocco | Adopted without a vote |
| A/HRC/RES/31/24<br>Situation of human rights in Myanmar | Netherlands | Adopted without a vote |
| A/HRC/RES/32/1<br>Youth and human rights | El Salvador, Portugal, Republic of Moldova | Adopted without a vote |
| A/HRC/RES/32/25<br>Situation of human rights in the Syrian Arab Republic | United Kingdom | 27 in favour, 6 against, 14 abstentions |
| A/HRC/RES/32/26<br>Situation of human rights in Belarus | Netherlands | 15 in favour, 9 against and 23 abstentions |
| A/HRC/RES/33/17<br>Assistance to Somalia in the field of human rights | United Kingdom | Adopted without a vote |
| A/HRC/RES/33/23<br>Situation of human rights in the Syrian Arab Republic | United Kingdom | 26 in favour, 7 against, 14 abstentions |
| A/HRC/RES/33/24<br>Situation of human rights in Burundi | Slovakia | 19 in favour, 7 against, 21 abstentions |

Source: United Nations, Human Rights Council.

## Human Rights Council: resolutions co-sponsored by Italy in 2016

| Resolution | Sponsor(s) of the Resolution | Outcome of the voting process |
|---|---|---|
| **31st session (29 February-24 March)** | | |
| A/HRC/RES/31/3<br>Protection of human rights and fundamental freedoms while countering terrorism: mandate of the Special Rapporteur on the promotion and protection of human rights and fundamental freedoms while countering terrorism | Mexico | Adopted without a vote |
| A/HRC/RES/31/5<br>Question of the realization in all countries of economic, social and cultural rights | Portugal | Adopted without a vote |
| A/HRC/RES/31/6<br>The rights of persons with disabilities in situations of risk and humanitarian emergencies | Mexico and New Zealand | Adopted without a vote |
| A/HRC/RES/31/8<br>Human rights and the environment | Costa Rica, Maldives, Slovenia | Adopted without a vote |
| A/HRC/RES/31/9<br>Adequate housing as a component of the right to an adequate standard of living, and the right to non-discrimination in this context | Finland | Adopted without a vote |
| A/HRC/RES/31/10<br>The right to food | Cuba | Adopted without a vote |
| A/HRC/RES/31/12<br>Promotion of the enjoyment of the cultural rights of everyone and respect for cultural diversity | Cuba | Adopted without a vote |
| A/HRC/RES/31/13<br>Rights of persons belonging to national or ethnic, religious and linguistic minorities | Austria | Adopted without a vote |
| A/HRC/RES/31/14<br>The role of good governance in the promotion and protection of human rights | Poland | Adopted without a vote |

| Resolution | Sponsor(s) of the Resolution | Outcome of the voting process |
|---|---|---|
| A/HRC/RES/31/15<br>The right to work | Egypt and Greece | Adopted without a vote |
| A/HRC/RES/31/16<br>Freedom of religion or belief | Netherlands | Adopted without a vote |
| A/HRC/RES/31/19<br>Situation of human rights in Iran | Sweden | 20 in favour, 15 against, 11 abstentions |
| A/HRC/RES/31/20<br>Situation of human rights in South Sudan | Albania, Paraguay, USA | Adopted without a vote |
| A/HRC/RES/31/23<br>Promoting human rights through sport and the Olympic ideal | Greece | Adopted without a vote |
| A/HRC/RES/31/27<br>Technical assistance and capacity-building to improve human rights in Libya | South Africa | Adopted without a vote |
| A/HRC/RES/31/28<br>Technical assistance and capacity-building for Mali in the field of human rights | South Africa | Adopted without a vote |
| A/HRC/RES/31/29<br>Strengthening technical cooperation and advisory services for Guinea | South Africa | Adopted without a vote |
| A/HRC/RES/31/31<br>Torture and other cruel, inhuman or degrading treatment or punishment: safeguards to prevent torture during police custody and pre-trial detention | Denmark | Adopted without a vote |
| A/HRC/RES/31/32<br>Protecting human rights defenders, whether individuals, groups or organs of society, addressing economic, social and cultural rights | Norway | 33 votes in favour, 6 against, 8 abstentions |
| A/HRC/RES/31/37<br>The promotion and protection of human rights in the context of peaceful protests | Costa Rica, Switzerland, Turkey | 31 votes in favour, 5 against, 10 abstentions |

| Resolution | Sponsor(s) of the Resolution | Outcome of the voting process |
|---|---|---|
| **32nd session (13 June-1 July)** | | |
| A/HRC/RES/32/2<br>Protection against violence and discrimination based on sexual orientation and gender identity | Chile, Brazil and Uruguay | 23 votes in favour, 18 against, 6 abstentions |
| A/HRC/RES/32/3<br>Trafficking in persons, especially women and children: protecting victims of trafficking and persons at risk of trafficking, especially women and children in conflict and post-conflict situations | Philippines | Adopted without a vote |
| A/HRC/RES/32/4<br>Elimination of discrimination against women | Colombia | Adopted without a vote |
| A/HRC/RES/32/10<br>Business and human rights: improving accountability and access to remedy | Norway, Ghana, Russian Federation | Adopted without a vote |
| A/HRC/RES/32/11<br>Mandate of the Special Rapporteur on the human rights of internally displaced persons | Austria and Uganda | Adopted without a vote |
| A/HRC/RES/32/13<br>The promotion, protection and enjoyment of human rights on the Internet | Sweden | Adopted without a vote |
| A/HRC/RES/32/17<br>Addressing the impact of multiple and intersecting forms of discrimination and violence in the context of racism, racial discrimination, xenophobia and related intolerance on the full enjoyment of all human rights by women and girls | Brazil | Adopted without a vote |
| A/HRC/RES/32/18<br>Mental health and human rights | Brazil and Portugal | Adopted without a vote |

| Resolution | Sponsor(s) of the Resolution | Outcome of the voting process |
|---|---|---|
| A/HRC/RES/32/19 Accelerating efforts to eliminate violence against women: preventing and responding to violence against women and girls, including indigenous women and girls | Canada | Adopted without a vote |
| A/HRC/RES/32/20 Realizing the equal enjoyment of the right to education by every girl | United Arab Emirates | Adopted without a vote |
| A/HRC/RES/32/21 Elimination of female genital mutilation | South Africa | Adopted without a vote |
| A/HRC/RES/32/22 Right to education | Portugal | Adopted without a vote |
| A/HRC/RES/32/29 Cooperation with and assistance to Ukraine in the field of human rights | Ukraine | 22 in favour, 6 against, 19 abstentions |
| A/HRC/RES/32/30 *Capacity-building and technical cooperation with Côte d'Ivoire in the field of human rights* (translation of French original name) | South Africa | Adopted without a vote |
| A/HRC/RES/32/31 Civil society space | Ireland and Sierra Leone | 31 in favour, 7 against, 9 abstentions |
| A/HRC/RES/32/32 The rights to freedom of peaceful assembly and of association | Maldives and USA | Adopted without a vote |
| A/HRC/RES/32/33 Human rights and climate change | Bangladesh, Philippines, Vietnam | Adopted without a vote |
| **33rd session (13-30 September)** | | |
| A/HRC/RES/33/1 Special Rapporteur on contemporary forms of slavery, including its causes and consequences | United Kingdom | Adopted without a vote |
| A/HRC/RES/33/2 The safety of journalists | Austria | Adopted without a vote |
| A/HRC/RES/33/5 The human rights of older persons | Brazil and Argentina | Adopted without a vote |

| Resolution | Sponsor(s) of the Resolution | Outcome of the voting process |
|---|---|---|
| A/HRC/RES/33/6<br>The role of prevention in the promotion and protection of human rights | Ukraine | Adopted without a vote |
| A/HRC/RES/33/8<br>Local government and human rights | Republic of Korea | Adopted without a vote |
| A/HRC/RES/33/9<br>The right of everyone to the enjoyment of the highest attainable standard of physical and mental health | Brazil | Adopted without a vote |
| A/HRC/RES/33/10<br>The human rights to safe drinking water and to sanitation | Germany | 42 in favour, 1 against, 4 abstentions |
| A/HRC/RES/33/11<br>Preventable mortality and morbidity of children under 5 years of age as a human rights concern | Ireland | Adopted without a vote |
| A/HRC/RES/33/12<br>Human rights and indigenous peoples: mandate of the Special Rapporteur on the rights of indigenous peoples | Mexico | Adopted without a vote |
| A/HRC/RES/33/15<br>National institutions for the promotion and protection of human rights | Australia | Adopted without a vote |
| A/HRC/RES/33/19<br>Human rights and transitional justice | Switzerland | 29 in favour, 1 against, 17 abstentions |
| A/HRC/RES/33/20<br>Cultural rights and the protection of cultural heritage | Cyprus | Adopted without a vote |
| A/HRC/RES/33/21<br>Protection of human rights and fundamental freedoms while countering terrorism | Mexico | 38 in favour, none against, 9 abstentions |
| A/HRC/RES/33/22<br>Equal participation in political and public affairs | Czech Republic | Adopted without a vote |

| Resolution | Sponsor(s) of the Resolution | Outcome of the voting process |
|---|---|---|
| A/HRC/RES/33/27<br>Technical assistance and capacity-building in the field of human rights in the Central African Republic | South Africa | Adopted without a vote |
| A/HRC/RES/33/28<br>Enhancement of technical cooperation and capacity-building in the field of human rights | Thailand | Adopted without a vote |
| A/HRC/RES/33/30<br>Arbitrary detention | France | 46 in favour, none against, 1 abstention |

Source: United Nations, Human Rights Council.

## Human Rights Council: resolutions not sponsored by Italy in 2016

| Resolution | Sponsor(s) of the Resolution | Outcome of the voting process |
|---|---|---|
| **31st session (29 February-24 March)** | | |
| A/HRC/RES/31/1<br>Composition of staff of the Office of the United Nations High Commissioner for Human Rights | Cuba | 33 in favour, 13 against, 1 abstention |
| A/HRC/RES/31/2<br>Integrity of the judicial system | Russian Federation | Adopted without a vote |
| A/HRC/RES/31/4<br>Commemoration of the thirtieth anniversary of the Declaration on the Right to Development | Iran | 34 in favour, none against, 13 abstentions |
| A/HRC/RES/31/11<br>The effects of foreign debt and other related international financial obligations of States on the full enjoyment of all human rights, particularly economic, social and cultural rights | Cuba | 33 in favour, 12 against, 2 abstentions |
| A/HRC/RES/31/22<br>The negative impact of the non-repatriation of funds of illicit origin to the countries of origin on the enjoyment of human rights, and the importance of improving international cooperation | South Africa | 32 in favour, none against, 15 abstentions |

| Resolution | Sponsor(s) of the Resolution | Outcome of the voting process |
|---|---|---|
| A/HRC/RES/31/25<br>Human rights in the occupied Syrian Golan | Pakistan | 31 in favour, none against, 16 abstentions |
| A/HRC/RES/31/26<br>Combating intolerance, negative stereotyping and stigmatization of, and discrimination, incitement to violence and violence against, persons based on religion or belief | Pakistan | Adopted without a vote |
| A/HRC/RES/31/30<br>Effects of terrorism on the enjoyment of all human rights | Egypt | 28 in favour, 14 against, 5 abstentions |
| A/HRC/RES/31/33<br>Right of the Palestinian people to self-determination | Pakistan | Adopted without a vote |
| A/HRC/RES/31/34<br>Human rights situation in the Occupied Palestinian Territory, including East Jerusalem | Pakistan | 42 in favour, none against, 5 abstentions |
| A/HRC/RES/31/35<br>Ensuring accountability and justice for all violations of international law in the Occupied Palestinian Territory, including East Jerusalem | Pakistan | 32 in favour, none against, 15 abstentions |
| A/HRC/RES/31/36<br>Israeli settlements in the Occupied Palestinian Territory, including East Jerusalem, and in the occupied Syrian Golan | Pakistan | 32 in favour, none against, 15 abstentions |
| **32nd session (13 June-1 July)** | | |
| A/HRC/RES/32/5<br>Human rights and arbitrary deprivation of nationality | Russian Federation | Adopted without a vote |
| A/HRC/RES/32/6<br>Enhancement of International cooperation in the field of human rights | Iran | Adopted without a vote |
| A/HRC/RES/32/7<br>The right to nationality: women's equal nationality rights in law and in practice | Mexico | Adopted without a vote |

| Resolution | Sponsor(s) of the Resolution | Outcome of the voting process |
|---|---|---|
| A/HRC/RES/32/8<br>Mandate of the Special Rapporteur on the right to food | Cuba | Adopted without a vote |
| A/HRC/RES/32/9<br>Human rights and international solidarity | Cuba | 33 in favour, 13 against, 1 abstention |
| A/HRC/RES/32/12<br>Impact of arms transfers on human rights | Ecuador and Peru | 32 in favour, 5 against, 10 abstentions |
| A/HRC/RES/32/14<br>Protection of the human rights of migrants: strengthening the promotion and protection of the human rights of migrants including in large movements | Mexico | Adopted without a vote |
| A/HRC/RES/32/15<br>Access to medicines in the context of the right of everyone to the enjoyment of the highest attainable standard of physical and mental health | Brazil and India | Adopted without a vote |
| A/HRC/RES/32/16<br>Promoting the right of everyone to the enjoyment of the highest attainable standard of physical and mental health through enhancing capacity-building in public health | China | Adopted without a vote |
| A/HRC/RES/32/23<br>Protecting the family: role of the family in supporting the protection and promotion of the human rights of persons with disabilities | Belarus, Egypt and Qatar | 32 in favour, 12 against, 3 abstentions |
| A/HRC/RES/32/24<br>Situation of human rights in Eritrea | Somalia | Adopted without a vote |
| A/HRC/RES/32/27<br>The Social Forum | Cuba | Adopted without a vote |
| A/HRC/RES/32/28<br>Declaration on the right to peace | Cuba | 34 in favour, 9 against, 4 abstentions |

| Resolution | Sponsor(s) of the Resolution | Outcome of the voting process |
|---|---|---|
| **33rd session (13-30 September)** | | |
| A/HRC/RES/33/3<br>Promotion of a democratic and equitable international order | Cuba | 30 in favour, 12 against, 5 abstentions |
| A/HRC/RES/33/4<br>The use of mercenaries as a means of violating human rights and impeding the exercise of the right of peoples to self-determination | Cuba | 32 in favour, 13 against, 2 abstentions |
| A/HRC/RES/33/7<br>Unaccompanied migrant children and adolescents and human rights | El Salvador and Nicaragua | Adopted without a vote |
| A/HRC/RES/33/13<br>Human rights and indigenous peoples | El Salvador and Nicaragua | Adopted without a vote |
| A/HRC/RES/33/14<br>The right to development | El Salvador and Nicaragua | 34 in favour, 2 against, 11 abstentions |
| A/HRC/RES/33/16<br>Technical assistance and capacity-building for Yemen in the field of human rights | Saudi Arabia and Yemen | Adopted without a vote |
| A/HRC/RES/33/18<br>Preventable maternal mortality and morbidity and human rights | Ireland | Adopted without a vote |
| A/HRC/RES/33/25<br>Expert mechanism on the rights of indigenous peoples | Ireland | Adopted without a vote |
| A/HRC/RES/33/26<br>Technical assistance and capacity-building to improve human rights in the Sudan | Algeria | Adopted without a vote |
| A/HRC/RES/33/29<br>Technical assistance and capacity-building for human rights in the Democratic Republic of Congo | Algeria | Adopted without a vote |

Source: United Nations, Human Rights Council.

In 2016, Italy also took part in the following special sessions:

– 25th special session of the Human Rights Council on the deteriorating human rights situation in the Syrian Arab Republic and the recent situation in Aleppo (21 October 2016); Italy was one of the countries which supported the request to convene the session, and also sponsored the concluding resolution (A/HRC/RES/S-25/1), adopted with 24 votes in favour, 7 against and 16 abstentions;

- 26th special session of the Human Rights Council on the human rights situation in South Sudan (14 December 2016): Italy was one of the countries that supported the request to convene the session, also sponsoring the concluding resolution (A/HRC/RES/S-26/1), adopted without a vote.

## B. Universal Periodic Review

Italy underwent its first Universal Periodic Review in 2010 (7th session): on that occasion, 92 recommendations were made to Italy, of which it fully accepted 78, partially rejected 2 and fully rejected 12. Detailed information on the outcome of the first Universal Periodic Review for Italy is contained in the 2011 edition of the *Italian Yearbook of Human Rights* (pp. 169–173).

In 2014, Italy underwent its second cycle of the UPR (20th session): during it, 186 recommendations were made to Italy, of which it fully accepted 176 and noted 12. Detailed information on the outcome of the second Universal Periodic Review for Italy is contained in the 2015 edition of the *Italian Yearbook of Human Rights* (pp. 161–164).

## C. Special Procedures

In 2016, the Human Rights Council activated two new thematic Special Procedures: Special Rapporteur on the Right to Development and Independent Expert on protection against violence and discrimination based on sexual orientation and gender identity. Consequently, all told, there were 43 thematic Special Procedures and 14 Country mandates in operation at the Council.

Special mention is made of the fact that in 2016 Maria Grazia Giammarinaro was Special Rapporteur on trafficking in persons, especially women and children.

In 2016 Italy was mentioned in the Report by the Working Group of Experts on People of African Descent (A/HRC/33/61/Add.1), following their visit to Italy in June 2015. In its Report, the Working Group recognises the Italian Government's efforts in response to the migrant crisis, particularly the increase in search and rescue operations on the high seas, which saved thousands of lives. At the same time, the Group urges Parliament to publicly condemn all racist and xenophobic acts, and to review legislation on parliamentary immunity, to ensure it is not granted for cases of racist propaganda or hate speech. Furthermore, the Working Group encourages the Government to:

- counter any tendency, especially by politicians, to stigmatise and negatively stereotype people of African descent, or to use racist propaganda for political purposes;
- collect disaggregated data on persons who self-identify as Italians of African descent or as Africans, with a view to promoting policies which protect their rights;
- ensure greater representation of people of African descent in the civil service (including the judiciary and law enforcement agencies), as well as in the mechanisms for determining refugee status;
- adopt laws that prohibit racial profiling by law enforcement agencies and ensure that detainees of African origin have access to all forms of legal, language and psychological support;
- ensure that the National Action Plan against racism and xenophobia explicitly includes the rights of people of African descent and appoint a focal point within the National Office against Discrimination;
- establish a National Human Rights Institution that is fully compliant with the Paris Principles;
- promote the teaching of the history of the trade in Africans and of colonialism in schools;
- adopt special measures for integrating refugees and migrants into Italian society, through appropriate educational, housing, healthcare and employment policies;
- ensure that evictions are carried out lawfully, only in exceptional circumstances and in full compliance with the relevant provisions of international human rights law;
- increase the number of territorial commissions to expedite the review of asylum claims and to decrease the waiting time in reception centres;
- reform the law regulating Italian citizenship in order to grant citizenship to children born in Italy of foreign citizens and minors entering Italy, as well as speeding up the process for adults;
- extend access to hospitals for emergency healthcare and to schools, as well as to other basic human rights, to undocumented migrants;
- ratify the International Convention on the Protection of the Rights of all Migrant Workers and Members of their Families, as well as Protocol XII to the European Convention on Human Rights, and to ensure respect for the rights of migrant workers enshrined in the bilateral agreements signed by Italy.

Listed below are the visits carried out, agreed (but not yet carried out) and simply those requested by the Special Rapporteurs.

*Visits carried out and reports*

- Special Rapporteur on the independence of judges and lawyers (11–14 March 2002): report E/CN.4/2002/72/Add.3.

- Special Rapporteur on the human rights of migrants (7–18 June 2004): report E/CN.4/2005/85/Add.3.
- Special Rapporteur on the right to freedom of opinion and expression (20–29 October 2004): report E/CN.4/2005/64/Add.1.
- Special Rapporteur on contemporary forms of racism (9–13 October 2006): report A/HRC/4/19/Add.4.
- Working Group on arbitrary detention (3–14 November 2008): report A/HRC/10/21/Add.5.
- Special Rapporteur on violence against women (15–26 January 2012): report A/HRC/20/16/Add.2.
- Special Rapporteur on the rights of migrants (30 September – 8 October 2012): report A/HRC/23/46/Add.3.
- Special Rapporteur on trafficking in persons (12–20 September 2013): report A/HRC/26/37/Add.4.
- Special Rapporteur on freedom of opinion and expression (11–18 November 2013): report A/HRC/26/30/Add.3.
- Working Group on arbitrary detention (7–9 July 2014): report A/HRC/30/36/Add.3.
- Special Rapporteur on the human rights of migrants (2–5 December 2014): report A/HRC/29/36/Add.2.
- Working Group of experts on people of African descent (1–5 June 2015): report A/HRC/33/61/Add.1.

*Agreed Visits*

- Special Rapporteur on extreme poverty and human rights (date to be agreed).

*Requested Visits*

- Special Rapporteur on the independence of judges and lawyers (visit requested in July 2013).
- Special Rapporteur on the human rights to safe drinking water and sanitation (visit requested in February 2015).
- Special Rapporteur in the field of cultural rights (visit requested in February 2016).

## III. High Commissioner for Human Rights (OHCHR)

The Office was established by the General Assembly in December 1993 with resolution 48/141.

The High Commissioner has a very broad mandate which includes the prevention of violations of human rights, ensuring the respect of all human rights, coordinating all United Nations activities involving human rights and strengthening national systems for protecting human rights and the rule of law. In this context, one of the crucial strategic activities for the High Commissioner's Office is supporting the introduction and development of independent human rights commissions at the national level.

In order to fulfil its mandate, the Office of the High Commissioner has consolidated its presence "on the ground", establishing 10 regional offices and the same number of national offices, sending its own experts on integrated United Nations peace missions or planning independent fact-finding operations, as well as mainstreaming the human rights component in United Nations teams' activities at Country or Programme level, and in those of specialised agencies of the United Nations (such as UNDP).

The High Commissioner for Human Rights in 2016 was Zeid Ra'ad Al Hussein (Jordan), in post since 2014.

The High Commissioner's Office is funded one-third by the ordinary budget of the United Nations, approved by the General Assembly every two years; the remaining two thirds of the budget comes from voluntary contributions, mostly from States, but also from international organisations, foundations, commercial enterprises and private citizens.

In 2016 Italy contributed to the budget of the High Commissioner's Office with funds for about 614,000 dollars (ranking 24[th] among donors), keeping its contribution substantially the same as in the previous year, when it ranked 21[st] (see graph below).

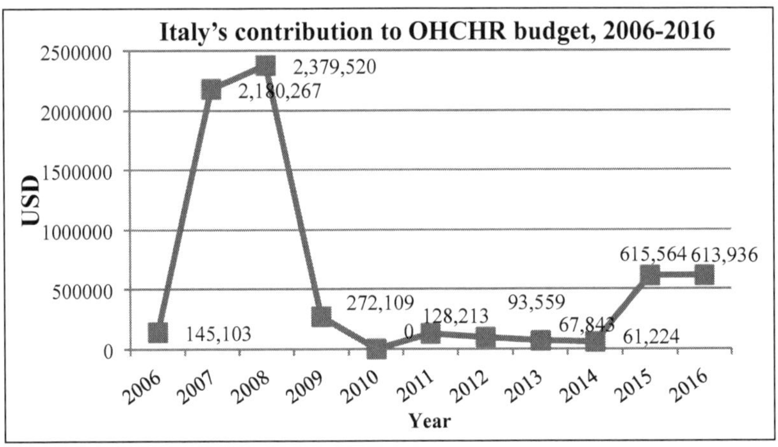


Source: OHCHR, *Voluntary contributions to OHCHR in 2016* (www.ohchr.org).

## IV. High Commissioner for Refugees (UNHCR)

This Office was established by the United Nations General Assembly on 14 December 1950, with resolution A/RES/428(V).

> The mandate of the Agency is to coordinate international action for the protection of refugees and the resolution of their problems all over the world. Its primary mission is the protection of the rights and wellbeing of refugees and to ensure that all of them can exercise their right to request asylum and seek safe refuge in another State, with the option to return voluntarily to their home Country, integrate locally or to resettle into a third Country. The remit of the UNHCR also includes assistance to stateless persons.

On 1 January 2016, the General Assembly of the United Nations appointed Filippo Grandi (Italy) High Commissioner for Refugees, for a five-year mandate.

The UNHCR has had its own office in Rome since 1953. The Italian Office participates in the procedures to determine refugee status in Italy and performs other duties regarding international protection, training, dissemination of information on refugees and asylum-seekers in Italy and in the various crisis areas all over the world, raising public awareness and fund-raising with Governments, companies and from individual donators. Since 2006, the Italian UNHCR Office has become a Regional Office, with responsibilities for Albania, Cyprus, Greece, Malta, Portugal, San Marino and the Holy See in addition to Italy. In 2016, Carlotta Sami was UNHCR Spokesperson in Italy.

According to data provided by UNHCR, 181,436 migrants arrived in Italy by sea in 2016, an increase of 18% on the figure for 2015 (153,842). These numbers include 25,846 minors either unaccompanied or separated from their parents, making up 14% of all arrivals by sea in 2016 (+7% compared to the previous year). Following the adoption by the Council of the European Union of the Decision on the mechanism for relocation and resettlement, (September 2015) and up to December 2016, 2,654 people were relocated outside Italy, equivalent to 6.7% of the target initially set (39,600 people).

The people arriving by sea in 2016 came mostly from Nigeria (21%), Eritrea (11%), Côte d'Ivoire, Guinea, Gambia (7% each), Senegal, Mali (6% each), Sudan, (5%), Bangladesh and Somalia (4% each).

The overwhelming majority of departures (around 90%) is from Libya; only 5.9% of people arriving in Italy by sea in 2016 left from Egypt, although that route is considered safer. A smaller number still of new arrivals had departed from Turkey, Algeria, Tunisia and Greece.

In 2016, 123,842 people submitted asylum claims in Italy. This represents a substantial increase compared to previous years: indeed, in 2015 there were only 83,970 claims for asylum and in 2014 63,456. The most common countries of origin of asylum-seekers are Nigeria, Pakistan, Gambia, Côte d'Ivoire, Senegal, Eritrea, Mali and Bangladesh.

Over 90,000 claims for asylum were processed by the territorial commissions all over Italy: 5% of asylum-seekers were granted refugee status, 12% were given subsidiary protection and 21% humanitarian protection.

In 2016, Italy contributed to the UNHCR budget with an allocation of about 31 million dollars, an increase of approximately 10 million dollars over the previous year (see graph below).

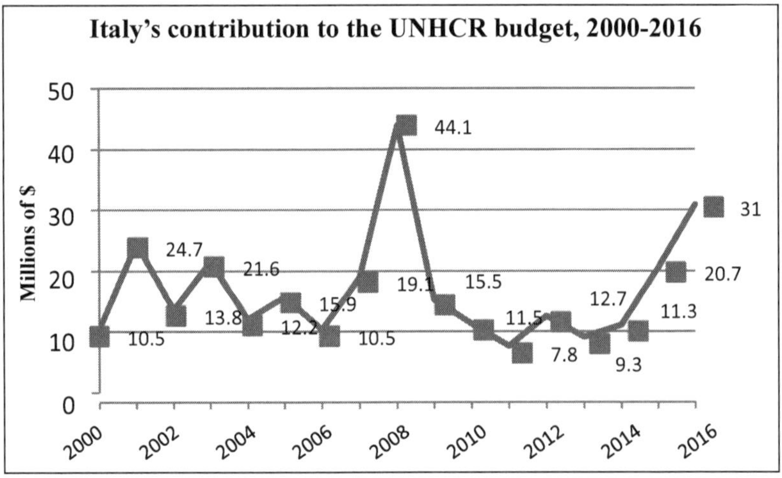


Source: *Contributions to UNHCR for the budget year 2016* (http://reporting.unhcr.org/donor-profiles?y=2016).

## V. Human Rights Treaty Bodies

Over the years, the United Nations have created an organic International Bill of Human Rights, whose core is made up of the nine conventions listed below: the Convention for the Elimination of All Forms of Racial Discrimination (ICERD, 1965); the Covenant on Civil and Political Rights (ICCPR, 1966); the Covenant on Economic, Social and Cultural Rights (ICESCR, 1966); the Convention on the Elimination of All Forms of Discrimination against Women (CEDAW, 1969); the Convention against Torture and other Cruel, Inhuman or Degrading Treatment or Punishment (CAT, 1984); the Convention on the Rights of the Child (CRC, 1989); the Convention on the Protection of the Rights of all Migrant Workers and Members of Their Families (ICRMW, 1990); the Convention on the Rights of Persons with Disabilities (CRPD, 2006); the Convention for the Protection of All Persons from Enforced Disappearance (CPED, 2006).

Italy has ratified eight conventions and their related optional protocols (as shown in the chart below). It has not yet signed the ICRMW.

| Convention | Ratification Law | Declarations/ Reservations | Recognition of competence of specific Committees |
|---|---|---|---|
| ICERD | l. 13 October 1975, No. 654 | Yes (art. 4) | Individual communications (art. 14): Yes |
| ICESCR | l. 25 October 1977, No. 881 | No | - |
| ICCPR | l. 25 October 1977, No. 881 | Yes (art. 15.1 and 19.3) | Inter-State communications (art. 41): Yes |
| OP – 1 | l. 25 October 1977, No. 881 | Yes (art. 5.2) | - |
| OP – 2 | l. 9 December 1994, No. 734 | No | - |
| CEDAW | l. 14 March 1985, No. 132 | Yes (general) | - |
| OP | Deposit date of ratification instrument: 22/09/2000 | No | Inquiry procedure (art. 8 and 9): Yes |
| CAT | l. 3 November 1988, No. 498 | No | Individual communications (art. 22): Yes<br>Inter-State communications (art. 21): Yes<br>Inquiry procedure (art. 20): Yes |
| CRC | l. 27 May 1991, No. 176 | No | - |
| OP – AC | l. 11 March 2002, No. 46 | Binding declaration in accordance with art. 3: 17 years old | - |

| Convention | Ratification Law | Declarations/ Reservations | Recognition of competence of specific Committees |
|---|---|---|---|
| OP – SC | l. 11 March 2002, No. 46 | No | - |
| CRPD | l. 3 March 2009, No. 18 | No | - |
| OP | l. 3 March 2009, No. 18 | No | Inquiry procedure (art. 6 and 7): No |

Legend:

OP = Optional Protocol

OP – AC = Optional Protocol to the Convention on the Rights of the Child on the Involvement of Children in Armed Conflict

OP – SC = Optional Protocol to the Convention on the Rights of the Child on the Sale of Children, Child Prostitution and Child Pornography

OP – IC = Optional Protocol to the Convention on the Rights of the Child on a Communications Procedure

Besides enunciating fundamental rights therein, the United Nations have set up control mechanisms for each treaty, the so-called Committees or Treaty Bodies, each comprising from 10 to 23 independent experts, selected on the basis of their high moral character and recognised expertise in the field of human rights.

In 2016, Mauro Politi was a member of the Human Rights Committee (civil and political rights); Biancamaria Pomeranzi was a member of the Committee on the Elimination of Discrimination against Women; Alessio Bruni was a member of the Committee against Torture and Maria Rita Parsi member of the Committee on the Rights of the Child.

> The principal duty of the Committees is to examine the periodic reports on the implementation in States Parties of the terms of the internationally binding rules, which the States Parties are under obligation to submit regularly (normally every 4 or 5 years). In addition to this procedure, some Committees can monitor implementation through three further mechanisms: conducting Country enquiries (in the field), examining inter-State communications and examining individual complaints. Finally, the Committees publish their interpretation of the contents of provisions on human rights, the so-called General Comments (for further detail on these functions, see *2011 Yearbook*, p. 180).

Italy is subject to monitoring by eight Committees, as shown in the table below. Italy did not submit any reports in 2016. However, it received the concluding observations from the Committee for the Elimination of Racial Discrimination, the Committee on the Rights of Persons with Disabilities and the report from the Sub-committee on the Prevention of Torture following their visit in September 2015.

**Italy's cooperation with United Nations Treaty Bodies**

| **Committee** | **Total No. of reports presented** | **Latest report presented** | **Latest concluding observations** | **Reporting status** |
|---|---|---|---|---|
| CERD | 20 | February 2015 | December 2016 | XXI report: to be submitted in February 2019 |
| CESCR | 5 | August 2012 | October 2015 | VI report: to be submitted in October 2020 |
| CCPR | 6 | October 2015 | - | VI report: submitted and awaiting discussion |
| CEDAW | 7 | October 2015 | - | VII report: submitted and awaiting discussion |
| CAT | 6 | October 2015 | - | VI report: submitted and awaiting discussion |
| CRC | 4 | January 2009 | October 2011 | Combined V and VI reports to be submitted in April 2017 |
| *OP – AC* | 2 | January 2009 | October 2011 | Information on the implementation of the Protocol to be included in the combined V and VI report |
| *OP – SC* | 2 | January 2009 | October 2011 | Information on the implementation of the Protocol to be included in the combined V and VI report |
| CRPD | 1 | November 2012 | September 2016 | Combined II, III and IV report to be submitted in May 2023 |
| CED | - | - | - | I report: date of submission to be confirmed |

## A. Committee on Economic, Social and Cultural Rights

In 2016, the Committee held three sessions: the 57th (22 February – 4 March), the 58th (6–24 June) and the 59th (19 September – 7 October). In the 57th session, reports from Canada, Kenya and Namibia were considered; in the 58th, those of Angola, Burkina Faso, France, Honduras, Sweden, the Former Yugoslav Republic of Macedonia and the United Kingdom; in the 59th those from Costa Rica, Cyprus, Dominican Republic, Lebanon, Philippines, Poland and Tunisia. Two General Comments were adopted during the year: No. 22 on the right to sexual and reproductive health (art. 12 ICESCR) and No. 23 on the right to just and favourable conditions of work (art. 7 ICESCR). Italy's latest periodic report was considered by the Committee in September 2015, in the course of its 56th session (see *2016 Yearbook*, pp. 162–164). Italy is to submit its sixth report in 2020.

## B. Human Rights Committee (Civil and Political Rights)

In 2016, the Committee held three sessions: the 116th (7–31 March), 117th (20 June – 15 July) and 118th (17 October – 4 November). In the 116th session, reports from Costa Rica, Namibia, New Zealand, Rwanda, Slovenia, South Africa and Sweden were considered; in the 117th, reports from Argentina, Burkina Faso, Denmark, Ecuador, Ghana, Kazakhstan and Kuwait were considered; and in the 118th, those from Azerbaijan, Colombia, Jamaica, Morocco, Poland, Republic of Moldova and Slovakia. No General Comments were adopted in 2016.

Italy submitted its latest report in October 2015, but it has not yet been considered (see *2016 Yearbook,* pp. 164–165).

## C. Committee against Torture

In 2016, the Committee held three sessions: the 57th (18 April – 13 May), the 58th (25 July – 12 August) and the 59th (7 November – 7 December). The 57th session examined the reports from France, Israel Philippines, Saudi Arabia, Tunisia and Turkey; the 58th examined the reports from Burundi, Honduras, Kuwait and Mongolia; and the 29th those of Armenia, Cabo Verde, Ecuador, Finland, Monaco, Namibia, Sri Lanka and Turkmenistan. No General Comments were adopted in 2016.

Italy submitted its latest report in October 2015 (see *2016 Yearbook,* pp. *2016*, pp. 165–166) but it has not yet been considered.

Moreover, in February 2016, the Subcommittee on the Prevention of Torture published the report on its first visit to Italy, from September 16–

22 2015, made in order to verify the respect of the norms and principles enshrined in the Convention in situations of migrant detention (Doc. CAT/OP/ITA/1). In the report, the Subcommittee made recommendations to Italy in four main areas:

– *National Preventive Mechanism (NPM).* The Subcommittee urges Italy to put this mechanism in place, pointing out that under the terms of Articles 3 and 17–23 of the Optional Protocol to the International Convention against Torture, it is compulsory for an NPM to be established.
– *Legal Framework.* In this area, the Subcommittee recommends that Italy should:

  consider de-criminalising all instances of irregular re-entry or stay;

  consider narrowing its definition of what circumstances constitute a "risk of absconding";

  ensure that detention of immigrants is only applied as a measure of last resort, following the determination, on a case by case basis, that it is strictly necessary, proportionate, lawful, non-arbitrary and is imposed for the shortest time possible;

  exclude vulnerable persons from detention;

  ensure that readmission agreements do not lead to unnecessary and disproportionate use of detention;

  reinforce its legislation to ensure the protection of migrants against all forms of torture and ill-treatment, in particular in the collection of fingerprints;

  avoid detention of migrants for the sole purpose of identification;

  introduce, as a matter of urgency, the crime of torture into the Penal Code;

  ensure that the legal framework, and its application in practice, provide for effective preventive safeguards against all forms of pushback (*refoulement*), starting from the introduction of an automatic suspensive effect of removal orders if legal procedures to challenge them are still ongoing.
– *Institutional Framework.* In this area, the Subcommittee recommends that Italy:

  re-examine the current system for the detention of migrants, in order to define clearly, and without overlapping, the roles and responsibilities of all authorities involved;

  establish procedures to ensure that migrants are informed, in a language accessible to them, of their situation, of the availability of specific services and how to access them, of the procedures that will be followed, of their rights and obligations during the procedure, the possible consequences of their non-compliance and the remedies available to them;

  cooperate with NGOs and the bar association providing support to migrants;

  provide independent monitoring of detention facilities and of all stages of processes, to guarantee that all actions undertaken are compliant with international human rights law, with special reference to the prevention of torture.

- *Overarching issues pertaining to immigration detention*

  The Subcommittee made specific recommendations that Italy should:

  take all necessary steps to avoid separating families during disembarkation procedures;

  ensure that the human rights and need for protection of refugees take precedence over border control and migration management objectives;

  provide adequate training to all staff working in structures involved in the management of migratory flows and immigrants;

  provide access to water, food and healthcare;

  ensure that child migrants are not held in detention, as it is never in the best interest of the child and constitutes a violation of the rights of the child;

  provide effective protection for women in reception facilities from all forms of sexual and gender-based violence;

  reconsider the process of militarisation of CARAs.

In November 2016, Italy submitted its reply to the Subcommittee, giving a detailed description of the actions undertaken and those planned in order to implement the recommendations made (Doc. CAT/OP/ITA/1/Add.1).

## D. Committee on the Elimination of Racial Discrimination

In 2016, the Committee held three sessions: the 89th (25 April – 13 May), 90th (2–26 August) and 91st (21 November – 9 December). During the 89th session, reports from the following countries were considered: Azerbaijan, Georgia, Namibia, Oman, Rwanda, Spain; during the 90th, reports from Greece, Lebanon, Pakistan, Paraguay, South Africa, Sri Lanka, Ukraine and the United Kingdom were considered; and during the 91st, those of Argentina, Italy, Portugal, Togo, Turkmenistan and Uruguay. No General Recommendations were adopted during the year.

**Latest Report submitted by Italy**

| | |
|---|---|
| **Reporting round** | Combined XIX and XX periodic report |
| **Date report due** | 04/02/2015 |
| **Date report actually submitted** | 06/02/2015 |
| **Report** | CERD/C/ITA/19–20 |
| **List of themes** | CERD/C/ITA/Q/19–20 |

| | |
|---|---|
| **Summary of the debate** | CERD/C/SR.2504, CERD/C/SR.2505 |
| **Concluding observations** | CERD/C/ITA/CO/19–20 |
| **Date the report was considered** | 1–2 December 2016, during the 91st session of the Committee (21 November – 9 December 2016) |

The Committee considered Italy's combined XIX and XX report during its 91st session (21 November – 9 December 2016), also drawing on the reports sent in by NGOs (specifically Amnesty International, Associazione 21 July Onlus (NGO supporting Roma and Sinti minorities, *TN)*, Comitato per la promozione e protezione dei diritti umani (*Committee for the Promotion and Protection of Human Rights)*, European Roma Rights Centre, Gruppo di Lavoro per la Convenzione sui diritti dell'infanzia e dell'adolescenza (*Working Group on the Rights of Children and Adolescents)*, Unione Forense per la tutela dei diritti umani (*Bar Association for the protection of human rights*) and by the European Union Agency for Fundamental Rights. After consideration, the following concluding observations and recommendations were adopted:

- *Legal framework.* Italy is requested to adopt all necessary measures to ensure that its domestic anti-discrimination legislation prohibits all forms of discrimination, in accordance with article 1 of the Convention, and that these legislative guarantees be applied in full to non-citizens, regardless of their immigration status, as specified in the Committee's general recommendation No. 30 (2004).
- *National human rights institutions.* Recalling its general recommendation No. 17 (1993) on the establishment of national institutions to facilitate the implementation of the Convention, the Committee recommends that Italy establish, without further delay and with the effective participation of civil society actors, a national human rights institution in accordance with the Paris Principles. Furthermore, the Committee requests that the independence of UNAR be guaranteed by the allocation of sufficient human and financial resources to carry out its mandate effectively.
- *Racist hate speech.* Taking into account its general recommendation No. 35 (2013) on combating racist hate speech, the Committee requests Italy to: ensure that all individuals, including politicians at all levels, are held accountable and sanctioned for the dissemination of ideas based on racial superiority or hatred, or for other violations of art. 4 of the Convention, including by lifting parliamentary immunity, in conformity with general recommendation No. 7 (1985) relating to the implementation of art. 4; ensure that victims of hate speech are provided with effective remedies; establish a data collection mechanism to systematically record incidents of hate speech, application of relevant legislation, penalties imposed on the perpetrators and remedies provided to victims; condemn unequivocally at the highest political level the dissemination of hate speech and engage in promoting a culture

of tolerance and respect; ensure that the prohibition of racist hate speech extends to the Internet, ratifying the Additional Protocol to the Convention on Cybercrime concerning the criminalising of acts of a racist and xenophobic nature committed through computer systems; encourage public and private media to adopt and abide by codes of professional ethics which incorporate respect for the principles of the Convention and other fundamental human rights standards, including avoidance of stereotyping and unnecessary references to race, religion and other group characteristics which may promote intolerance.

- *Racist hate crimes*. Taking into account its general recommendation No. 31 (2005) on the prevention of racial discrimination in the administration and functioning of the criminal justice system, the Committee recommends Italy: investigate all reported acts of racist hate crimes, prosecute and punish those found responsible with sanctions commensurate with the gravity of the offence and provide effective remedies to victims; adopt concrete measures to increase the reporting of hate crimes, providing transparent and accessible reporting mechanisms; strengthen the law on aggravating circumstances to extend its application to ordinary crimes when racial hatred is one of the main motivations.
- *Mixed migratory flows: migrants, asylum-seekers and refugees*. The Committee recommends that Italy should: ensure that immigration detention is only applied as a measure of last resort, after it has been determined, on a case-by-case basis, that it is a necessary, proportionate, lawful and non-arbitrary measure and is imposed for the shortest period of time; decriminalise all instances of irregular re-entry or stay; ensure that migrants and asylum-seekers deprived of their liberty are not held beyond the legally permitted duration of 48 hours; adopt individual screening and identification procedures which are gender appropriate and culturally and age sensitive, to ensure the rapid and appropriate identification of international protection needs or any situations of vulnerability; safeguard the physical integrity of migrants and asylum-seekers; ensure that migrants and asylum-seekers receive adequate legal support and that law enforcement officers observe the principle of the minimum use of force when taking their fingerprints; strictly observe the principle of non-refoulement and amend expulsion procedures to ensure that no individual is expelled without an individualised assessment.
- *Roma, Sinti and Travellers*. Recalling its general recommendation No. 27 (2000) on discrimination against Roma, the Committee recommends that Italy: halt any plans to carry out further evictions of Roma, Sinti and Traveller communities, or to establish new segregated camps which separate them from larger society; review housing policies at national, regional and municipal level, to ensure they do not discriminate against Roma, Sinti and Travellers in the enjoyment of their rights, with particular reference to access to social housing and other forms of housing benefits; prioritise efforts to ensure that Roma, Sinti and Travellers' children are able to access quality education that is culturally and linguistically appropriate, at schools that are geographically accessible and that they will not suffer any form of segregation or ill-treatment; ensure that the National Strategy for the Inclusion of Roma, Sinti and Traveller

Communities 2012–2020 leads to concrete and tangible improvement in the enjoyment of their human rights by the members of these communities; provide effective remedies to Roma, Sinti and Travellers who have suffered human rights violations, including as a result of the implementation of the so-called Nomad Emergency Decree, taking into account the Council of State's Judgment No. 6050 of 16 November 2011.

- *Situation of migrant workers.* The Committee recommends that Italy: ensure the effective implementation in practice of the new law approved by the Chamber of Deputies on 18 October 2016, to combat undeclared work and labour exploitation in agriculture (the so-called "legge sul caporalato" – *law against gangmasters*); adopt further measures to strengthen the Labour Inspectorate's power to act; ensure that all migrants have access to justice and effective remedies, and that they can lodge complaints of violations of their rights without fear of arrest, detention or deportation; provide access to basic services to all migrants regardless of their immigration status, in accordance with international human rights standards.
- *People of African descent.* Recalling its general recommendation No. 34 (2011) on racial discrimination against people of African descent, the Committee recommends that Italy: investigate all acts of racial discrimination against people of African descent, both citizens and non-citizens, prosecuting those who committed the violations and providing effective remedies to victims; collect and publish data on incidents of discrimination against people of African descent, on the application of pertinent legislation, penalties imposed on those responsible and remedies provided to the victims; ensure that there are teachers of African descent in schools, and that all teachers and other staff working in educational institutions receive adequate training on the principles of equality and non-discrimination and on ways to deal with instances of racial discrimination in schools; ensure that the school curriculum includes study of Italy's colonial past in order to convey appropriate awareness of the consequences and of the continuing impact of racially discriminatory policies.
- *Criminal justice system.* Italy is requested to provide clarification on the reasons behind the disproportionate representation of non-citizens in its prisons, and on the measures adopted to rectify this situation.
- *Ratification of international instruments.* Italy is requested to ratify the International Convention on the Protection of the Rights of All Migrant Workers and Members of their Families.

Italy is due to present its next report in February 2019.

## E. Committee on the Elimination of Discrimination against Women

In 2016, the Committee held three sessions: the 63rd (15 February – 4 March), 64th (4–22 July) and 65th (24 October – 18 November). The 63rd session considered the reports from the Czech Republic, Haiti, Iceland,

Japan, Mongolia, Sweden, Tanzania, Vanuatu; the 64th those from Albania, France, Mali, Myanmar, Philippines, Trinidad and Tobago, Turkey and Uruguay; and the 65th those from Argentina, Armenia, Bangladesh, Belarus, Bhutan, Burundi, Canada, Estonia, Honduras, the Netherlands and Switzerland. Furthermore, General Recommendation No. 34 was adopted, on the rights of rural women.

Italy submitted its latest report in October 2015 but it has not yet been considered (see *2016 Yearbook,* p. 167).

## F. Committee on the Rights of the Child

In 2016, the Committee held three sessions: the 71st (11–29 January), 72nd (17 May – 3 June) and 73rd (13–30 September). The 71st session considered the reports from Benin, Brunei Darussalam, France, Haiti, Iran, Ireland, Kenya, Latvia, Maldives, Oman, Peru, Senegal, Zambia and Zimbabwe; the 72nd those from Bulgaria, Gabon, Nepal, Pakistan, Samoa, Slovakia and the United Kingdom; the 73rd considered reports from Nauru, New Zealand, Saudi Arabia, Sierra Leone, South Africa and Suriname. General Comment No. 20 was also adopted, on the implementation of the rights of the child during adolescence.

The Committee discussed Italy's latest periodic report in September 2011, during its 58th session (see *2012 Yearbook*, pp. 195–199). Italy is due to present its combined fifth and sixth report in 2017.

## G. Committee on the Rights of Persons with Disabilities

The Committee held two sessions in 2016, the 15th (29 March – 21 April) and the 16th (15 August – 2 September). During the 15th session reports from Chile, Lithuania, Portugal, Serbia, Slovakia, Thailand and Uganda were considered, whereas the 16th session considered reports from Bolivia, Colombia, Ethiopia, Guatemala, Italy, United Arab Emirates, and Uruguay. Two General Comments were adopted during the year: No. 3 on women and children with disabilities (art. 6 of the Convention) and No. 4 on the right to inclusive education (art. 24 of the Convention).

**Latest Report submitted by Italy**

| | |
|---|---|
| **Reporting round** | 1st report |
| **Date report due** | 15/06/2011 |
| **Date report actually submitted** | 22/01/2013 |
| **Report** | CRPD/C/ITA/1 |

| | |
|---|---|
| **List of issues** | CRPD/C/ITA/Q/1 |
| **Replies to the list of issues** | CRPD/C/ITA/Q/1/Add.1 |
| **Summary of the debate** | CRPD/C/SR.283, CRPD/C/SR.284 |
| **Concluding observations** | CRPD/C/ITA/CO/1 |
| **Date the report was considered** | 24–25 August 2016, during the Committee's 16th session (15 August – 2 September) |

The Committee considered Italy's initial report during its 16th session (15 August – 2 September), basing its findings also on the reports submitted by civil society organisations (*Forum Italiano Sulla Disabilità* – Italian Forum on Disabilities – and *Coordinamento Nazionale Famiglie Disabili* – National Coordinating Network between Families of people with Disabilities). After the debate, the following concluding observations and recommendations were adopted:

- *General principles and obligations* (arts. 1–4). The Committee recommends adopting a concept of disability in line with the Convention and ensuring that Italian legislation incorporates the new concept in a homogeneous manner across all levels of government. Italy should also establish a permanent consultative body that will allow persons with disabilities to participate effectively and meaningfully, through their organisations, in the development of laws, policies and programmes.
- *Equality and non-discrimination* (art. 5). The Committee recommends that Italy immediately adopt a definition of "reasonable accommodation" aligned with the Convention, and enact legislation which explicitly recognises the denial of reasonable accommodation as disability-based discrimination across all areas of life, including within public and private sectors. Furthermore, Italy should enact appropriate legislation and policies to introduce enforcement mechanisms to address multiple and intersectional discrimination.
- *Women with disabilities* (art. 6). The Committee recommends that gender be mainstreamed in disability policies and that disability be mainstreamed in gender policies, both in close consultation with women and girls with disabilities and with their representative organisations.
- *Children with disabilities* (art. 7). The Committee recommends immediate support to the data collection system, to ensure early detection, intervention and service provision to all children with disabilities, particularly those in the 0–5 age group. Furthermore, policies aimed at tackling child poverty should specifically include children with disabilities through their representative organisations.
- *Awareness-raising* (art. 8). The Committee recommends adopting measures to raise public awareness, using mass media campaigns and by training people who work in the media on the negative impact of stereotypes and the importance of portraying the positive contributions made by persons with disabilities, in particular women and girls with disabilities.

- *Accessibility* (art. 9). Italy should increase its efforts to ensure that accessibility standards are observed, with particular reference to the accessibility of websites, emergency services, public transport, buildings and infrastructure. The Committee also recommends adopting an action plan to ensure that all public sectors can provide services of live assistance and intermediaries, including guides, readers and professional sign language interpreters and augmentative and alternative communications methods. In particular, augmentative and alternative communication must be provided free of charge in the education sector.
- *Equal recognition before the law* (art. 12). The Committee requests Italy to repeal all laws that permit substituted decision-making by legal guardians, including the mechanism of administrative support and the enactment and implementation of supported decision-making provisions, including the training of professionals in the justice, health and social sectors.
- *Liberty and security of the person* (art. 14). The Committee recommends: a reform of legislation and of policies so as to prohibit detention, including involuntary hospitalisation and/or treatment, on the grounds of disability; repealing criminal laws which allow persons with intellectual or psychosocial disabilities to be declared unfit to institute court proceedings, thus permitting the full application of the principle of fair trial; the provision of reasonable accommodation, in prisons or other centres of detention, to prisoners with disabilities, to ensure their participation in and access to all services and activities on an equal basis with other detainees.
- *Freedom from exploitation, violence and abuse* (art. 16). The Committee recommends that Italy enact legislation, including appropriate monitoring mechanisms, to detect, prevent and combat violence within and outside the homes of persons with disabilities, particularly that against women and children with disabilities, and to draw up an action plan to implement the Council of Europe Convention on preventing and combating violence against women and domestic violence (the Istanbul Convention), which specifically addresses women and children with disabilities. It is also considered necessary for Italy to set up training mechanisms for members of the police, the judiciary and health and social services, and to provide accessible and inclusive support services to victims of violence.
- *Protecting the integrity of the person* (art. 17). It is recommended that Italy ensure that during their childhood or adolescence, no one is subjected to medical or surgical treatment not supported by scientific evidence and that Italy guarantee the bodily integrity, autonomy and self-determination of the children concerned by such medical procedures.
- *Living independently and being included in the community* (art. 19) The Committee recommends that Italy: enact safeguards to retain the right to autonomous independent living across all regions; redirect resources from institutionalisation to community-based services, increasing budget support to enable persons with disabilities, throughout Italy, to live independently and have equal access to all services, including personal assistance.

- *Freedom of expression and access to information and communication* (art. 21). The Committee recommends that Italy: expedite the enactment of legislation on the proposed "provisions to remove communications barriers and to recognise Italian sign and tactile languages (*LIS* and *LIST*)"; promote inclusion for deaf and deaf-blind people and for those with hearing disabilities in general, significantly increasing the use of sign language in public broadcasting; adopt concrete measures to ensure the teaching of standardised Braille to blind persons and tactile communications to deaf-blind persons.
- *Respect for home and family* (art. 23). The Committee recommends that Italy: allocate specific financial, social and other resources fairly across all regions to ensure that all families with members with disabilities can access all the support they require, to safeguard their right to home and family and to inclusion and participation in their local communities, avoiding recourse to institutionalisation; review current laws, policies and practice relating to adoption and provide support to parents with disabilities to retain full parental responsibility for their children.
- *Education* (art. 24). The Committee recommends that Italy: implement an action plan, with sufficient allocation of resources, timelines and specific goals, to monitor the implementation of laws, decrees and regulations regarding improvement of the quality of inclusive education in classrooms, providing support and quality teacher training at all levels; ensuring equal access to all levels of education and vocational training; building or adapting education facilities to make them safe and suitable for students with disabilities; providing highly qualified sign language interpreters to any deaf child requesting this type of assistance, and to desist from recommending general communications assistants as the sole alternative; guarantee, through legislative and other measures, the availability of accessible learning materials and the provision of assistive technology, including the recent decrees to implement educational reforms, to ensure inclusive and quality education in mainstream schools.
- *Health* (art. 25). The Committee recommends that Italy: ensure accessibility of facilities, equipment, information and communications regarding health services, organising training for staff on the rights of persons with disabilities, in close collaboration with the organisations representing them; abolish all laws that permit medical treatment, including sterilisation, authorised by a third party (legal guardian or parent), without the free and informed consent of the person; expedite the adoption, funding and implementation of Minimum Standards of Health Care so that all children have access to early identification and intervention, according to their needs.
- *Work and employment* (art. 27). Italy is invited to remove any legislation limiting the rights of persons with disabilities to perform any profession on the grounds of their disability and to implement specific measures to address the low level of employment for women with disabilities.
- *Adequate standard of living and social protection* (art. 28). The Committee recommends that Italy: homogenise social protection interventions and policies throughout the Country; expedite the adoption and implementation of the Minimum Standards of Social Assistance; conduct assessments on the

impact of austerity measures on children and adults with disabilities and avoid any further reductions in funding that could increase levels of poverty.

- *Participation in political and public life* (art. 29). The Committee recommends that Italy: provide support and facilitation services to ensure all persons with disabilities can exercise their right to vote, including persons with intellectual and/or psychosocial disabilities; repeal art. 48 of the Constitution and also law No. 62/04, which restricts the right of persons with disabilities to vote at the polling stations of their choice; harmonise the regulatory framework on assistance with voting for persons with disabilities, in compliance with the Convention.
- *Participation in cultural life, recreation, leisure and sport* (art. 30). Italy is requested to ratify the Marrakesh Treaty to Facilitate Access to Published Works for Persons who are Blind, Visually Impaired or otherwise Print Disabled.
- *National human rights institutions* (art. 33). The Committee recommends that Italy immediately establish and implement an adequately funded, independent monitoring mechanism in conformity with the Paris Principles, and ensure that the organizations representing persons with disabilities are fully involved in its work.

Italy is due to present its combined second, third and fourth report in May 2023.

## H. Committee on Enforced Disappearances

In 2016 the Committee held two sessions, the 10th (7–18 March) and the 11th (3–14 October), in the course of which concluding observations were adopted concerning Burkina Faso, Kazakhstan, Tunisia (10th session), Bosnia Herzegovina and Colombia (11th session).

The date for Italy to submit its first periodic report has not yet been established.

## I. Committee on Migrant Workers

The Committee held two sessions in 2016: the 24th (11–22 April) and the 25th (29 August – 7 September), during which the concluding observations were adopted relative to Lesotho, Mauritania, Senegal and Turkey (24th session), Honduras, Nicaragua, Niger and Sri Lanka (25th session). No *General comments* were adopted in the course of the year.

Italy has not ratified the Convention on the Protection of the Rights of all Migrant Workers and Members of their Families and, consequently, is not subject to monitoring by the Committee.

# VI. Specialised United Nations Agencies, Programmes and Funds

## A. *International Labour Organisation (ILO)*

Established by the Treaty of Versailles in 1919, the ILO became the first specialised agency of the United Nations in 1946.

The ILO is devoted to promoting decent and productive work for men and women in conditions of freedom, equality, safety and dignity. Its chief objectives are: to promote rights at work, to encourage decent employment opportunities, to enhance social protection and to strengthen dialogue on work-related issues. The ILO is the only United Nations agency which has a tripartite structure: representatives of Governments, employers and workers jointly elaborate the policies and programmes of the Organisation. 185 States are members of the ILO.

Since its foundation, the ILO has adopted 189 conventions. Of these, the ILO has identified 8 which it defines as "fundamental" or "core" (No. 29 on Forced Labour, 1930; No. 87 on Freedom of Association and Protection of the Right to Organise, 1948; No. 98 on the Right to Organise and Collective Bargaining, 1949; No. 100 on Equal Remuneration for Men and Women Workers for Work of Equal Value, 1951; No. 105 on the Abolition of Forced Labour, 1957; No. 111 on the Elimination of All Forms of Discrimination in Employment, Occupation, Vocational Training and Terms and Conditions of Employment, 1958; No. 138 on the Minimum Age for Admission to Employment or Work, 1973; and No. 182 on the Elimination of the Worst Forms of Child Labour, 1999) and 4 defined as "priority" (or "governance": No. 81 on Labour Inspection, 1947; No. 122 on Employment Policy, 1964; No. 129 on Labour Inspection [Agriculture], 1969; and No. 144 on Tripartite Consultation [International Labour Standards], 1976).

Italy has been a member of the ILO since 1919 (it is one of the founding members); it withdrew from the Organisation in 1937 but joined again permanently in 1945. The ILO is present in Italy with its offices in Rome, which have been operating since 1920, and the International Training Centre, established in Turin in 1965.

Italy has ratified 113 conventions adopted by the ILO (of which 82 in force and 31 denounced), including the 8 fundamental ones, the 4 priority ones and 101 of the 177 technical conventions.

The complete list, updated to December 2016, of ILO conventions and of Italy's acceptance status (ratification, signature, no initiative is available online at: www.italianhumanrightsyearbook.eu, in the section "attachments".

> In order to monitor the application of conventions ratified by States, in 1926 the ILO established the Committee of Experts on the Application of Conventions and Recommendations, a body made up of twenty eminent jurists and social professionals, who are independent of Governments and appointed on individual merits. The monitoring mechanism requires each Member State to submit periodic reports on the steps they have taken, in law and in practice, to apply each of the conventions it has ratified. At the same time, Governments are required to submit copies of their reports to employers' and workers' organisations, which are entitled to make comments and supply further information. Government reports are initially examined by the Committee of Experts, which can make two different kinds of comments: observations and direct requests. The observations contain comments on fundamental questions raised by the application of a particular convention by a State, and are published in the Committee's annual report. On the other hand, direct requests relate to more technical requests or requests for further information; they are not published in the report but are communicated directly to the Governments concerned.
>
> Upon conclusion of its considerations, the Committee presents an annual report to the International Labour Conference, the most representative body of the ILO, comprising representatives from all the ILO Member States and including all its observations and recommendations, which are carefully examined by the Conference Committee on the Application of Standards, a tripartite standing committee made up of Government, employer and worker delegates. This Committee selects a number of observations from the report for more in-depth discussion. The Governments referred to in these comments are invited to respond before the Conference Committee to provide information on the situation in question. In many cases, the Conference Committee adopts conclusions recommending that Governments take specific steps to remedy a problem or to invite the ILO to come on a mission to their Country or to request technical assistance.

In 2016, Italy received eight direct requests and one observation from the Committee of Experts on the Application of Conventions and Recommendations.

The Committee's direct requests were made in order to obtain further information on Italy's legislative, administrative and political instruments with regard to the implementation of the following Conventions: No. 29 – Forced Labour; No. 105 – Abolition of Forced Labour; No. 139 – Occupational Cancer; No. 159 – Vocational Rehabilitation and Employment (persons with disabilities); No. 167 – Health and Safety in Construction; No. 170 – Chemicals Convention; MLC – Maritime Labour Convention; No. 189 – Domestic Workers.

The observation was relative to Convention No. 181 – Private Employment Agencies.

*Convention No. 181 on Private Employment Agencies.*

The Committee requested that the Italian Government provide information on the following: the impact of the measures taken to ensure adequate protection of workers employed by private employment agencies, in accordance with arts. 11 and 12 of the Convention; the measures taken to promote cooperation between the public employment service and private employment agencies, and also on the activities of the National Agency for Active Employment Policies; on the application of the Convention in practice, with particular reference to the number of workers covered by the measures benefiting from the measures enshrined in the Convention (specifying the type and the duration of their employment arrangements), and the number and nature of infringements reported in relation to the activities of private employment agencies.

The overall budget of the ILO is structured through three main funding sources: the regular budget, voluntary contributions in addition to the regular budget (the Regular Budget Supplementary Account) and the resources for technical cooperation. In line with previous years, in 2016 Italy again contributed 4.5% of the ILO regular budget, an amount equivalent to approximately 17 million Swiss francs. Over the two-year period 2016–2017, Italy made a further voluntary contribution to the regular budget equivalent to 223,000 dollars, making Italy one of the eight donor countries, in addition to Belgium, Denmark, Germany, Luxemburg, the Netherlands, Norway and Sweden.

## B. United Nations Educational, Scientific and Cultural Organisation (UNESCO)

The human rights which fall under the responsibility of UNESCO are the right to education, the right to benefit from scientific progress, the right to participate freely in cultural life and the right to information, including freedom of opinion and expression. In connection with these, the right to freedom of thought, conscience and religion, the right to seek, receive and impart information and ideas through any instrument and across borders, the right to protection of the moral and material interests resulting from any scientific, literary or artistic production are pertinent, as are the right to freedom of assembly and association.

Italy has been a Member State of UNESCO since 1948. In 2016, H.E. Vincenza Lomonaco was Italy's Permanent Representative to UNESCO. Since its inception, UNESCO has adopted 28 Conventions, of which Italy has ratified 20.

The complete list, updated to December 2016, of UNESCO conventions and of Italy's acceptance status (ratification, signature, no initiative is available online at: www.italianhumanrightsyearbook.eu, in the section "attachments".

In the field of education, in 1991 the 26th General Conference of UNESCO established the International Programme for University Cooperation (IUC). The Programme is working to foster the creation of a network of centres of excellence (UNESCO Chairs) which will implement advanced teaching and research programmes in fields related to UNESCO policies, with special reference to the areas of peace, human rights, democracy and intercultural dialogue. There are over 680 UNESCO chairs worldwide; in 2016 Italy had 25 chairs (+4 compared to 2015) of which 3 are specifically devoted to human rights and include these words in their name: the Chair in "Human rights, Democracy and Peace", established in 1999 at the University of Padova (holder: Antonio Papisca); the Chair in "Human Rights and Ethics of International Cooperation", established in 2003 at the University of Bergamo (holder: Stefania Gandolfi); and the Chair in "Bioethics and Human rights", established in 2009 at the "Regina Apostolorum" Pontificial Athenaeum, European University of Rome (holder: Alberto García Gómez).

There are two committees on bioethics operating in UNESCO: the International Bioethics Committee (IBC) and the Intergovernmental Bioethics Committee (IGBC).

The IBC was established in 1993, particularly thanks to the efforts of Director-General of UNESCO at that time, and it is a body made up of 36 independent experts coming from different geographical and disciplinary backgrounds. Its mission is to follow progress in life science and its applications in order to ensure respect for human dignity and human rights and to promote reflection on the ethical and legal issues raised by research in the life sciences and their applications. To this end, over the years it has published a number of recommendations and other documents, the most significant of which is the Universal Declaration on Bioethics and Human Rights, adopted by the UNESCO General Conference in 2005. The Committee convenes once a year upon invitation from the UNESCO Director-General. The 2013 session (twentieth) was held in Seoul from June 19–21 and debated the issue of non-discrimination and non-stigmatisation, as set forth in art. 11 of the Declaration. In 2013 the Chairperson of the Committee was Stefano Semplici, full professor of Moral Philosophy at Rome "Tor Vergata» University and member of the Committee since 2008.

The IGBC was created in 1998 pursuant to art. 11 of the IBC Statute. It is comprised of 36 Member States who are elected by the UNESCO General Conference, and meets at least once every two years to examine the proposals and recommendations of the IBC and to forward these proposals, accompanied by its own opinions, to the other UNESCO Member States.

As in previous years, Italy contributed to about 4.5% of UNESCO's regular budget (which covers ongoing expenses for personnel and the main activities of the Organisation), a sum equivalent to approximately 14.4 million dollars, placing it seventh among the main contributors to the Organisation. Moreover, in 2016, did not make voluntary contributions, which fund multiannual cooperation programmes managed by UNESCO (in 2015 the voluntary contribution of Italy was 4.5 million dollars),

*UNESCO Machinery*

Italy was not involved with any of the organisation's monitoring mechanisms in 2016.

## C. The Food and Agriculture Organisation of the United Nations (FAO)

The FAO was established in 1945 in Ville de Quebec, Canada, and has its headquarters in Rome. José Graziano da Silva (Brazil) has been the Director-general of the Organisation since 1 January 2012. The Organisation budget for the biennium 2016–2017 has amounted to 2.6 billion dollars.

As at 31 March 2017, Italy was the seventh largest donor to the FAO, contributing almost 12 million dollars. Italy also cooperates with the FAO through the FAO/Italy Cooperative Programme, the main components of which are: the Traditional Programme, the Italian Trust Fund for Food Security and the Decentralised Cooperation Programme.

## D. The World Health Organisation (WHO)

The primary objective of the Organisation, established in 1948, is the attainment by all peoples of the highest possible level of health, understood not as the absence of disease but as a state of complete physical, mental and social well-being.

In Italy there is one office of the WHO (Venice) and currently 27 accredited collaborating centres. The latter, specialised institutions which receive no funding from the WHO, are identified by the Director General of the WHO and are part of a worldwide network to support the Organisation in various medical and scientific fields. In Italy their activity is coordinated by the Ministry of Health.

On 15 November 2016, the WHO Regional Office for Europe launched the European Knowledge Hub on Health and Migration, with the financial support of the Sicilian regional health council, which should serve as a repository for scientific evidence on the health-related aspects of migratory flows.

## E. The United Nations Development Programme (UNDP)

The United Nations Development Programme (UNDP) was established by the General Assembly in 1965 and has the role of central agency for the coordination and funding of development cooperation of the United Nations system.

UNDP action pursues the general objective of "human development", understood as not only economic growth but also as social development, based on gender equality and respect for human rights. UNDP conducts research and analysis, preparing studies and reports. Of the most significant, worth noting are the Annual Report on Human Development and the report on the state of achievement of the Sustainable Development Goals.

Italy contributed approximately 5.5 million dollars to the ordinary budget of the UNDP in 2016, which made it the 16th largest contributing Country.

## F. The United Nations Environment Programme (UNEP)

The UNEP's mission is to coordinate and facilitate the realisation of a global partnership for development projects and environmental protection activities so that nations and peoples may improve their quality of life without jeopardising that of future generations.

Since 13 May 2016, the current Director General is Erik Solheim. The Permanent Representative to the UNEP and also head of the Italian Embassy mission in Nairobi is H.E. Mauro Massoni.

## G. The United Nations Children's Fund (UNICEF)

UNICEF is the permanent United Nations Fund mandated to protect and promote the rights of boys, girls and adolescents with the aim of improving their living conditions. Anthony Lake (USA) has been the Executive Director since 1 May 2010.

Italy hosts the UNICEF Research Centre at the Istituto degli Innocenti in Florence. Moreover, the Italian Committee for UNICEF, a non-governmental organisation whose activity is regulated by a cooperation agreement signed with UNICEF International, has been operating in Italy since 1974. Chairperson of the Committee is Giacomo Guerrera, who has held the post since November 2011.

According to UNICEF's Annual Report for 2015, published in June 2016, Italy ranked 18th among donor countries for the two-year period 2014–2015, with 7.6 million dollars. Furthermore, the Italian Committee for UNICEF contributed over 18 million dollars to the Fund in 2015.

## VII. International Organisations with Permanent Observer Status at the General Assembly

### *A. The International Organisation for Migration (IOM)*

Established in 1951, the IOM is the major inter-governmental organization which deals with migrant issues. Its mission is to promote orderly migration based on respect for human dignity; to this end, it collaborates with Governments and civil society.

The IOM Coordination Office for the Mediterranean countries is based in Rome and the main activities of the IOM offices in Italy concern: providing assistance to vulnerable groups and minors, migration and employment; migration and health; migration, climate and development, reuniting families; supporting voluntary return; relocation and resettlement. Two events of note in 2016 were the launch of the information campaign "Aware Migrants" – jointly developed with the Ministry for Internal Affairs, and the presentation of the results of the "Study on Migrants' Profiles, Drivers of Migration, and Migratory Trends", commissioned by the U.K. Department for International Development and carried out by the International Organisation for Migration's Coordination Office for the Mediterranean in collaboration with the European University Institute in Fiesole (Florence).

# Council of Europe

Established on 5 May 1949, the Council of Europe (CoE, 47 Member States) is the first and most advanced system of promotion and protection of human rights at the regional level. The Permanent Representative of Italy to the Council of Europe was, until September 2016, H.E. Amb. Manuel Jacoangeli, who was succeeded by H.E. Amb. Marco Marsilli. The Italian Gabriella Battaini-Dragoni is currently serving her second term as Deputy Secretary-General of the organisation. Italy is home to one of the external offices of the CoE, with the CoE Programme Office in Venice, whose activities focus on themes relative to culture, cultural heritage and hosting training courses on human rights and democracy.

In 2016, Italy contributed an overall total of 34,721,576 euro to the activities of the Council of Europe, of which 27,332,430 euro for the ordinary budget (in 2015 the overall total was 35,900,364 euro, 27,369,609 of which for the ordinary budget). In 2016, Italy made voluntary contributions for 587,980 euro (583,980 euro in 2015).

The following pages will illustrate, with reference to Italy, the activities of the Parliamentary Assembly and the Committee of Ministers; those of six bodies established by a treaty: the European Court of Human Rights, the Committee for the Prevention of Torture, the European Committee of Social Rights, the Advisory Committee on the Framework Convention for the Protection of National Minorities, the Group of Experts on Action against Trafficking in Human Beings and Group of Experts on Action against Violence against Women and Domestic Violence; and of four bodies established by the Committee of Ministers: Commissioner for Human Rights, the European Commission against Racism and Intolerance, the European Commission for Democracy through Law and the Group of States against Corruption.

## I. Parliamentary Assembly

In the Parliamentary Assembly of the Council of Europe (PACE), made up of delegations from the national Parliaments of the Member States of the CoE, 18 members of the Senate and the Chamber of Deputies sit for Italy; there are an equal number of alternate members.

The following are the members and the alternate members (a) of PACE in 2016: Ferdinando Aiello (a), Francesco Maria Amoruso (a), Anna Ascani, Deborah Bergamini, Anna Maria Bernini, Maria Teresa Bertuzzi, Tamara Blazina (a), Nunzia Catalfo, Elena Centemero, Massimo Cervellini (a), Khalid Chaouki (a), Vannino Chiti, Eleonora Cimbro (a), Paolo Corsini, Luca D'Alessandro (a), Cristina De Pietro (a), Manlio Di Stefano, Sergio Divina, Claudio Fazzone (a), Giuseppe Galati (a), Adriana Galgano (a), Adele Gambaro, Florian Kronbichler, Francesco Maria Giro, Carlo Lucherini (a), Emanuela Munerato (a), Michele Nicoletti, Luis Alberto Orellana (a), Laura Puppato (a), Lia Quartapelle Procopio (a), Andrea Rigoni, Vincenzo Santangelo, Milena Santerini, Maria Edera Spadoni (a), Francesco Verducci (a), Sandra Zampa (a).

The President of the Italian delegation is Michele Nicoletti. Adele Gambaro is one of the 20 Vice-Presidents of the Assembly. As to the role of Italian members of Parliament in the various PACE parliamentary committees, Elena Centemero is Chairperson of the Committee on Equality and Non-Discrimination; Andrea Rigoni is Chairperson of the Sub-Committee on Cooperation with non-European Countries of Origin and Transit (Committee on Migration, Refugees and Displaced Persons).

As concerns the actions of the Italian members of the Parliamentary Assembly in 2016, four reports are highlighted, all of which were submitted to the appropriate committees and on the basis of which the PACE adopted resolutions: Maria Elena Spadoni's report to the Equality and Non-Discrimination Committee on the *Systematic collection of data on violence against women,* (submitted on 17 February, resolution 2101, adopted on 4 March 2016); two reports by Manlio Di Stefano to the Committee on Migration, Refugees and Displaced Persons on *The need to eradicate statelessness for children,* (submitted on 16 February, resolution 2099, adopted on 4 March 2016) and on *Harmonising the protection of unaccompanied minors in Europe,* (report submitted on 26 September, resolution 2136, adopted on 13 October); and the report by Andrea Rigoni to this same committee, on *Violence against migrants* (report submitted on 20 May, resolution 2128, adopted on 24 June 2016).

## II. Committee of Ministers

On the subject of human rights, the Committee of Ministers (CM) relies on the work of the Steering Committee for Human Rights, an inter-governmental body composed of representatives of the 47 Member States which performs, among other things, standard-setting and follow-up.

The CM adopts recommendations regarding the Member States and on matters for which a common policy is agreed upon – in accordance with its role in the implementation of the European Social Charter (art. 29) – with the aim of asking some States to adapt their laws and public policies with the provisions contained in the Charter. In addition, it is ultimately responsible for monitoring the Framework Convention on National Minorities (art. 26). In this context, it adopts specific resolutions by Country based on the opinions of the Advisory Committee of the Framework Convention.

With regard to its role in relation to the European Court of Human Rights, the CM has the function of supervising the execution of judgments of the Court, ensuring that Member States act in accordance with the rulings issued by the same. The Committee terminates each case by adopting a final resolution. Finally, the CM may apply to the Court for a ruling on issues related to difficulties of interpretation of the judgments of the Court itself which would impede their implementation and if it believes that a Member State is refusing to comply with a final judgment, it may refer the issue to the Court.

In 2016, the CM adopted 11 final resolutions on the execution by Italy of ECtHR judgments: CM/ResDH(2016)358 on *Di Bonaventura and 74 other cases*, CM/ResDH(2016)315 on *Silvestri and one other case*, CM/ResDH(2016)276 on *Costa and Pavan,* CM/ResDH(2016)252 on *Calcagno and 11 other cases*, CM/ResDH(2016)221 on *Hirsi Jamaa and others,* CM/ResDH(2016)119 on *Patrono, Cascini and Stefanelli and 3 other cases,* CM/ResDH(2016)95 on *Cecere Enrico*, CM/ResDH(2016)63 on *Panetta*, CM/ResDH(2016)28 on *Torreggiani and others and 1 other case*, CM/ResDH(2016)27 on *Roda and Bonfatti and two other cases* and CM/ResDH(2016)13 on *Alikaj and others.*

As concerns ongoing monitoring of the implementation of ECtHR judgments against Italy, the Committee of Ministers adopted five decisions in 2016.

On 9 June 2016, during its 1259th session, the CM adopted a decision on the case *Di Sarno and others* (CM/Del/Dec(2016)1259/H46-16), concerning waste collection and treatment in the region of Campania (see *2013 Yearbook,* pp. 365–366). Therein the Committee recognises the various measures progressively adopted by the Italian authorities to resolve the problems relative to the treatment and disposal of waste in the region of Campania, as well as the introduction of mechanisms for monitoring waste management. The CM observes that the situation on the ground has improved, since there have been no further instances of uncollected waste accumulating on the streets for over four years and that encouraging results have also been achieved as far as disposal of refuse is concerned. Consequently, the Committee requests that Italy continue to provide information on the impact of the measures implemented and expedite the rapid adoption of the remaining additional measures envisaged, to ensure that the situation criticised in the judgment of the European Court does not recur. Moreover, the Italian authorities are requested to provide information on the monitoring mechanisms established to this end, and particularly whether they have the authority to make recommendations and if so, on the type of actions that follow such recommendations. The CM also requested the Italian authorities to provide information on the effective domestic remedies available to citizens to obtain redress for the damage caused them by poor management of waste collection and treatment.

On 22 September 2016, during its 1265th session, the CM adopted a decision on the case *Sharifi and others* (CM/Del/Dec(2016)1265/H46-16), in which the Strasburg Court censured the practice of automatic readmission of irregular migrants arriving from Greece at ports on Italy's Adriatic coast (see *2015 Yearbook*, p. 303). In its decision, the CM encouraged the Italian authorities to provide additional information on the steps taken to clarify the current situation of some of the applicants, who have not been granted international protection in Italy. The Committee took note with interest of the measures adopted by the Italian authorities to ensure that migrants arriving in ports on the Adriatic have effective access to international protection procedures and observed in this respect that there is still some uncertainty as to the effectiveness of these measures. Consequently, the CM invited the Italian authorities to provide them with information on the current organisation and functioning of the reception system and on the financial and human resources allocated thereto. The Committee further took note of the assurances provided by the Italian authorities according to which the readmission agreement concluded between Italy and Greece is now being applied within the limits specified in article 6 and in keeping with the requirements of the ECHR. The CM noted, however, that the available information relates to 2012–2013 and invited the authorities to provide the Committee with clarifications on the current procedure being followed from the arrival of these persons, on how their effective access to the services provided by NGOs in the Adriatic ports is assured, and on the time-frames and arrangements for sending them back. While noting the significant reduction in the numbers returned to Greece reported by the authorities, the Committee considered that a series of statistical clarifications are necessary in order to be able to evaluate fully the extent of the same.

On 8 December 2016, during its 1273rd session, the CM adopted a decision on the *Ledonne* case (CM/Del/Dec(2016)1273/H46-15). Therein, the Committee noted with interest the criminal law reform bill currently being examined by the Senate and invited the authorities to inform the Committee of the outcome of the legislative process and, where appropriate, of any other measure adopted, since June 2013, or in the process of being adopted, aimed at solving the problem of the excessive length of criminal proceedings. Furthermore, the CM invited the authorities to provide, by April 2017, a thorough evaluation of the situation on the ground together with statistical data for the period 2011–2016 particularly as regards the average length of criminal proceedings, the ratio between incoming cases and cases solved and the number of cases pending at the end of each year by level of jurisdiction.

On the same date, the CM also adopted a decision on the group of cases *Agrati and others* (CM/Del/Dec(2016)1273/H46-14, see *2012 Yearbook*, pp. 346–347). Therein, regarding the individual measures, the Committee invited the authorities to clarify, first, the procedures available under national law to determine and remedy the consequences stemming from the retroactive application of law No. 266/2005 for the applicants in the cases *Agrati and others, De Rosa and others* and *Bordoni and others,* for the period subsequent to 31 December 2011 and, secondly, the possibility of ensuring that the benefit of the internal decision in favour of *Ms Peduzzi* and *Mr Arrighi,* which was delivered prior to the application of the disputed legislation, is retained. The Committee also invited the authorities to clarify whether the other applicants suffered pecuniary damage and, where appropriate, if it is possible to seek compensation in this respect at domestic level.

With respect to the general measures, the CM noted that the practice of the national courts concerning the application of the disputed provisions of Law No. 266/2005 does not appear to be aligned with the requirements of Article 6 ECHR highlighted in these cases and so invited the authorities to provide the Committee with their assessment in this respect as well as clarification as to how they envisage, if necessary, solving this problem. Moreover, the CM invited the authorities to provide information on the measures adopted or envisaged to ensure that laws with retroactive effect are adopted in strict conformity with the requirements of the Convention, to provide the Committee of Ministers with a revised action plan containing clarifications on the outstanding questions identified in this group of cases.

Again on 8 December 2016, the CM adopted a decision on the *Abenavoli* group of cases (CM/Del/Dec(2016)1273/H46-13) concerning the excessive duration of administrative proceedings and the issues relative to the "Pinto" act. In its decision, the CM noted the significant measures adopted by the Italian authorities, which show their determination to continue their efforts to solve the problem of the excessive length of administrative proceedings. They also noted with satisfaction that the positive trend observed with respect to reducing the backlog of cases has consolidated since 2011 and that encouraging results have been attained regarding the average length of certain proceedings before the Council of State. Consequently, in the light of these positive developments, the CM decided to end the monitoring of the execution of 75 cases in which the question of individual measures has been settled (see final resolution CM/ResDH(2016)358). However, the Committee decided that it would continue to monitor the issues still unresolved since the first level of proceedings. Finally, the CM invited the Italian authorities to provide the Committee with their analysis of the current situation based on complete statistics as soon as possible, to enable it to assess fully the status of execution of this group of cases.

On 6 July 2016, the CM adopted a resolution (CM/ResChS(2016)3) on the decision by the European Committee of Social Rights regarding the collective complaint against Italy lodged on 17 January 2013 by the *Confederazione Generale Italiana del Lavoro* (CGIL) (91/2013) (see Part in this Part, Council of Europe, V). In its resolution, the CM took note of the information provided on the follow-up to the decision of the European Committee of Social Rights and welcomed the positive developments therein.

Finally, on 6 July, the CM adopted a resolution CM/ResCSS(2016)10 on the application of the European Code of Social Security (with reference to the period 1 July 2014–30 June 2015). Basing itself on the report submitted by the Italian Government, the Committee made a series of observations and requests for further information.

These included, with reference to Part V of the Code (Old-age benefits), a request from the CM that the authorities calculate the level of the old age pension of a standard beneficiary who has paid 30 years of contributions, under both the old and the new rules, in order to show that the 40% replacement rate requested by the Code will be reached in all of the above-mentioned cases. Concerning reduced benefits after 15 years of insurance, considering the above-mentioned gap in social protection in Italy (minimum twenty years of contributions, and considering that the amount of the pension must be no less than 1.5 times the minimum monthly social pension) is incompatible with both the letter and the spirit of the Code, the CM invites Italy to re-establish the right of all persons protected under Part V to a reduced social insurance pension after 15 years of contributions. Concerning Part XI (Standards to be complied with by periodical payments), the Committee requests Italy to include more detailed information in its next report on, among other things, the process of determining the reference wage, the index of contractual wages, wage variation by gender and the description of the tasks performed by level I and III workers in metal industries. With reference to Part IV of the Code (concerning the adjustment of the benefits in payment), the CM asks the Italian authorities to explain its policy of maintaining the purchasing power of the benefits in payment as well as giving the pensioners a fair share of the growth of the national economy after the crisis. Taking into account that in comparison with the base year of 2010, the consumer price index for families of workers and employees had increased at the end of 2014 by 7.2 per cent, the CM requests the Italian Government to provide full information and statistics in the next report on the adjustment of pensions. Finally, as concerns the adequacy of social security benefits, the CM invites the Italian authorities to update and supplement the statistical information in the "Technical Note", sent to the Government, also including, for the same time basis, updated statistics on social security coverage, amount of the reference wage and calculations of the replacement rate of benefits.

## III. European Court of Human Rights

The European Court of Human Rights (ECtHR), the first international court specifically designed for the protection of human rights in a particular region of the world, guarantees the respect of the commitments laid down in the ECHR and its protocols by Member States of the CoE.

The Italian judge who now sits at the Court is Guido Raimondi, appointed President of the ECtHR in September 2015. Of the 679 members of the Registry, which provides legal and administrative support to the Court in exercising its functions, 23 are Italian.

The statistical data provided by the Court and updated to December 2016, show that the total number of complaints pending against Italy amounts to 6,200, constituting about 7.8% of the total. In a worse situation are Ukraine with 18,150 pending complaints, equivalent to 22.8% of the total, Turkey (12,600/15.8%), Hungary (8,950/11.2%), Russia (7,800/9.8%) and Romania (7,400/9.3%). In 2016, the Court received 1,409 valid applications by individuals who complained of a violation by Italy of the rights enshrined in the ECHR (1,885 in 2015 and 5,490 in 2014). Over the same period, 2,695 were declared inadmissible or struck from the register, 15 led to a decision on the merits (relative to 35 applications), 10 of which identified at least one violation of the Convention; 763 applications were communicated to the relevant Country in view of a hearing on their merits. The ECtHR also received 39 requests for temporary measures pursuant to article 39 of the rules of Court, mostly regarding the suspension of deportation proceedings for as many applicants, only two of which were granted by the ECtHR.

An analysis of the Court's 2016 judgments concerning Italy is made in Part IV, Italy in the Case-law of the European Court of Human Rights.

## IV. Committee for the Prevention of Torture

The European Committee for the Prevention of Torture and Inhuman or Degrading Treatment or Punishment (CPT) was established by the 1987 Convention of the same name, conceived as complementary to the regulations under art. 3 ECHR which sets forth an absolute ban on torture. The CPT is a body composed of independent experts and has one member for each State Party to the Convention for the Prevention of Torture. The members of the Committee are elected by the Committee of Ministers. The independent expert for Italy from 20 December 2011 to 19 December 2015 was Andreana Esposito. On 7 October 2015, the CM elected Elisabetta Zamparutti as Italy's new member of the CPT (CM/ResCPT(2015)3). She will remain in post until 19 December 2019.

> Over the course of 2016, the CPT made 19 visits to 15 countries: Azerbaijan, Belgium, Greece (2 visits, of which one focusing on the hot spots for migrants), the former Yugoslav Republic of Macedonia, Russian Federation (2, of which one focusing on the Northern Caucasus), Italy, Lichtenstein, Latvia, Lithuania, the Netherlands, Portugal, the United Kingdom, Spain (2, of which one focusing on the treatment of foreign citizens during a "removal by air" operation), Turkey (2, of which one focusing on Imrali Island) and Ukraine. During the year, the CPT published 14 reports relative to previous visits to the following CoE member states: Albania, Armenia, Belgium, Bosnia-Herzegovina, the Former Yugoslav Republic of Macedonia, Greece, Kosovo, Malta, Netherlands, Republic of Moldova, Serbia, Sweden, Switzerland and Hungary.

The CPT has visited Italy 12 times overall (seven scheduled periodic visits and five ad hoc visits). The latest visit took place on 8–21 April 2016 and focused on evaluating the conditions and the treatment of detainees, with a special focus on the measures recently introduced by the Italian authorities to tackle the issue of prison overcrowding. During the visit, the CPT delegation also examined the situation of prisoners assigned to the strictest security measures as per the provisions of the "regime 41-*bis*" in Ascoli Piceno and Sassari prisons. Furthermore, the delegation examined the treatment and safeguards by law enforcement officers enjoyed by persons deprived of their personal freedom. For the first time, the CPT delegation also examined the situation of forensic psychiatric patients housed in "REMS", residential buildings for the execution of security measures following the closure of criminal psychiatric hospitals in Italy in application of law 81/2014. In connection with this specific area, the CPT also visited one of the remaining psychiatric hospitals, the department of civil psychiatry in a generalist hospital, a psychiatric observation unit in a prison and a secure unit in a general hospital. Over the course of their visit, the CPT delegation attended meetings with, among others, the Minister of Justice, Andrea Orlando, the National Ombudsperson for the Rights of Persons in Prison or Deprived of their Liberty, Mauro Palma, as well as representatives of law enforcement agencies, regional authorities and NGOs with expertise in this area.

Furthermore, in 2016, on request of the Government, the CPT published the report on its previous ad hoc visit, together with the answers provided by the Italian authorities. This visit took place from 16–18 December 2015, centred on examining the way foreign nationals were treated during a joint removal operation from Italy by air, coordinated and co-financed by the European agency FRONTEX. The CPT delegation specifically observed the organisation and carrying out of a charter flight to Lagos (Nigeria) which also involved, apart from Italy as the organising member State, Belgium and Switzerland as participating member states (see *2016 Yearbook*, p. 187).

On a general level, the CPT remarked that the level of cooperation provided by the Italian authorities was excellent, that the members of the escort behaved professionally, and that no instances of ill-treatment towards the people being removed by air were observed. Despite this, some specific aspects were a cause of concern for the Committee delegation, leading them to make a series of recommendations to the Italian authorities.

As concerns the organisation of the operation, the CPT reports that, according to the information gathered by the delegation in Rome, the repatriation of some women held at the Ponte Galeria Centre for Identification and Expulsion had been decided while the appeals against the rejection of their asylum requests were still ongoing. Since this information was not shown on the repatriation files of these people, the CPT recommends that the Italian authorities should take steps to ensure that the removal files of all persons detained in CIE Ponte Galeria are updated and contain all the relevant information, including on pending legal procedures.

Furthermore, in order to reduce the risk of violating the principle of *non-refoulement* during these repatriation operations, the CPT issued a series of recommendations relative to cases in which foreign citizens should not be removed: for example, when a court has suspended such removal or when a request for suspension of a removal is pending before a court. On this issue, the CPT suggested adopting measures to improve the flow of information (informing people subject to a removal operation and their lawyers about the operation concerning them) and ensuring an opportunity for people who are scheduled for repatriation to access a "last call procedure".

As regards the removal operation itself, the CPT states that it is not fully convinced by the policy of the Italian authorities not to inform detainees of their imminent repatriation until the actual day of departure. Indeed, according to the delegation, leaving a person who is to be repatriated uninformed of this decision, rather than facilitating the process, as the Italian authorities say, increases the risk that the person may violently resist their removal. Preparing the person concerned well in advance, on the other hand, has proven the most humane and efficient approach.

The Committee recommends that all detainees undergo a medical examination prior to a removal operation and that, should an operation of this type fail, the detainee should be examined again prior to being readmitted to the detention centre.

As regards the staff taking part in the removal by air, the CPT delegation notes that their jobs are quite stressful. Consequently, they recommend that the Italian authorities pay due attention to the psychological aspects of their jobs during staff selection and training processes. The delegation also recommended that escorts in this type of operation should wear a clearly visible identification tag.

Concerning the use of force during removals by air, in the CPT's opinion, FRONTEX and its State Parties should apply more specific, common rules on the use of means of restraint. The CPT also feels that an effective complaints procedure should be set up and made accessible in practice to detainees up to the moment of their arrival in their destination Country and asks the Italian Government to provide further information on the mandate, the powers and the instruments at the disposal of the National Ombudsperson for the Rights of Persons in Prison or Deprived of their Liberty.

## V. European Committee of Social Rights

The European Committee of Social Rights (ECSR) was established pursuant to art. 25 of the European Social Charter of 1961 in order to determine whether the legislation and practice of States Parties comply with the provisions of the European Social Charter, its Protocols and the European Social Charter (revised) (ESC-R). Currently, the Committee is composed of 15 independent experts elected by the Committee of Ministers for a period of six years, renewable only once. Between 10 November 2010 and 31 December 2016, an Italian expert, Giuseppe Palmisano, has been a part of the Committee.

Italy ratified the European Social Charter in 1965 and the revised European Social Charter in 1999, accepting 97 of its 98 numbered paragraphs. The only provision not accepted is article 25 ESC-R, which protects the right of workers in the event of the insolvency of their employer. In 2002, the CM decided that, every five years, countries must also inform the European Committee of Social Rights on the status of rights protected under provisions that they have not accepted. Italy's most recent communication on this issue dates from 2014 (see *2016 Yearbook*, pp. 188–189); the Committee's next assessment of art. 25 ESC-R is scheduled for 2019.

As concerns the analysis of provisions it has accepted, from 1967 to 2016 the Italian Government submitted 20 annual reports on the application of the 1961 Charter and 15 on that of the revised Charter. Based on these, the Committee adopted its conclusions each year on the status of protection of social rights in Italy. Their most recent *Conclusions* on Italy were published in January 2017. The document refers to the fifteenth report, submitted on 15 December 2015 and covering the provisions of the Revised Charter in the thematic group 1 "Employment, training and equal opportunities" (arts. 1, 9, 10, 15, 18, 20, 24 and 25 ESC-R). The report submitted by the Italian Government also provides the information the Committee requested in its *2014 Conclusions* on thematic group 3 "Workers' rights" referring to the conclusions of non-conformity due to the continuing failure to provide the information required in the previous reports periodically submitted by the Italian authorities (see *2015 Yearbook*, pp. 201–205).

Overall, the 2016 *Conclusions* refer to the Italian situation in relation to 23 articles or paragraphs of the revised Charter. The Committee found 12 situations of conformity, often emphasising the fact that these assessments were made while awaiting additional information on the issues examined, and 5 situations of non-conformity. For 6 situations, the Committee decided to postpone their conclusions while awaiting more detailed information from the Italian authorities in their next annual report.

**Summary table of 2016 Conclusions on Italy by paragraph**

| ESC-R Article | Conclusions of conformity | Conclusions of non-conformity | Requests for further information |
|---|---|---|---|
| Art. 1 ESC-R (The right to work) | | Para. 1 (achieve full employment) | Para. 2 (occupation freely entered into)<br>Para. 3 (free employment services)<br>Para. 4 (vocational guidance, training and rehabilitation) |
| Art. 2 ESC-R (The right to just conditions of work) | | Para. 4 (eliminate risks in inherently dangerous or unhealthy occupations) | |
| Art. 6 ESC-R (The right to bargain collectively) | | | Para. 4 (collective action) |

| ESC-R Article | Conclusions of conformity | Conclusions of non-conformity | Requests for further information |
|---|---|---|---|
| Art. 9 ESC-R (Right to professional guidance) | The whole of the one-paragraph article. | | |
| Art. 10 ESC-R (Right to vocational training) | Para. 1 (technical and vocational training; access to higher technical and university education)<br>Para. 2 (apprenticeships)<br>Para. 5 (full use of facilities available) | | Para. 3 (training and retraining of adult workers)<br>Para. 4 (long-term unemployed) |
| Art. 15 ESC-R (Right of persons with disabilities to independence, social integration and participation in the life of the community) | Para. 1 (professional training for persons with disabilities)<br>Para. 2 (employment of persons with disabilities)<br>Para. 3 (social integration and participation in the life of the community for persons with disabilities) | | |
| Art. 18 ESC-R (Right to engage in gainful occupation in the territory of other States Parties) | Para. 2 (simplify existing formalities and reduce dues and taxes)<br>Para. 4 (right of nationals to leave the Country) | Para. 1 (applying existing regulations in a spirit of liberality).<br>Para. 3 (liberalising regulations) | |

| ESC-R Article | Conclusions of conformity | Conclusions of non-conformity | Requests for further information |
| --- | --- | --- | --- |
| Art. 20 ESC-R (Right to equal opportunities and equal treatment in matters of employment and occupation without discrimination on the grounds of sex) | The whole of the one-paragraph article. | | |
| Art. 21 ESC-R (Right of workers to be informed and consulted) | The whole of the one-paragraph article. | | |
| Art. 22 ESC-R (Right to take part in the determination and improvement of working conditions and working environment) | The whole of the one-paragraph article. | | |
| Art. 24 ESC-R (Right to protection in cases of termination of employment) | | The whole of the one-paragraph article. | |

Looking at the *conclusions* in detail, as concerns art. 1 (Right to work), the Committee considered the situation in Italy not in conformity with para. 1 (achieve full employment) on the grounds that employment policy efforts to combat unemployment and promote job creation have not been adequate. With reference to the other three paragraphs, the Committee has postponed its decision while awaiting further information. As concerns para. 2 (occupation freely entered into) the information requested was the actual and tangible impact of the various measures introduced by the Italian Government over the period 2011–2015 on non-discrimination in employment, and on all regulatory and legal developments concerning the access of foreign citizens to employment in the public sector; on steps the State has taken to ensure that employers give due care to the private lives of workers when organising work and that all interference be prohibited and, where necessary, incur penalties. Concerning para. 3 (free employment services), the Committee's requests for information regarded the total number of jobseekers and unemployed persons registered with the public employment service, the number of vacant positions notified to the service, the number of people employed through this service, the employment ratio, the average time the service took to fill a vacancy, the number of jobs as a percentage of recruitment in the overall jobs market, and the respective market shares of the public and private sector. Further data requested by the Committee in order to make a decision on the conformity of the situation were on the number of people working in public job centres, the number of advisers working in employment services and the ratio of employment services staff to people registered as job seekers. Finally, they also requested information on the participation of the trade unions and employers' associations in organising and managing employment services. As concerns para. 4 (vocational guidance, training and retraining), the Committee asked the authorities to provide information on the provisions for training and professional retraining of workers and persons with disabilities.

With reference to art. 2 ESC-R (Right to just conditions of work), the Committee examined only the situation in relation to para. 4 (elimination of risks in dangerous or unhealthy occupations), in accordance with the new reporting system (adopted by the CM in April 2014) which requires member states to report within a short timeframe on those provisions for which the conclusion of a situation of non-conformity had been reached because of the persistent lack of required information. In its *2016 Conclusions*, based on the partial information received from the Italian Government, the Committee confirmed a situation of non-conformity of the provision monitored, on the ground that the right of workers exposed to residual occupational health risks to appropriate compensatory measures is not adequately guaranteed.

The same reporting system is applicable to para. 4 (collective action) of art. 6 ESC-R (Right to bargain collectively), on which a situation of non-conformity had been found in the *2014 Conclusions* (see *2015 Yearbook*, p. 204). The Committee found that the information provided, particularly on the power of the Government to issue injunctions which restrict strikes in essential public services, was insufficient to assess the conformity of these restrictions with art. G ESC-R (restrictions). Consequently, they requested detailed information on the injunctions issued during the reference period of Italy's report and, while awaiting this information, deferred its conclusions on the provision in question.

The Committee found that Italy was in conformity with art. 9 ESC-R (Right to professional guidance, an article consisting of just one paragraph), although it requested the Italian Government to provide, as of its next report, systematic, quantified information as to the levels of funding and staffing and the number of beneficiaries of the vocational guidance services in the labour market.

With reference to art. 10 ESC-R (Right to vocational training) the Committee concluded that the situation in Italy is in conformity with para. 1 (technical and vocational training; access to higher technical and university education), pending receipt of information on the implementation of the 2014 national guidelines for vocational training and the resulting National Qualifications Framework; on para. 2 (apprenticeships) and on para. 5 (full use of facilities available), while still waiting, however, for information on the measures introduced to evaluate the vocational training programmes for young workers. The Committee made a different assessment on para. 3 (training and retraining of adult workers), and it postponed its conclusion while awaiting information on the total number of unemployed people taking part in continuing training and on the activation ratio of the latter (the ratio between the average annual number of previously unemployed participants in active measures divided by the registered number of unemployed persons and participants in active measures). The Committee also deferred its conclusions on para. 4 (long-term unemployed). In this area, the information requested by the Committee to be able to make its assessment concerns the types of training and retraining offered within the labour market, the number of people undertaking this type of training and the impact of the measures adopted by the Government in reducing long-term unemployment.

As concerns art. 15 ESC-R (Right of persons with disabilities to independence, social integration and participation in the life of the community), the Committee concluded that the situation in Italy is in conformity with all three numbered paragraphs making up this article. However, on para. 1 (vocational training for persons with disabilities), the Committee requested further information, some of which had already been requested in the *2012 Conclusions* (see *2013 Yearbook*, pp. 252–253); on the practical impact of the 2013–2015 Action Plan to promote the rights and integration of persons with disabilities in terms of integration of students with disabilities in higher education institutions; on the percentage of students with disabilities who dropped out of school and how that compared to the total population; and on the vocational training of persons with disabilities in mainstream education. On para. 2 (employment of persons with disabilities), the Committee requested the authorities to provide information on the steps taken to ensure the effective conformity of the Italian situation with the compulsory reserved quota system for persons with disabilities and the results achieved in this respect. On the other hand, no further information was requested on para. 3 (social integration and participation in the life of the community for persons with disabilities).

As concerns art. 18 ESC-R (Right to engage in a gainful occupation in the territory of other States Parties), the Committee found both para. 2

(simplifying existing formalities and reducing dues and taxes) and para. 4 (right of nationals to leave the Country) in conformity with the Charter. However, for para. 2 the conclusion of conformity was maintained pending receipt of further information on the following: a) the average time needed to obtain residence permits for work purposes and the permits and certificates issued by the various Italian institutions and authorities involved in these procedures and b) the regulatory criteria applied when the amount of charges is set, clarifying, for instance, whether the charges correspond to the actual cost of processing the residence permit application and whether there are plans to introduce measures to reduce costs for workers or employers. On the other hand, the Committee found Italy in a situation of non-conformity with para. 1 (applying existing regulations in a spirit of liberality) on the ground that the report submitted by the Italian Government does not establish that the existing regulations are applied in the spirit required by the Charter. A conclusion of non-conformity was also reached for para. 3 (liberalising regulations). In this case, the Committee's conclusion was reached on the grounds that the regulations governing access to the labour market for foreign workers who are nationals of non-EEA States Parties to the European Social Charter (revised) are too restrictive.

A situation of conformity was found as concerns art. 20 ESC-R (Right to equal opportunities and equal treatment in matters of employment and occupation without discrimination on the grounds of sex). However, in this area the Committee asked the Italian Government to provide further information on the position of women in employment and training, on the gender pay gap and on all positive measures promoting gender equality, in particular equal pay for equal value.

As regards art. 21 ESC-R (Right of workers to be informed and consulted), again the Committee found a situation of conformity. However, in this case too, the Italian authorities were reminded that additional information was needed in order to make a full assessment. The specific requests from the Committee were: to confirm that Legislative decree 25/2007 (Implementation of directive 2002/14/CE which establishes a general framework for informing and consulting with workers) is applied even when there is no worker representation (RSU) in a company and also requests information as to what percentage of the workforce is guaranteed information and consultation rights.

The Committee also found a situation of conformity relative to art. 22 ESC-R (Right of workers to take part in the determination and improvement of working conditions and working environment). The additional information requested on this provision include more concrete information on the participation rights of employees in the determination and improvement of the working conditions, work organisation and working environment for example relevant legislation and collective agreements.

Finally, the Committee found a situation of non-conformity with art. 24 ESC-R (Right to protection in cases of termination of employment), on the grounds that employees subject to a six-month trial period have no protection in cases of dismissal.

The next report Italy had to submit to the Committee was on thematic group 2, "Health, social security and social protection" (arts. 3, 11, 12, 13, 14, 23 and 30 ESC-R) and the submission was due by 31 October 2016.

As regards the collective complaints procedure established by the 1995 Additional Protocol, in 2016 the conclusions of the Committee on case No. 91/2013, adopted on 12 October 2015, were published. The collective complaint, lodged by the *Confederazione Generale Italiana del Lavoro* (CGIL), requested that the Committee declare art. 9 of law 194/1978, which governs the right to conscientious objection of medical personnel in relation to abortion services, in violation of articles 11 ESC-R (Right to health), 1 (Right to work), 2 (Right to just conditions of work), 3 (Right to safe and healthy working conditions), 26 (Right to dignity at work) and E (Non- discrimination). According to the CGIL, shortcomings in the Italian legal framework, combined with the high number of conscientious objectors among doctors in public health structures, not only failed to protect women's right to access abortion services, in violation of the European Social Charter, but also damaged non-objecting medical practitioners, on whom the whole workload associated with protecting the aforementioned right falls (on the same issue, although it highlighted partially different reasons for non-conformity, see the complaint against Italy No. 87/2012, *2015 Yearbook,* pp. 198–199).

On the first point, the Committee found a lack of availability of abortion services due to the high numbers of objecting practitioners and the health structures inefficient in filling these gaps, as well as a worrying lack of action on the part of the regional authorities charged with overseeing and providing proper implementation of relevant legislation. The Committee considered that these factors cause considerable risks for women's health, as they find themselves having to apply to other health structures, in Italy or abroad, with the consequent effect of discouraging abortions. The Committee also accepted the second point, finding a violation of arts. 1(2) and 26(2) ESC-R. The insufficient application of section 9 of law 194/1978 and the high percentage of objecting medical practitioners do, in effect, lead to a difference in the way the two categories of health workers are treated. The few non-objecting doctors find themselves forced to cover the whole workload of abortions, with significant repercussions on the advancement of their careers. The Committee found that this forces them to carry out repetitive abortions, often outside the doctors' own specialism, with serious repercussions on their opportunities for training and achieving further useful qualifications.

On 16 November 2016 the European Committee of Social Rights' decision on the complaint lodged by the *Associazione Nazionale dei Giudici di Pace* (National Association of Justices of the Peace) against Italy was published (complaint No. 102/2013). In the complaint, submitted in August 2013, the Association alleged that Italian law does not provide any social security protection for Justices of the Peace, in violation of art. 12 ESC-R (Right to social security), specifically paragraphs 3 and 4b. The Association also alleged that there is a discrimination of Justices of the Peace in matters of social security in comparison with tenured judges and other categories of lay judges. After examining the merits of the complaint, the European Committee of Social Rights upheld the complaint and concluded unanimously that Italy had violated art. 12(1) of the Charter ESC-R, in conjunction with article E (Non discrimination).

Finally, three new collective complaints were lodged against Italy in 2016. The first (complaint No. 122/2016) was lodged by the *Movimento per la libertà della psicanalisi – Associazione culturale* (Movement for freedom to practise psychoanalysis) and concerned the alleged violation of art. 1(2) ESC-R (Right of the worker to earn his living in an occupation freely entered upon) because it is impossible to freely practise the profession of psychoanalyst, since such a profession can only be practised by physicians or psychologists enrolled on professional registers. On 6 September 2016 the Italian Government submitted its observations as to the admissibility of the complaint.

The second case (complaint No. 133/2016), was a collective complaint lodged by the association University Women of Europe (UWE) against 15 States concerning the alleged violation of the provisions of the European Social Charter (revised) on fair and equal remuneration between men and women. All the complaints lodged allege violation of art. 1 on the right to work, art. 4(3) ESC-R on fair remuneration and art. 20 ESC-R on equal opportunities, in conjunction with art. E on non-discrimination. On 2 November 2016 the Italian Government submitted its observations as to the admissibility of the complaint.

The third and last complaint (No. 140/2016) was lodged by the *Confederazione Generale Italiana del Lavoro* (CGIL) and related to the alleged violation of art. 5 (Union rights) and 6 (Right to bargain collectively) ESC-R, as these rights are denied to employees of the *Guardia di Finanza* (militarised finance & customs police, TN)

## VI. Commissioner for Human Rights

The Commissioner for Human Rights is an independent non-judicial institution created by the Committee of Ministers' resolution (99)50 of 7 May 1999. Nils Muižnieks (Latvia) is the present Commissioner for Human Rights of the Council of Europe (in office since 1st April 2012).

In 2016 the Commissioner visited Andorra, Croatia, Greece, Ireland, Iceland, Latvia, Lithuania, Poland, United Kingdom, Turkey and Ukraine, and he published reports concerning Country visits made (in 2015 and 2016) to the following countries: Belgium, Cyprus, Croatia, Georgia, Latvia, Poland, United Kingdom, Turkey and Ukraine. He also cancelled a planned visit to Russia following the restrictions the Russian authorities wished to impose on his schedule.

The Commissioner has visited Italy five times. The most recent visit was from 3 to 6 July 2012. The purpose of the visit was to re-examine a series of critical issues relating in particular to the excessive length of legal proceedings and to the protection of the rights of Roma, Sinti, migrants and asylum-seekers. The resulting report was published on 18 September 2012 (CommDH (2012)26) (see *2013 Yearbook*, pp. 256–260). Over the course of 2016, the Commissioner sent a series of letters to the governments of Albania, Bulgaria, France, Italy, Sweden and Hungary on the human rights situation of these minority groups, an issue which is a constant cause of concern to his office Europe-wide.

In his letter to the Italian Prime Minister, Matteo Renzi, dated 27 January 2016, the Commissioner expressed his serious concern over the continuing practice of evicting Roma families, taking place in several different Italian towns, as referred in a number of statements received by his office over the period 2015–16. While underlining once again that any eviction carried out without due process and without offering suitable alternative accommodation constitutes a violation of Italy's international obligations, particularly if these practices make the evicted people homeless. The Commissioner recalls a series of recommendations which several Council of Europe bodies have made to the Italian authorities over the past few years. Highlighted in particular are the decisions of the European Committee of Social Rights in two collective complaints – *European Roma Rights Centre v. Italy* (complaint 27/2004) and *Centre of Housing Rights and Evictions v. Italy* (complaint 58/2009) which found Italy in violation of art. 31 ESC-R on the grounds of the unsuitable housing conditions and the forced evictions of Roma and Sinti in Italy (see *2011 Yearbook*, pp. 218–220). His letter also refers to the most recent visit to Italy (2012), during which the Commissioner was able to witness first-hand the low standard of living conditions suffered by members of these communities, and to stress the fact that the kind of segregation typical of Roma settlements in Italy (whether formal or informal) was undermining the very foundations of any prospects for people living in such structures to access education programmes, get a paid job, interact with people outside the Roma community and, more generally, to integrate into mainstream society.

In view of the information continually received on the practice of evicting Roma in Italy – in contrast with the objectives of the National Inclusion Strategy for Roma and Sinti adopted by the Cabinet in February 2012 – the Commissioner noted with disappointment what he called a "continuation of past policies" and expressed his concern over the lack of the resources necessary for the implementation of the strategy at a national level, with particular reference to the responsibilities of UNAR (the National Anti-Racial Discrimination Office), the national focal point for its implementation.

The Commissioner ends his letter requesting information as to the concrete measures the Government intends to take to avoid making Roma homeless, to put an end to forced evictions and to close the settlements occupied exclusively by Roma, offering the families involved the alternative of ordinary and truly integrated housing solutions.

The Government's answer, dated 10 February 2016 and signed by the Under-Secretary Benedetto della Vedova, firstly goes into a detailed account stressing the heterogeneous characteristics of Roma and Sinti communities, their scattered distribution over the whole of Italy and the challenges this presents for Italy's efforts to manage the issues relating to them in a uniform manner. He reiterates the commitment of central and local authorities to carrying out evictions in the best interests of the people involved and providing satisfactory alternative housing solutions. The letter also draws attention to the initiative taken by UNAR to publish and distribute the Italian translation of the United Nations Guidelines on forced evictions. Finally, concerning the Inclusion Strategy for Roma and Sinti, the letter claims that the lack of funds for its implementation is due to the broader economic crisis Italy is undergoing. In this perspective, della Vedova points out that in the Planning for European funds 2014–2020, for the first time, there is an objective concerning the inclusion of Roma.

Among his other activities, in 2016 the Commissioner for Human Rights published a number of *Human Rights Comments* online, which are short articles from a blog in which the Commissioner examines and comments briefly on significant current issues relating to the human rights situation in Europe. He published 11 *Comments* in 2016 (14 in 2014 and 9 in 2015). Three of these contain explicit references to the human rights situation in Italy:

*Human rights of refugee and migrant women and girls need to be better protected* (7 March 2016); the Commissioner starts by noting that for the first time since the migrant crisis began in Europe, the number of women and children migrants exceeded those of adult men, making up 60% of the total. He then examines the main areas of vulnerability and the risks of violence, discrimination and exploitation to which female migrants are exposed and discusses the recommendations made in this area by the United Nations and the Council of Europe. One of the issues mentioned in this comment was on the increased use of detention of female migrants, including pregnant ones, together with men who are not part of their families, an issue on which the Strasbourg court has found a number of human rights violations. In this particular area, the Commissioner voices his concern that the "hotspots" in Italy and Greece, originally envisaged as reception and registration centres for migrants may in fact become additional detention centres, with all the risks they carry for the female migrant population.

*Business enterprises begin to recognise their human rights responsibilities* (4 April 2016); in this *Comment*, the Commissioner recognises that business enterprises are finally starting to take notice of the need to protect human rights. He then gives an overview of the main standards developed by the United Nations (Guiding Principles on Business and Human Rights) and, building on these, those at European regional level (CoE and EU). Italy is mentioned as one of the nine European states which have adopted a National human rights action plan intended as a political strategy developed by a State to combat the negative impact of businesses on human rights.

*Protect women's sexual and reproductive health and rights* (21 July 2016); the Commissioner observes a resurgence of threats to women's rights and gender equality and in this area feels it is necessary to redouble efforts to protect the sexual and reproductive health of women, where human rights are frequently violated and at the same time, protecting them is a precondition for realising other human rights. Italy is mentioned in the part of the *Comment* which reaffirms the obligation to provide access to safe and legal abortion services. The Commissioner specifically mentions the decision of the European Committee on Social Rights (in the complaint *IPPF EN v. Italy*, No. 87/2012; see *2015 Yearbook* pp. 206–207) under which Italy was found to be in violation of the right to health enshrined in the European Social Charter (revised), as the Italian authorities had failed to adopt the measures necessary to ensure that, as required by law, abortions requested in accordance with the applicable regulations are always performed, even when there is a high number of medical staff and physicians who are "conscientious objectors".

Finally, attention is drawn to the publication by the Commissioner's Office of two *issue papers,* documents made available to give more information to the general public, the authorities and NGOs working in the human rights field, on the following subjects: *Time for Europe to get migrant integration right* and *Missing persons and victims of enforced disappearance in Europe.*

## VII. European Commission against Racism and Intolerance

The European Commission against Racism and Intolerance (ECRI), established in 1993, is a monitoring body of the Council of Europe specialised in combating any form of racism, xenophobia, anti-semitism and intolerance in a human rights perspective. The members of ECRI remain in office for five years. They are selected for their moral authority and their recognised experience in the field of combating racism, xenophobia, anti-semitism and intolerance; they act on an individual basis and independently. The Commission is composed by a member and, if a Government so wishes, a deputy member for each State of the Council of Europe. The expert in respect of Italy during 2016 has been Vitaliano Esposito. An Italian official, Stefano Valenti, is responsibe for the External Relations of the Commission Secretariat, part of the Directorate-general Human Rights and the Rule of Law of the Council of Europe.

In 2016, the Commission published the reports on the fifth monitoring cycle concerning Armenia, Azerbaijan, Cyprus, the former Yugoslav Republic of Macedonia, France, Georgia, Italy, Lithuania, Principality of Monaco, the United Kingdom and Turkey. The ECRI also published its conclusions on the priority recommendations made to the following countries in relation to the previously published reports on the fourth cycle: Russian Federation, Finland, Ireland, Liechtenstein, Malta, the Netherlands, Poland, Republic of Moldova and San Marino. Still in the fifth monitoring cycle, in 2016 the ECRI also visited Andorra, Bosnia-Herzegovina, Denmark, Iceland, Luxemburg, Montenegro, Serbia and Ukraine.

The report on Italy relative to the fifth monitoring cycle, adopted on 18 March 2016 and published on 7 June (CRI(2016)19) was produced following the ECRI delegation's visit to Italy from 13–18 September 2015 (see *2016 Yearbook,* p. 196). As done for the other countries in this monitoring cycle, the report concentrates on four common themes for all CoE member states (legislative issues, hate speech, violence and integration policies) as well as on a number of specific issues relative to the Country being monitored. The latter are on the recommendations from the fourth monitoring cycle on Italy which were subject to interim follow-up (evictions of Roma and right to housing; strengthening of UNAR; respecting the principle of *non-refoulement*; see *2015 Yearbook,* pp. 211–212), and the policies to combat discrimination and intolerance towards LGBT people. In order to prepare this report, the delegation held meetings in Rome, Venice, Treviso and Padova with representatives of the Government, local authorities and members of the judiciary, and with a number of NGOs. In Rome, the delegation visited two housing centres for Roma and in Treviso a reception centre for asylum-seekers.

According to the ECRI report, progress has been made in some areas covered in the previous report, from 2011 (see *2012 Yearbook,* pp. 208–216). The progress recognised includes the draft laws, still being discussed, for the ratification of Protocol XII to the ECHR (bill 1633 from 2014) and the additional Protocol to the Convention on cybercrime (bill 3084 del 2015), handing down harsher penalties when racist propaganda and public incitement to hate crimes are based on Holocaust denial, the decision to consider homophobia an aggravating circumstance in any offence, the measures to combat hate speech and racist, homophobic and transphobic violence included in the new National Action Plan against racism, xenophobia and intolerance, and the creation of the Observatory for protection against discriminatory acts (OSCAD). Further positive signs in Italian legislation mentioned by ECRI were the results of the implementation, as of 2012, of a compulsory individual integration programme, based on an "integration agreement" aiming to facilitate the integration of foreigners, the introduction of a bill (No. 2092) to amend law 91/1992 governing citizenship and which, if enacted, will make the acquisition of Italian citizenship significantly easier for large numbers of foreign minors in Italy, and the approval by the Senate (in February 2016, now law 76/2016) of the bill regulating the situation of same-sex couples. ECRI also welcomed the fact that law 107/2015 lists as one of the objectives of the "good schooling" programme supporting schools which commit to enrolling a significant number of foreign pupils, as well as appreciating the organisation of training programmes for law enforcement agents and public servants as part of the national LGBT Strategy 2013–2015. The Commission also expresses satisfaction over the considerable efforts made by national and local authorities to offer a proper welcome to the numerous asylum-seekers landing on Italian shores.

Despite these positive developments, ECRI finds that several causes for concern still remain. One of these is the fact that Italian law does not criminalise discrimination based on grounds of colour or language, and the penalties envisaged do not always represent an effective, proportionate and dissuasive response to offences involving racism and racial discrimination. UNAR, the independence of which is subject to interim monitoring by ECRI, continues to be non-compliant with the principle of independence of national bodies specialised in the fight against racism, and it does not have sufficient powers to cover all the areas of discrimination. Moreover, on the question of hate speech, the Italian authorities have proven unable at times to collect data on hate speech or other hate-motivated offences in a systematic and coherent manner. As concerns the situation of members of Roma communities, ECRI found substantial geographical disparities in their integration into Italian society and highlighted the considerable delays suffered in the implementation of the Roma Inclusion Strategy. Furthermore, as already raised by the Commissioner for Human Rights (see, in this Part, Council of Europe, VI), the Commission also regretted the continuation of forced evictions of Roma from unauthorised settlements, often carried out without procedural guarantees and without providing alternative housing solutions for those evicted. Finally, ECRI expressed concern over the question of sex education in schools, particularly on gender identity and on sexual orientation, still controversial and met with strong opposition, especially in Veneto and Lombardy regions.

In the light of this general overview, ECRI asked the Italian authorities to undertake further initiatives in a certain number of fields and it made a series of recommendations on specific issues.

On the theme of legislation against racism and racial discrimination, ECRI recommends that Italy complete the legislative process for the ratification of Protocol XII to the European Convention on Human Rights and the additional Protocol to the Convention on cybercrime concerning the criminalisation of acts of racism and xenophobia committed through computer systems as soon as possible. It hopes that, in line with the provisions of ECRI's *General Policy Recommendation No. 7*, the authorities make sure that colour and language are expressly included in the grounds of racist behaviour and racial discrimination punishable under the Criminal Code and that the public dissemination or public distribution, or the production or storage aimed at public dissemination or public distribution, with a racist aim, of written, pictorial or other material inciting to racial discrimination and racial violence are treated as criminal offences.

As was already the case in the previous report, ECRI once again recommends that the Italian authorities assess the effectiveness of the provisions for combating the dissemination of racist ideas as well as incitement to commit and the commission of discriminatory acts motivated by hatred. They should make sure it is not too difficult for the judicial authorities to prove the existence of grounds and proceed with criminal prosecution of conduct aimed at disseminating racist ideas, and that the penalties for the offences concerned are effective, proportionate and dissuasive. Again on the legislative front, the Commission recommends that the Italian authorities introduce provisions into the Criminal Code penalising public insults and defamation or threats against a person or group of people on the grounds of their race, colour, language, religion, nationality, or national or ethnic origin, in keeping with its *General Policy Recommendation No. 7*. ECRI also recommends that the Italian authorities complete approval, as soon as possible, of bill 54 from 2015, the criminal law on the prevention and repression of genocide, crimes against humanity and war crimes, so that the denial, gross minimisation, and public justification or condoning of these crimes for racist motives are made criminal offences. Still concerning the legislative framework, the Commission reiterates its recommendations to the authorities a) to introduce legal provisions prohibiting discrimination based not only on grounds such as "race", religion and ethnic origin but also language, colour and nationality, and b) to ensure that all organisations active in the field of combating racism and racial discrimination are able to take legal action on behalf of alleged individual victims of these phenomena or in cases of collective discrimination.

As concerns the situation of UNAR, ECRI reiterates its recommendation (made in the report on the fourth monitoring cycle and subject to interim monitoring) to ensure that UNAR's full independence is secured both in law and in fact; the Commission also recommends extending its powers so that the relevant legislation clearly covers discrimination based not only on ethnic origin and race but also on colour, language, religion, nationality and national origin; and to grant it the right to bring legal proceedings. The authorities should also ensure that any move to merge UNAR with an independent body with a broader remit – for example the creation of an independent National institution for human rights in line with the Paris Principles – guarantees the full implementation of the above recommendations and provides for all the human and financial resources necessary to fulfil its mission.

On the theme of hate speech, ECRI recommends that the Italian authorities set in place, without delay, a method of collecting data on incidents related to hate speech, broken down into the different categories of racist motivation and of victims, and that they regularly publish the results, with information on the number of prosecutions, any reasons for not prosecuting and the outcome of the legal proceedings concerned. The issue becomes particularly important among the younger generation and the use of communications technology: here the Commission urges the Government to do more to raise awareness among young people of tolerance and mutual respect and alert them to the dangers of using the Internet to spread hate speech and offensive content. In particular, they should provide all young people with the information and support they need in order to make responsible use of social media and social networks.

Again to assist in combating hate speech, ECRI recommends that the Italian authorities take the necessary legislative steps to provide the victims of hate crimes with specialised support, if necessary by adapting the services which already exist for victims of other crimes. It also recommends appointing a contact person in each police district to deal with questions of racism and homophobia/transphobia, as well as a contact person in the corresponding public prosecutor's office, to ensure they work together as a network, with good communication between the police contact persons and those in the prosecutors' offices. ECRI also reiterates its recommendation to the Italian authorities to establish a body independent of the police and the prosecution service to investigate allegations of human rights violations by the police, including all allegations of racial discrimination or racially motivated misconduct.

With the aim of making naturalisation easier for foreign nationals born in Italy or who have been to school there, ECRI recommends that the Italian authorities complete the legislative process to reform the legislation on the granting of citizenship as soon as possible and also ensuring that the legislation on naturalisation is in conformity with the provisions of the European Convention on Nationality. The Italian authorities should also ensure that the extension of the national "Identity and Encounter" Plan involves an assessment of all the integration projects set launched in recent years, based on accurate data on the integration rates achieved in the different sectors of social life.

On the issue of Roma integration, ECRI recommends completing the collection of statistical data in all areas relating to Roma integration in order to establish an order of priority for the implementation of the National Roma Integration Strategy for the members of these communities; setting quantifiable objectives in every field of intervention of the Strategy; completing the setting up of regional working groups; allocating special funding to the Strategy; and providing UNAR with the resources it needs to be able to coordinate, monitor and assess the Strategy effectively.

Furthermore, considering that there are thousands of Roma children in Italy who were born in Italy to parents originating from countries formerly part of Yugoslavia, who have no identity documents and are therefore invisible to the law due to their condition of "*de facto* statelessness" (see *2012 Yearbook*, p. 35), ECRI strongly recommends that the authorities enact a new law or reform the law on access to citizenship so that no children born in Italy are stateless.

ECRI's recommendations also focus on the issue of housing rights for Roma. Here, ECRI recommends that the authorities ensure that all Roma who may be evicted from their homes enjoy the full protection of the guarantees of international law in such matters. In particular sufficient prior notice should be given of any decision to evict Roma; they should be entitled to proper legal protection; and they should not be evicted without the possibility of being re-housed in suitable accommodation.

Moving on to the issues concerning LGBT rights, firstly ECRI urges the authorities, practically reiterating a recommendation subject to interim monitoring, to broaden UNAR's powers so that the relevant legal provisions clearly cover discrimination based, inter alia, on sexual orientation and gender identity. ECRI then turns to reforms in education and recommends that the authorities implement in schools at every level, be it in the framework of the implementation of Act No. 107/15 "on good schooling" or in the context of the continuing National LGBT Strategy, measures to promote mutual tolerance and respect at school, regardless of sexual orientation or gender identity. In particular these measures should provide all pupils and students with the information, the protection and the support they need in order to be able to live in harmony with their sexual orientation and their gender identity.

The latter is one of the two recommendations on which ECRI requests priority implementation and which will be subject to interim monitoring. The other covers the recommendations made on UNAR and particularly, the necessity of guaranteeing its total independence and extending its powers to cover all possible fields in which discrimination may occur.

In 2016, ECRI adopted one new general policy recommendation, No. 16 (CRI(2016)16). This recommendation, on safeguarding irregularly present migrants from discrimination, was adopted on 16 March 2016. The purpose of the recommendation, as stated in the relative text, "is to address a pressing issue of discrimination which is causing grievous hardship to a substantial number of migrants who are irregularly present in member States" of the Council of Europe. It deals exclusively with the question of ensuring access by all persons in this particularly vulnerable group to those human rights which are guaranteed to them in international human rights instruments, in particular as concerns education, health care, housing, social security and assistance, labour protection and justice, while they are within the jurisdiction of a member State. To this end the recommendation calls for the creation of effective "firewalls" to prevent State and private sector actors from denying human rights to irregularly present migrants by prohibiting the sharing of the personal data of, or other information about, persons suspected of irregular presence or work, with the immigration authorities for purposes of immigration control and enforcement. Indeed, in this area, the document recommends that the national authorities decouple immigration control and enforcement from the provision of services and assurance of rights of irregularly present migrants within their jurisdiction in order to ensure that those rights are guaranteed to such migrants and to relieve authorities whose primary responsibilities lie elsewhere from interference by immigration enforcement policies and institutions.

## VIII. Advisory Committee on the Framework Convention for the Protection of National Minorities

The Committee is a monitoring body instituted pursuant to art. 26 of the Council of Europe Framework Convention for the Protection of National Minorities. It is composed of 18 independent experts with recognised expertise in the field of the protection of national minorities. They shall serve on the Committee in their individual capacity, for a period of four years. Between 2012 and 2016 Italian expert Francesco Palermo has been a member of the Advisory Committee.

> The Advisory Committee serves to assist the CM in evaluating the implementation of the Framework-Convention in States Parties, through the examination of periodic State Reports. The results of this evaluation are expressed in a detailed opinion which serves as a basis for the preparation of the CM's conclusive resolutions on the Country in question. Follow-up meetings are generally organised by the Advisory Committee with a view to bringing together all actors – governmental and non-governmental – interested in the implementation of the Convention and to examine ways of implementing the results of the monitoring procedure.
>
> In 2016, as part of the respective monitoring cycles, the Advisory Committee on the Framework Convention visited the following countries: Armenia, Austria, Kosovo, Norway, United Kingdom, Republic of Moldova and Ukraine; it adopted, but, in line with the principle of confidentiality, has not yet published, opinions on Armenia, Austria, Malta, Norway, United Kingdom and Republic of Moldova, whereas it has published opinions on the situation of national minorities in Croatia, Finland, Georgia, Italy, Czech Republic, San Marino and Hungary.

Italy is currently undergoing its fourth monitoring cycle of the Framework Convention. On 12 March 2014, the Italian Government submitted a report to the Advisory Committee on measures adopted to protect national minorities, with special attention devoted to the priority recommendations received during the third cycle (see *2015 Yearbook*, pp. 213–214). The Committee's opinion on this report, based also on its visit to Italy from 29 June to 3 July 2015, was adopted on 19 November 2015 (ACFC/OP/IV(2015)006) and published on 12 July 2016, together with the comments made by the Italian Government in response to the observations made by the Advisory Committee.

In its opinion, the Advisory Committee observes that since the adoption of the previous opinion (see *2012 Yearbook*, pp. 264–268), Italy has continued its efforts to protect persons belonging to national minorities, who are referred to in the domestic legal order as "historical linguistic minorities". Considering the decentralised structure of the Italian Republic, minority rights are protected and implemented in a very asymmetric way in different parts of the Country and not all minorities have benefited on an equal basis from the rights laid down in the Framework Convention. In particular, the Committee highlights the fact that protection of rights guaranteed by law 482/1999 (Regulations governing the protection of historical linguistic minorities) is further strengthened in some Regions such as Valle d'Aosta, Friuli Venezia-Giulia and Trentino-Alto Adige, by their autonomous Statutes and by other national and regional laws.

As concerns Roma, Sinti and Travellers, the Advisory Committee notes that the implementation of the 2012 Inclusion Strategy has to date been rather slow and no dedicated funds have been allocated to advancing it. Moreover, no legislation has yet been enacted to protect the members of these communities from discrimination, despite the bills submitted to Parliament (see *2015 Yearbook*, pp. 15–16). Consequently, the Roma, Sinti and Travellers continue to be socially and economically marginalised in Italy and those who live in segregated housing, particularly the so-called "nomad camps", are still living in deplorable conditions, despite a number of judgments confirming that assigning housing in prefabricated containers surrounded by fences constitutes discrimination.

Reflecting this situation, although a general climate of openness and tolerance prevails in Italy towards people who belong to recognised, long-established linguistic minorities, the Committee found a visible increase in xenophobia and anti-Gypsyism within Italian society in recent years. The use of discriminatory, intolerant and racist language in political discourse and in certain media has become commonplace and there have been a number of violent verbal and physical attacks on asylum-seekers. Furthermore, as reiterated by the European Commission against Racism and Intolerance (see in this Part, Council of Europe, II, G), the autonomy and independence of UNAR are not guaranteed.

After a detailed analysis of the situation of minority groups in relation to each article of the Framework Convention, the Committee formulated a series of recommendations to the Italian authorities, some of which were considered priority recommendations. Specifically, the Advisory Committee reiterated its call on the authorities to take urgent steps to elaborate and adopt without further delay a specific legislative framework, at national level, for the recognition and protection of Roma, Sinti and Travellers with due consultation of representatives of these communities at all stages of the process; the authorities should also adopt more resolute and effective measures to prevent, combat and sanction the inequality and discrimination suffered by these communities, particularly women and girls, improve their living conditions, especially the conditions which would allow the residents to move from settlements (whether authorised or unauthorised) to suitable social accommodation. The Italian authorities are requested to ensure that all Roma, Sinti and Traveller children, regardless of their status, have full access and are effectively included in the formal education system; they should also adopt robust measures to reduce the dropout rate of these children and to address the problems related to underachievement in school.

The Advisory Committee reiterates its call on the authorities to review the mandate and status of UNAR with a view to strengthening its competencies and continue to make available all the resources needed for it to operate efficiently and independently, in accordance with the Paris Principles. The Advisory Committee also encourages the authorities to improve the access of persons belonging to national minorities, including the numerically smaller ones, to radio and television programmes of particular interest for them, as well as to provide high-speed Internet to favour media access from remote areas, and to continue a sustainable development of minority language newspapers.

Another of the priority recommendations of the Advisory Committee is for the authorities to allocate sufficient funds for teaching of and in minority languages and to ensure sufficient availability of school books and qualified teachers, paying special attention to the needs of people belonging to the numerically smaller minorities.

In addition to the above, the Committee's *opinion* also contains other significant recommendations:

- promote tolerance and respectful attitudes amongst the majority population and increase efforts to combat all forms of intolerance, racism, xenophobia and hate speech; take further legislative measures and implement policies to combat racist manifestations, including in the media, at sporting events and in the political arena;
- consult representatives of the Roma, Sinti and Travellers communities, including women, in all projects and activities concerning them, in particular those implemented in the framework of the National Inclusion Strategy at national, regional and local levels;
- increase funding for projects aiming to maintain and develop the cultural heritage of linguistic minorities; pay particular attention to the actual needs of persons belonging to the numerically smaller minorities;
- make sustained efforts to promote the use of minority languages by persons belonging to minorities in dealings with the local administrative authorities; ensure that linguistic help desks are opened in all the municipalities concerned and that these help desks are given the human and financial resources they need to operate effectively;
- review the procedures for appointment of representatives of national minorities in the work of the technical committee set up to implement

the aforementioned law No. 482/1999 to ensure that legitimate interests of all recognised historical linguistic minorities are represented; review the composition of the technical committee with the aim of giving greater say to representatives of minorities on issues affecting them and ensuring gender balance within the committee.

## IX. European Commission for Democracy through Law

The Commission, also known as the Venice Commission, is the Council of Europe's advisory body on constitutional issues; it was established in 1990 and receives financial support by a law of the Region of Veneto.

The Commission is composed of independent experts with extensive experience in the area of democratic institutions or excellence in the legal and political domains. Members are designated for four years by the participating countries which, as well as the 47 Member States of the CoE, include Algeria, Brazil, Chile, South Korea, Israel, Kazakhstan, Kyrgyzstan, Morocco, Mexico, Peru, United States and Tunisia. Belarus is an associate member, while Argentina, Canada, Japan, the Holy See and Uruguay participate in the work of the Commission as observer countries. The European Commission, Palestinian National Authority, South Africa and the Association of Constitutional Courts using the French Language have a special co-operation status.

Since 2009 Gianni Buquicchio has been President of the *Venice Commission*. Two Italian experts participate in the Commission's activities as alternate members: Sergio Bartole and Guido Neppi Modona.

One of the Commission's activities is the production of reports and opinions on topics within its mandate, some of which on request from other bodies such as the Parliamentary Assembly of the Council of Europe, and it also organises seminars on specific issues. During 2016, the Venice Commission adopted 29 opinions relating to the adoption of laws or bills of constitutional interest in the following countries: Armenia (4), Azerbaijan, Bulgaria, Former Yugoslav Republic of Macedonia, France, Georgia (3), Kazakhstan, Kyrgyzstan, Poland (2), Republic of Moldova (4), Tunisia, Turkey (6), and Ukraine.

The Venice Commission's most recent activity directly concerning Italy was the opinion it adopted on 18 June 2015, on the citizens' bill "On the regulation of public participation, citizens' bills, referendums and popular initiatives and amendments to the provincial electoral law of the autonomous Province of Trent" (CDL-AD(2015)009, see *2016 Yearbook*, pp. 199–200).

## X. Group of experts on Action against Trafficking in Human Beings

The Group of Experts (GRETA) was established pursuant to art. 36 of the Council of Europe Convention on Action against Trafficking in Human Beings (Warsaw Convention) and is charged, together with a Committee made up of the representatives in the CM of the States Parties to the Convention (Committee of the Parties), with monitoring the implementation of the obligations contained in the Convention.

> The Group is made up of 15 independent experts known for their recognised competence in the fields of human rights, assistance and protection of victims of trafficking in human beings or having professional experience in the areas covered by the Convention. The monitoring procedure is divided into 4-year rounds. The Group of Experts starts the dialogue with the Party under evaluation by sending out a questionnaire, which may be followed by requests for further information. If the Group of Experts deems it necessary, additional information may be requested from civil society organisations or gathered by organising a visit to the Country concerned. The draft report is sent to the relevant Government for comments. On receiving them, GRETA prepares its final report and conclusions and transmits it to the Country concerned and to the Committee of the Parties, which can adopt recommendations on the basis of the contents of the document. Each Party to the Convention appoints a contact person to co-operate with the Group of Experts. The contact person for Italy is Michele Palma from the Equal Opportunities Department under the Prime Minister's Office.

In 2016, the Group of Experts published its reports assessing the state of implementation of the Convention in Albania, Bulgaria, Croatia, Denmark, Georgia, Kosovo, Montenegro, United Kingdom, Republic of Moldova and Romania.

The first evaluation round on Italy's implementation of the Warsaw Convention was completed with the recommendation by the Committee of Parties (CP(2014)16), adopted on 5 December 2014, which confirmed the initial recommendations made by the Group of Experts (GRETA(2014)18, see *2015 Yearbook*, p. 216–219). The second monitoring cycle is expected in May 2017. However, in 2016, the Group of Experts once again directed its attention to trafficking in Italy after receiving disturbing information, in the course of the 25th plenary meeting (7–11 March 2016), to the effect that Italy had removed possible victims of trafficking through forced return flights to Nigeria, as part of the joint removal operations organised and coordinated by FRONTEX (on the implications of these operations, see also in this Part, Council of Europe, IV). This issue, which was closely monitored by members of civil society at the national level, goes directly against some of the recommendations GRETA made to Italy during the first monitoring cycle, specifically the need to adopt a clear legislative and political framework concerning the removal of victims of trafficking, so as to guarantee that these operations are carried out with due attention to their rights, their safety and their personal dignity; the victims of trafficking must be informed of the existing programmes to protect them from re-victimisation, and compliance with the obligation of *non-refoulement* must be assured.

Alarmed by this information, GRETA began by requesting information from the Italian authorities as to the measures adopted relative to these procedures. As they considered the information received only partial, the Group of Experts decided to organise a visit to Italy, which took place on 21–23 September 2016. During the visit, the GRETA delegation, in addition to meeting with representatives from the Ministry of the Interior, the Prefecture of Rome, commissions for recognition of international protection, from the IOM and from civil society, also visited the Ponte Galeria CIE near Rome (where one of the main incidents which had caused concern to GRETA had taken place) and the Pozzallo first reception centre in Sicily.

The report on this visit (GRETA(2016)29) was adopted in December 2016 and published on 30 January 2017, after receiving the response of the Italian authorities (attached to the report). After presenting a summary of the trends of migratory flows and trafficking in Italy, the most recent legislative developments at the national level and the various procedures for identification, referral to assistance and removal currently operating in Italy, GRETA makes a series of recommendations to the Italian authorities. The Group of Experts acknowledges the extreme difficulties that Italy is facing due to the unprecedented increase in the arrivals of migrants and refugees and the significant efforts made by the Italian authorities to cope with them, with the assistance of international organisations and civil society. However, as already stated by other CoE bodies (specifically, in the *Khlaifia and others vs. Italy* case, see *2016 Yearbook*, pp. 265–267), GRETA recognises that such factors cannot exempt Italy from guaranteeing conditions that are compatible with respect for human dignity to all individuals. In particular, the immigration policies and procedures applied by Italy must not prejudice the application of the protection and assistance measures provided by the CoE Convention on Action against Trafficking in Human Beings.

According to GRETA, many of the concerns raised by this visit echo those contained in the Group's first evaluation report, but are magnified by the substantial increase in the number of victims and potential victims of trafficking arriving in Italy. Indeed, from what they have observed, it emerges that the victims who are granted refugee status or subsidiary protection in Italy, particularly the youngest ones, continue to be at risk of re-trafficking in Italy and elsewhere in the EU, which requires urgent action at both domestic and European level to ensure effective protection of the rights of migrant and asylum-seeking children and young people. These problems are further exacerbated by delays in relocating asylum-seekers from Italy to other EU member states, caused, among other things, by the fact that the Italian authorities do not allow thorough security vetting by receiving countries prior to relocation.

On this point, GRETA once again urges the Italian authorities to improve the system for identifying victims of trafficking among migrants and asylum-seekers by setting up clear and binding procedures to be followed and providing proper and systematic training to staff working in all types of migrant centres; providing frontline staff with operational indicators for proactively identifying victims of trafficking; strengthening multi-agency involvement in victim identification by introducing a National Referral Mechanism, involving specialised civil society bodies; ensuring that there are appropriate facilities for holding confidential interviews in order to identify victims of trafficking in hotspots and other places where migrants and asylum-seekers are held.

GRETA also urges the Italian authorities to mainstream prevention of trafficking in the training of all staff working with unaccompanied minors and separated children, providing them with training on relevant indicators. The Italian authorities should also increase efforts to identify child victims of trafficking and set up child-specific identification procedures which involve child specialists and take into account the special circumstances and needs of child victims of trafficking.

The Group of Experts once again urges the Italian authorities to take steps to address the problem of the disappearance of unaccompanied children in Italy, also by providing enhanced safeguarding in reception facilities specialising in children, with adequately trained staff, and ensuring that unaccompanied children are assigned a suitably trained legal guardian as quickly as possible, protecting the best interests of the child.

GRETA considers that the Italian authorities should review their age assessment procedure to ensure that the best interests of the child are effectively protected, that the benefit of the doubt is given in cases of age disputes and that special protection measures are provided.

Finally, without prejudice to the right of victims of trafficking to seek and enjoy international protection, GRETA urges the Italian authorities to ensure that, when there are reasonable grounds to believe that a person is a victim of trafficking, he/she be granted a recovery and reflection period of at least 30 days, during which expulsion orders cannot be enforced and they can benefit from the right to obtain a renewable residence permit under art. 18 of the Consolidated Immigration Act (l. 286/1998 and subsequent amendments). Furthermore, victims should be provided with assistance in accordance with art. 12 of the Warsaw Convention, and the Italian authorities should as a matter of priority consider strengthening the capacity of victim support programmes for both adults and children.

## XI. Group of States against Corruption

The Group of States against Corruption (GRECO) was established in 1999 in order to monitor the compliance of CoE Member States with the anti-corruption standards and rules of the Organisation. These benchmarks are contained in the legal instruments adopted by the Council of Europe on actions against corruption – the Criminal Law Convention on Corruption with its Additional Protocol and the Civil Law Convention on Corruption – as well as the recommendations and resolutions adopted by the Committee of Ministers (in particular resolution (97)24 on the 20 Guiding Principles for the Fight against Corruption).

> The Group comprises 49 States (47 Member States of the CoE plus Belarus and the United States). GRECO's main objective is to improve the capacity of its members to fight corruption by monitoring their compliance with Council of Europe anti-corruption standards through a dynamic process of mutual evaluation and peer pressure. It helps to identify shortcomings in national anti-corruption policies, prompting the necessary legislative, institutional and practical reforms. GRECO also provides a platform for sharing best practices.

Italy has been a member of GRECO since 30 June 2007 and has undergone three evaluation rounds to date. The first two rounds were dealt with jointly and concluded in 2013 with the adoption by the Group of States of an *addendum* to the compliance report (see *2014 Yearbook*, p. 253). On 23 June 2014, on the basis of information previously provided by the Italian Government, GRECO adopted the compliance report (Greco RC-III (2014) 9E) on the measures adopted by the Italian authorities to implement the 16 recommendations received in the course of the third monitoring round regarding two themes: I) incriminations for corruption and II) transparency of party funding (see *2015 Yearbook*, p. 220).

In 2016, GRECO adopted two reports on Italy: the second compliance report, relative to the third monitoring cycle, adopted and published on 2 December 2016, and the evaluation report on Italy after the fourth evaluation round, adopted on 28 October 2016 and published in January 2017.

In the former report, GRECO assesses the measures taken by the Italian authorities to implement the recommendations made on Incriminations and on the Transparency of party funding which were still pending after the examination of the first compliance report (see *2015 Yearbook*, p. 220). GRECO concluded its analysis of this monitoring cycle recognising that Italy has implemented, or at least dealt with in a satisfactory manner, eight of the sixteen recommendations made in the third round evaluation report. Of the remaining eight, seven have been partially implemented and one has not been implemented.

On the issue of incrimination for corruption, the Italian Government is currently examining various legislative proposals concerning the bribery of foreign officials and jury members, and to criminalise the active and passive bribery of foreign arbitrators. GRECO's assessment is that progress has been made towards criminalising corruption in the private sector. Parliament has given the Government the power to adopt a legislative decree containing the measures necessary to meet the requirements of articles 7 and 8 of the Criminal Law Convention on Corruption. The Italian Government has also submitted a proposal for new legislation on the statute of limitation. Alongside the potential developments on the legislative front, commendable, but yet to be adopted, GRECO welcomes the only relevant law adopted by Italy since the first compliance report, law No. 69/2015 (Provisions on offences against the public administration, mafia-type associations and fraudulent accounting) increasing prison sentences for corruption in the public sector. Furthermore, GRECO takes a positive view of the fact that the Italian Government is considering the ratification of the Additional Protocol to the Criminal Law Convention on Corruption.

The Group of States recognises that Italy's convention-derived obligations to deal with certain shortcomings of domestic legislation in respect of the Criminal Law Convention on Corruption are reduced by the reservations Italy made at the time it ratified this legal instrument. Nevertheless, in line with its established practice towards states which have made reservations, GRECO requests the Italian authorities to reconsider the recommendations made to them in order to fully comply with the provisions of the Convention and to withdraw, or not renew, the reservations on articles 5–8, 12 and 17.

With regard to political financing, GRECO notes significant progress, including a general ban on anonymous donations, increased transparency of donations and a review of sanctions for infringing the rules on political financing. However, as regards the establishment of an independent supervisory mechanism over the financing system and the coordination of the same, the solutions put forward by Italy are not considered satisfactory. Further efforts are required on the publication of information concerning financing of parties and election campaigns. Concluding its analysis, GRECO consequently asks the Italian authorities to provide additional information on the recommendations which are still pending, on both Incriminations and Transparency of Party Funding.

With reference to the latter report, the Evaluation Report on the fourth evaluation round, GRECO examined the Italian situation as concerns the corruption prevention in respect of members of parliament, judges and prosecutors. In this area, the main issues examined in this round were: ethical principles, rules of conduct and conflicts of interest; the prohibition or restriction of certain activities; the declaration of assets, income, liabilities and interests; the enforcement of current legislation; and awareness issues. The report was drawn up based on the Italian Government's answers to the evaluation questionnaire (GrecoEval4(2016)1), data provided by civil society and information gathered by the GRECO delegation which visited Rome on 25–29 April 2016. Following its analysis, the Group of States made 12 recommendations to Italy.

Regarding members of parliament, GRECO recommends:

i. strengthening the integrity framework for parliamentarians, including through (i) the formalisation of the Code of Conduct in the Rules of Procedures of the Chamber of Deputies; (ii) its further refinement through detailed guidance on its provisions; and (iii) the establishment of an effective enforcement and accountability regime. The same measures are recommended for the Senate;

ii. that (i) clear and enforceable conflict of interest rules be adopted for parliamentarians, including through a systematisation of the currently dispersed ineligibility and incompatibility regime; and (ii) the process of verification of ineligibility/incompatibility be further streamlined and thereby performed in an effective and timely manner;

iii. establishing a robust set of restrictions concerning donations, gifts, hospitality, favours and other benefits for parliamentarians, and ensuring that the future system is easily understood and enforceable;

iv. that (i) a study be carried out in order to identify post-employment restrictions for members of Parliament which might be required to avert conflicts of interests; and (ii) post-employment restrictions in such cases be introduced, as necessary;

v. further developing the applicable rules on how members of Parliament engage with lobbyists and other third parties who seek to influence the parliamentary process, including by developing detailed guidance on the matter and securing its effective monitoring and enforcement. The same measures are recommended for the Senate;

vi. that practical measures be put in place to support the implementation of clear parliamentary integrity rules including through the development of dedicated training activities.

Regarding judges and prosecutors, GRECO's recommendations are:

vii. that (i) a deliberate policy for preventing and detecting corruption risks and conflicts of interests be developed within the fiscal jurisdiction; (ii) appropriate measures be taken with a view to enhancing supervision of the professional behaviour and integrity of members of fiscal courts, *inter alia,* by introducing a system of periodic assessment and regular training, including on questions of ethics, expected conduct, corruption prevention and related matters; (iii) drawing up a set of clear standards/code of professional conduct, accompanied by explanatory comments and/or practical examples;

viii. that (i) the authorities continue in their endeavours to ensure efficiency of the justice system through a prompt adoption of the planned reforms in civil and criminal matters, including the reform of the appeal system and of the statute of limitation; (ii) an analysis be carried out of the budgetary and staff situation in courts and prosecution offices, with a view to ensuring that the resources necessary are available and efficiently used across the judicial system;

ix. that (i) a Code of Judicial Ethics, which covers all magistrates, whether associated or not, is further developed and complemented by explanatory comments and/or practical examples, including guidance on conflicts of interest, gifts, etc.; (ii) the proper application of the rules of conduct is ensured via an effective supervisory mechanism and accompanied by dedicated and regular training, advice and counselling for both professional magistrates and lay judges;

x. (i) that a restriction on the simultaneous holding of the office of magistrate and that of a member of local government be laid down in law; and more generally, (ii) that the issue of political activity of magistrates be dealt with in all its aspects at legislative level, given its impact on the fundamental principles of independence and impartiality, both real and perceived, of the judiciary;

xi. to strengthen the follow-up of the financial declaration forms filed by magistrates, notably, by ensuring a more in-depth scrutiny of the declarations and subsequently sanctioning the identified violations;

xii. that the supervisory role of the High Council of the Judiciary over organisational programmes of prosecutorial offices is strengthened with the aim of enhancing transparency and objectivity in case management.

The Italian Government is to submit a report on the measures taken to implement the recommendations from GRECO by the end of April 2018.

## XII. Group of Experts on action against Violence against Women and Domestic Violence

The Group of Experts (GREVIO) is the body responsible for monitoring the implementation of the Council of Europe Convention on Preventing and Combating Violence against Women and Domestic

Violence (Istanbul Convention) by the Parties which have ratified it. The Group held its first meeting on 21 September 2015.

> GREVIO's main purpose is to draw up and publish reports evaluating legislative and other measures taken by the Parties to give effect to the provisions of the Convention. If necessary, in the event of serious and persistent acts of violence covered by the Convention, GREVIO may initiate a special inquiry procedure. It can also adopt general recommendations on themes and concepts of the Convention.

GREVIO currently has 10 members (with increases in the number of ratifications of the Istanbul Convention, this can go up to 15) with multidisciplinary expertise in the area of human rights, gender equality, violence against women and domestic violence or in the assistance to and protection of victims. The first ten members of GREVIO were elected by the Committee of the Parties at its first meeting of 4 May 2015. The Italian expert Simona Lanzoni is one of them.

In 2016 GREVIO made its first two evaluation visits, to Austria and the Principality of Monaco, after receiving the reports from the two countries on their respective levels of implementation of the Istanbul Convention.

# European Union

## I. European Parliament

The European Parliament (EP), together with the Commission and the Council of the European Union, exercises a fundamental role in the promotion and protection of human rights within the overall framework of EU activities.

Among the permanent EP Committees prominent in human rights issues the following are highlighted: the Subcommittee on Human Rights (Chair: Pier Antonio Panzeri; other Italian member: Ignazio Corrao) within the Committee on Foreign Affairs (Italian members: Goffredo Maria Bettini, Mario Borghezio, Fabio Massimo Castaldo, Lorenzo Cesa and Pier Antonio Panzeri).

Other Committees with significant involvement in human rights issues are the Committee on Civil Liberties, Justice and Home Affairs (Italian members: Caterina Chinnici, Laura Ferrara, Lorenzo Fontana, Cécile Kashetu Kyenge, Barbara Matera and Alessandra Mussolini); the Committee on Constitutional Affairs (Vice Chair: Barbara Spinelli; other Italian members: Mercedes Bresso and Fabio Massimo Castaldo); the Committee on Legal Affairs (Vice Chair Laura Ferrara; other Italian member Enrico Gasbarra); the Committee on Employment and Social Affairs (Italian members: Laura Agea, Tiziana Beghin, Brando Benifei, Mara Bizzotto and Elena Gentile); the Committee on the Environment, Public Health and Food Safety (Italian members: Marco Affronte, Simona Bonafè, Alberto Cirio, Elisabetta Gardini, Giovanni La Via, Massimo Paolucci, Piernicola Pedicini and Damiano Zoffoli); the Committee on Development (Italian members: Ignazio Corrao and Elly Schlein); the Committee on Women's Rights and Gender Equality (Vice-Chair: Barbara Matera; other Italian members: Daniela Aiuto and Pina Picierno and the Committee on Petitions, of which more below.

In 2016, the Sacharov Prize for Freedom of Thought was awarded to Nadia Murad and Lamiya Aji Bashar, Yazidi Iraqi human rights activists.

Among the European Parliament acts adopted in 2016 containing specific references to Italy, the following are recalled: the resolution of 10 March 2016 on Egypt, specifically regarding the case of Giulio Regeni (P8_TA(2016)0084); the legislative resolution of 15 September 2016 on the proposal for a Council decision amending Council Decision (EU)

2015/1601 of 22 September 2015 establishing provisional measures in the area of international protection for the benefit of Italy and Greece (P8_TA(2016)0354); the resolution of 1 December 2016 on the situation in Italy after the earthquakes (P8_TA(2016)0476).

*Committee on Petitions*

The Committee on Petitions' task is to examine petitions presented by citizens (a right enshrined in art. 44 of the CFREU, as well as in articles 24 and 227 TFEU) and to work to resolve possible infringements of the rights conferred on them by EU law. The Italian members of the Committee are Alberto Cirio, Andrea Cozzolino and Eleonora Evi.

## II. European Commission

The European Commission plays a central role in the development and implementation of European Union policies on human rights both within the Union and as regards third countries.

Of the 28 Commissioners it comprises, particularly important are: Frans Timmermans, First Vice-President responsible for the quality of legislation, inter-institutional relations, the rule of law and the Charter of Fundamental Rights; Dimitris Avramopoulos, Commissioner for Migration, Home Affairs and Citizenship; Marianne Thyssen, Commissioner for Employment, Social Affairs, Skills and Labour Mobility; Christos Stylianides, Commissioner for Humanitarian Aid and Crisis Management; and Věra Jourová, Commissioner for Justice, Consumers and Gender Equality.

A vital financial resource for European Union human rights activities is the European Instrument for the Promotion of Democracy and Human Rights (EIDHR) which supports, among other things, the activities of the European Inter-university Centre for Rights and Democratisation (EIUC) and the European Master in Human Rights and Democratisation (E.MA).

Further details on the Commission's activities are provided in the section on EU Legislation in 2016 (see Part I, International Human Rights Law, IV, B).

Among the Commission's activities in 2016 which are particularly relevant to Italy is a Commission report on the progress made in Greece and Italy with respect to the European Agenda on Migration. The Commission noted that of the six hotspots identified by the Italian authorities (in Lampedusa, Pozzallo, Porto Empedocle/Villa Sikania, Trapani, Augusta and Taranto), only two are fully functional (those on Lampedusa and in Pozzallo). As concerns recollocation outside Italy, the Commission noted that this is proceeding at a much slower pace than is necessary in order to reach the objective set. Finally, in the Commission's opinion, the Italian reception system is plenty large enough to meet the needs of the Italian asylum system. However they note evident and serious shortcomings in the provision of pre-relocation housing: indeed there are only 420 places available as compared to the 1,252 planned in the schedule submitted to the Commission.

Still concerning the European Agenda on Migration, on 8 December 2016, the European Commission published its eighth report on relocation and resettlement. Regarding Italy, the Commission noted that as of 6 December 2016, a total of 1,950 people had been relocated, against the 34,953 forecasted. However the Commission also mentions that Italy has made considerable efforts to remove the barriers hampering the speeding-up of relocations, such as for example the non-application of the EURODAC Regulation. The rate of fingerprinting of third-country citizens subject to fingerprinting procedures, who entered the EU in an irregular manner through Italy's external borders is close to 100%.

On 28 June 2016 the Commission adopted its 2016 report on Roma integration. As concerns Italy, it points out that Italy made limited progress in 2015 towards implementing the commitments made under the EU Framework for National Roma Integration Strategies. The most critical issue in this area is the lack of strategic direction and coordination at the national level. According to the Commission, progressing beyond the system based on "camps" should be part of an integrated approach aiming to tackle the challenges in the areas of education, employment and health all together. To this end, the Commission hopes that a monitoring mechanism will be established.

Finally, following the earthquakes which hit central Italy at the end of August 2016 and again in October, on 30 November 2016, the Commission announced an initial aid disbursement for the sum of 30 million euro under the EU Solidarity Fund, and proposed to fully fund reconstruction operations under Structural Funds programmes.

## III. Council of the European Union

Within the Council there are the Human Rights Working Group (COHOM), the Working Party on Fundamental Rights, Citizens' Rights and Free Movement of Persons (FREMP), the Working Group "Asylum" and the Working Group of Public International Law (COJUR), within which a sub-group devoted to the International Criminal Court operates (COJUR-ICC).

Of the decisions the Council adopted in 2016 containing specific references to Italy, mention is made of that amending decision (UE) 2015/1601 establishing provisional measures in the area of international protection for the benefit of Italy and Greece.

## IV. Court of Justice of the European Union

Following the entry into force of the Treaty of Lisbon, which made the Charter of Nice legally binding, the Court of Justice plays an ever more vital role for the promotion of human rights within the scope of EU law.

Italian members of the Court are currently Antonio Tizzano, as a judge and Vice-President, and Paolo Mengozzi, as an advocate-general.

According to data provided by the CJEU, in 2016 Italy was the Country with the second-highest number of requests for a preliminary ruling (art. 267 TFEU) submitted to the Court (62 out of 453), preceded only by Germany.

For a selection of the CJEU case-law regarding Italy in 2016, see Part IV, Italy in the Case-law of the Court of Justice of the European Union.

## V. European External Action Service

The European External Action Service (EEAS) assists the High Representative of the Union for Foreign Affairs and Security Policy in upholding the CFSP/CSDP and ensuring the consistency of EU external actions in her functions both as President of the Foreign Affairs Council and as Vice-President of the Commission. Since November 2014, Federica Mogherini has been the High Representative.

No significant actions concerning Italy took place in 2016.

## VI. Special Representative for Human Rights

Appointed by EU Council decision 2012/440/CFSP of 25 July 2012, the mandate of the European Union Special Representative for Human Rights involves enhancing dialogue with all relevant stakeholders concerning EU human rights policy, including international organisations, States as well as civil society organisations. Stavros Lambrinidis was appointed on 1 September 2012 as the first incumbent. His first mandate has been extended until 28 February 2019.

No significant actions concerning Italy took place in 2016.

## VII. Fundamental Rights Agency (FRA)

The FRA, an advisory body established in 2007, is the main technical instrument for the EU charged with supporting European and national institutions in the promotion and protection of human rights. Michael O'Flaherty (Ireland) has been director of the Agency since 16 December 2015 and since July 2015, Filippo di Robilant has been on the FRA Management Board for Italy.

The research element of FRA's work consists mainly of the gathering and comparative analysis of data concerning the fundamental rights situation in the various EU member states, including Italy. In this area, a brief summary is given below of some of the reports drawn up by the FRA in 2016, followed by some comments on the most significant facts that emerged concerning Italy:

*Professionally speaking: challenges to achieving equality for LGBT people* (March 2016): according to the report, the fundamental rights of lesbian, gay, bisexual and transgender (LGBT) people are frequently infringed throughout the EU. Public officials and other education, health and law enforcement professionals have a duty to ensure that the fundamental rights of all people are protected and promoted. The report examines the difficulties these people encounter in their work. Drawing on extensive interviews with public officials, teachers, health professionals and law enforcement officers in 19 EU Member States, it analyses their views and experiences, identifying persisting hurdles – such as perceptions of homosexuality as a pathological condition – and encouraging trends – including considerable commitment to improving the situation.

According to the report, Italy is one of the countries in which public servants believe that the main obstacles to effective implementation of the laws and policies on equality are a hostile social climate, some forms of political opposition and a range of different approaches at the regional level. Furthermore, according to those interviewed, many healthcare professionals in Italy still consider homosexuality a pathological condition. Finally, according to Italian teachers, although the situation for LGBT people has improved overall, harassment of LGBT youngsters at school, such as verbal abuse, cyber-bullying and physical violence, remains an issue.

*Ensuring justice for hate crime victims: professional perspectives* (April 2016): according to the report, most hate crimes, whether against Roma, LGBT people or members of the Muslim or Jewish communities, go unreported and consequently remain invisible and unprosecuted, and often leave the victims without redress for their suffering. The aim of the report is to assist EU member states on one hand to encourage and support victims to report their experiences and on the other hand, to improve the responses of the police and the judiciary in dealing with hate crimes, thus ensuring access to justice for all victims.

In Italy, as in many other member states, hate speech by politicians is a serious issue, inasmuch as it can have a significant impact on the societal climate. Furthermore, these manifestations of hate often go unpunished because they very rarely lead to criminal proceedings. According to FRA research, the groups most subject to hate speech are the Roma and Sinti. The report notes that Italy has created systems and online platforms for reporting hate crimes or instances of discrimination. These are the OSCAD *(Osservatorio per la sicurezza contro gli atti discriminatori* – the Observatory for Security against Acts of Discrimination*)* and the UNAR (*Ufficio nazionale anti-discriminazioni razziali* – National Office against Racial Discrimination) platform.

*Criminal detention and alternatives: fundamental rights aspects in EU cross-border transfers (November 2016):* the report examines issues relative to detention and alternative punishments in EU states, updating the current level of implementation of the group of laws adopted by the EU in this area: framework decision No. 2008/909 on the application of the principle of mutual recognition of criminal judgments imposing custodial sentences or measures involving the deprivation of liberty; No. 2009/829 on the application of the principle of mutual recognition between member states of decisions on supervision measures as an alternative to provisional detention and No. 2008/947 on the application of the principle of mutual recognition of judgments and probation decisions with a view to the supervision of probation measures and alternative sanctions.

According to the data in this report, in Italy there are 108 detainees per 100 available places (EU average 95); the cost per day per detainee is 130 euro (EU average 95 euro). As concerns pre-trial detention, Italy has the highest number of detainees, well above the EU average, of whom there are 3,828 from other member states. Concerning these detainees, some critical aspects were identified concerning their right to an interpreter and the right to legal assistance during the transfer procedures.

## VIII. European Ombudsman

The European Ombudsman, an institution established in 1992 by the Treaty of Maastricht and provided for in articles 24 and 228 TFEU, examines the complaints lodged by European citizens about maladministration in the institutions and bodies of the European Union. Elected by the EP, the Ombudsman performs his duties with complete independence. Emily O`Reilly, previously the National Ombudsperson of the Republic of Ireland, has held this position since 1 October 2013.

According to the report on the European Ombudsman's activities in 2015 (published on 3 May 2016), over the course of that year, the Ombudsman's office received 2,077 complaints, of which 105 from Italy. Again in 2015, it opened 261 enquiries (of which 22 relative to complaints from Italy), and closed 277 cases overall. In that same year, 12 investigations were opened by the Ombudsman's office of its own initiative.

## IX. European Data Protection Supervisor

Established by Regulation 45/2001, the European Data Protection Supervisor is responsible for ensuring the right to the protection of individual privacy in the handling of personal data by EU institutions and bodies, as specified in articles 7–8 of the Nice Charter. It is an independent body elected by the Parliament and the Council of the EU and the current Supervisor is Giovanni Buttarelli, who was previously Secretary-General to the Italian Data Protection Authority.

# Organization for Security and Cooperation in Europe (OSCE)

Through a multi-dimensional approach to security, the OSCE (57 Participating States) operates in the fields of conflict prevention, crisis management and post-conflict rehabilitation. Among its specific bodies and mechanisms worth noting are the Office for Democratic Institutions and Human Rights (ODIHR), the High Commissioner on National Minorities, the Representative on Freedom of the Media and the Special Representative and Co-ordinator for Combating Trafficking in Human Beings. Lamberto Zannier from the Italian diplomatic service has been the Secretary General of the OSCE since 1 July 2011.

Head of the Italian mission to the OSCE is H.E. Amb. Alessandro Azzoni. 13 members of the Italian Chamber of Deputies and Senate sit in the OSCE Parliamentary Assembly. The head of the Italian parliamentary delegation is Paolo Romani and the other 12 members are: Marietta Tidei (rapporteur of the Second Committee), Ferdinando Aiello, Luigi Compagna, Cristina De Pietro, Sergio Divina, Emma Fattorini, Federico Fauttilli, Claudio Fava, Francesco Monaco, Guglielmo Picchi (Vice Chair of the First Committee), Emanuele Scagliusi and Francesco Scalia. The Italian official Roberto Montella took up his post as the new Secretary-General of the OSCE Parliamentary Assembly as of January 1st 2016.

Italy is one of the main contributors to the OSCE. In 2015 (the most recent data available), Italy's contribution to the budget was just under 15 million euro (about 10.4% of the overall budget), on a par with France and the United Kingdom, and only below that of Germany (11%). Italy also contributed towards 2.4% of the non-budgeted expenses, for an amount of approximately 600 thousand euro, ranking ninth in this area. In 2015, there were 57 Italian officials working in the Secretariat and the OSCE institutions.

## I. Office for Democratic Institutions and Human Rights (ODIHR)

This Office is the main OSCE institution which, since 1991, has been supporting Member States in meeting their human dimension commitments. Michael Georg Link (Germany) has been its Director since 1 July 2014.

In 2016, the ODIHR extended for a further two years the tenure of the panel of experts on freedom of religion or belief, which includes an Italian expert, Marco Venturi. The panel's mission is to discuss the challenges to and opportunities for furthering the protection of the aforementioned right throughout the OSCE area. Over the year being examined, there were no actions relating to or directly concerning Italy.

## II. High Commissioner on National Minorities

The office of the High Commissioner on National Minorities is the institution which is responsible for identifying, and as far as possible addressing, situations of inter-ethnic tension in the OSCE area. As well as serving as a conflict-preventing mechanism, the High Commissioner can also support quick solutions which can defuse processes of escalating violence. The term of the fourth High Commissioner. Astrid Thors (Finland), who had been in post since 2013, ended in 2016.

Over the year being considered, there were no activities relating to or directly concerning Italy.

## III. Representative on Freedom of the Media

Established in 1997 with a view to ensuring a high level of compliance with the rules and standards on freedom of expression and freedom of the media accepted by the States Parties to OSCE, the Representative on Freedom of the Media acts as an early warning instrument in cases of violation of the right to freedom of expression, with particular attention to any obstacles or impediments to the activities of journalists. This position has been held since March 2010 by Dunja Mijatovic (Bosnia-Herzegovina).

As in previous years (see *2016 Yearbook*, p. 211 and *2015 Yearbook*, p. 232), once again in 2016 the OSCE Representative focused on the issue of defamation in the press in Italy. Specifically, in a letter dated 26 May, Dunja Mijatovic urged the Italian Senate to consider the bill they were debating (the so-called "Defamation bill" S. 1119b) in light of the impact it would have on freedom of expression, as it would increase the maximum penalty for criminal defamation of elected officers and judges from six to nine years imprisonment. According to the Special Representative, who for years has supported and pressed for total decriminalisation of defamation offences in the OSCE area, adopting these measures would be damaging, because prison sentences are a disproportionate penalty for this type of offence. Furthermore, increasing penalties would have a negative impact on investigative journalism. Laws on defamation should not be tools for the benefit of politicians and others in a position of authority to stifle criticism, and public figures should be prepared for a higher level of scrutiny and criticism precisely on account of their public roles. After being informed that Parliament intended to remove the measure concerning harsher penalties, the Representative expressed satisfaction and confirmed that this decision was a step in the right direction.

## IV. Special Representative and Coordinator for Combating Trafficking in Human Beings

The Office of the Special Representative and Coordinator for Combating Trafficking in Human Beings is responsible for assisting OSCE States to progressively meet their commitments in this area under the 2003 Action Plan. It also serves as the body co-coordinating all OSCE activities combating trafficking. From September 2014, Madina Jarbussynova (Kazakhstan) is the OSCE Special Representative and Coordinator.

The last official visit to Italy by the Special Representative took place in the summer of 2013 and the relative report was published in July 2014 (see *2014 Yearbook*, pp. 266–267).

In 2016, the Special Representative published the 2016 Report on the survey of the efforts made to meet the commitments and implement the recommendations from OSCE on combating human trafficking. The survey, launched in 2015, aimed to get an overview on these issues throughout the whole OSCE area. The results will be used as a reference point to measure progress over the next four years, when the survey will be run again. The data on the situation in Italy as regards combating trafficking were provided by the Italian authorities and by six specialised NGOs and, together with those gathered in the 56 other participating OSCE countries, helped draw up a series of recommendations for combating trafficking in this region.

# Humanitarian and Criminal Law

## I. Adapting to International Humanitarian and Criminal Law

Italy is party to all the main international conventions on the law of armed conflict and international criminal law. In the armaments sector, the obligation to submit regular reports on the state of implementation of the provisions of the various conventions is particularly significant.

In this respect, in 2016 Italy submitted the annual report required by the Convention on Prohibitions or Restrictions on the Use of Certain Conventional Weapons (19 May 2016); the annual report established under art. 7 of the Convention against Anti-personnel Mines; the report required by the Protocol on Landmines, Booby Traps and Other Devices and that of the Protocol on Explosive Remnants of War; the annual report required by the Oslo Convention banning cluster munitions (March 2016); and the annual report required by the Arms Trade Treaty (31 May 2016).

Considering its relevance to this issue, it is worth mentioning the adoption in 2016 of the III National Action Plan for the period 2016–2019 to implement the United Nations Security Council resolution 1325(2000) (see Part II, National Bodies with Jurisdiction over Human Rights, III, A).

## II. The Italian Contribution to "Peacekeeping" and Other International Missions

In 2016 law 21 July 2016, No. 45 was adopted and is a framework law governing Italy's participation in international missions. This new law had been long awaited, so as to have a cohesive approach to a subject that until now had always been regulated by urgent decrees, and brings some welcome examples of synergy between domestic and international law; first of all, for the explicit and crystal-clear definition of the legislative framework within which the participation of the Italian armed forces, police and civil peace corps can be deployed in international missions. Indeed, article 1, para. 1 of the law specifies that they may be deployed only on condition that this deployment takes place "in line with the principles of article 11 of the Italian constitution, of general international law, of international human rights law, international humanitarian law and international criminal law". Another key point is that the objective of promoting the participation of women and a gender approach has been firmly written into the general principles of the law, as prescribed by the United Nations Security Council resolution No. 1325 in 2000 and subsequent resolutions, as well as by the relevant Action Plan 2014–2016. Finally, also to be highlighted is the part of the law concerning the criminal law applicable for personnel involved in international missions. Although, on the one hand, the applicability of the peacetime military criminal code is mentioned, despite the Government reserving the faculty to deliberate the application of the rules of the wartime criminal code, the law specifies that in international missions, crimes which fall under the responsibility of the International Criminal Court, i.e. genocide, crimes against humanity, war crimes and the crime of aggression will always be prosecuted.

In 2016, with law-decree 16 May 2016, No. 67, subsequently converted into law 14 July 2016 No. 131, Italy allocated funds for the extension of Italian military and civilian personnel on international missions.

The list below shows the military and police missions to which Italy contributed forces in the course of 2016.

| **Country/geographical area of Intervention** | **Italian Mission and Actions** |
|---|---|
| Asia | Deployment of military personnel to the Global Coalition against Daesh |
| Afghanistan | Military personnel deployed to Resolute Support Mission (RSM) (NATO) |
| | EUPOL AFGHANISTAN (military and police component) |
| Albania | Italian police in cooperation programmes in Albania and the Balkan states |
| Bosnia-Herzegovina | European Union Force named ALTHEA, within which the Integrated Police Unit (IPU) (military personnel) operates |
| Cyprus | United Nations Peacekeeping Force in Cyprus (UNFICYP) (military personnel) |
| United Arab Emirates/ Bahrain/ Qatar/Tampa, USA | Deployment of military personnel in support of missions in the Middle East and Asia |

| Country/geographical area of Intervention | Italian Mission and Actions |
|---|---|
| Kosovo/Balkans | Multinational Specialized Unit (MSU), European Union Rule of Law Mission in Kosovo (EULEX Kosovo), Security Force Training Plan in Kosovo (military, police and judiciary personnel), United Nations Mission in Kosovo (UNMIK) (police personnel) |
| | Operation Joint Enterprise (NATO) (military personnel) |
| Lebanon | Military contingent which is part of the United Nations Interim Force mission in Lebanon (UNIFIL), which includes the use of naval units in the UNIFIL Maritime Task Force, as well as training the Lebanese armed forces |
| Mali | Participation of military personnel in the European Union missions EUTM Mali and EUCAP Sahel Mali |
| | Participation of military personnel in the United Nations mission in Mali, called the United Nations Multidimensional Integrated Stabilization Mission in Mali (MINUSMA) |
| Mediterranean | Deployment of military personnel to the mission in the Mediterranean Operation Active Endeavour (NATO) |
| | Deployment of military personnel to the European Union military operation in the Southern Central Mediterranean EUNAVFOR MED operation SOPHIA |
| Niger | Participation in the European Union mission EUCAP Sahel Niger |
| Palestine | Participation of military personnel in the mission Temporary International Presence in Hebron (TIPH2) and deployment of military personnel to training activities for the Palestinian Security Forces |
| | Participation of police and judiciary personnel in the mission denominated European Union Police Mission for the Palestinian Territories (EUPOL COPPS) |
| Palestine/Egypt | Deployment of military personnel to the EU mission denominated Resolute Support Mission (RSM European Union Border Assistance Mission in Rafah (EUBAM Rafah) |

| **Country/geographical area of Intervention** | **Italian Mission and Actions** |
|---|---|
| Somalia/Indian Ocean | Participation of military personnel in the European Union military operation "Atalanta" combating piracy |
| | Participation of military personnel in the missions EUTM Somalia and EUCAP Nestor and in the other European Union initiatives for regional maritime capacity building in the Horn of Africa and the western Indian Ocean, as well as running the Italian military base in the Republic of Djibouti and for the extension of the use of military personnel in training activities for the Somali and Djibouti police forces |
| Uganda | Assignment of one officer from the *Carabinieri* as a Police Advisor to the Ugandan Police Force. |

# Part IV

# National and International Case-Law

# Human Rights in Italian Case-law

An overview of the case-law of the Italian courts in 2016 is given in this section to highlight the issue of human rights, focusing particularly on the case-law of the Constitutional Court and the Court of Cassation. The intent is not to provide an exhaustive examination, but rather to cite and note the guidance and the new paths that were recorded in 2016 within Italian judicial practice regarding human rights standards, with particular reference to those reflected in international law.

## I. Aspects of the Relationship Between the Italian Justice System and European Case-law

### *A. Relevance within Italy of ECtHR Case-law*

The Italian legal system is obligated to abide by the final judgments of the ECtHR (art. 46 ECHR). Due to this obligation, in some cases requests were made for the revision of final internal judgments that were in stark contrast to the legal principles established by ECtHR case-law. The issue was addressed in the Court of Cassation, civil division, sec. I, judg. No. 13435, 30 June 2016 – see also section XI. The judgment revoked a previous decision taken by the Court of Cassation based on, inter alia, the consistent case-law of the ECtHR concerning the declaration of the state of adoptability. Regarding the effectiveness of the ECtHR judgments for the Italian legal system, the Court of Cassation noted that "although officially limited to the single case decided, they are likely to provide guidelines for [the cases] to come, when the ascertained violation has been made either in virtue of a general and abstract internal provision or when faced with a repeatable factual situation". With this *obiter dictum* the Supreme Court seems to reiterate what was established by the Constitutional Court with judgment 49/2015, which only recognised the binding nature of the ECtHR decisions when an Italian court must rule on the same case decided by the ECtHR, as well as when the Court adopts a "pilot sentence" (see *2016 Yearbook*, p. 217).

## B. Ne Bis in Idem *as a Principle of EU Law*

The Court of Cassation, civil division (sec. II, ord. 13 October 2016, No. 20675, and 15 November 2016, No. 23232) raised a preliminary question before the CJEU in relation to legislation that forms part of EU law, yet also corresponds to a principle set forth by the ECHR. This regards the *ne bis in idem* rule, which prohibits any legal action from being taken for a fact that has already been the subject of a final judgment, a principle that applies to all criminal proceedings, pursuant to, inter alia, art. 4, Protocol VII ECHR and art. 50 CFREU. The question was raised in connection with appeals lodged by persons and companies that had been subjected to criminal proceedings for having committed crimes of market manipulation and insider trading (punished by articles 184 and 185 of lgs.d. 24 February 1998, Consolidated Act on Finance – TUF) concerning transactions in a publicly traded company. The Italian Companies and Stock Exchange Commission (CONSOB), an independent authority, had requested the application of a fine for the same persons and actions under art. 187-*bis* TUF. The complainants believed that the duplication of the criminal penalty and fine permitted under Italian legislation was a violation of the principle of *ne bis in idem*, also in consideration of the potential severity of the fine the above law provided for, which was comparable to a criminal penalty. The ECtHR had already ruled on a similar issue in the judgment *Grande Stevens v. Italy* in 2014 (see *2015 Yearbook,* pp. 308–309). The ECtHR in finding Italy guilty had also found a general problem of incompatibility of the penalty system for market abuse crimes under the TUF with the principle of *ne bis in idem*. Concerning this ECtHR judgment, also see the decision taken by the Constitutional Court, found below in this section, XII.A. In regard to the orders in question, the Court of Cassation found that, since the prevention and repression of financial market abuse fall within the competence areas of EU law, doubts concerning the legitimacy of Italian law (introduced within the framework of transposing a community directive) should be resolved by making reference to the parameter of art. 50 CFREU, as well as art. 4 Protocol VII ECHR. The EU rule of law, while reproducing the contents of the ECHR Protocol, is open to a novel interpretation, in particular when considering the purposes of guaranteeing the effective implementation of EU objectives. Indeed, for the purposes of guaranteeing the precise application of EU law, some CJEU judgments found it legitimate for member States to punish certain conduct with a "double" penalty, both with a fine and subsequent criminal penalty (Case C-617/10, *Fransson*, 26 February 2013). The proposal of a preliminary ruling at the CJEU is therefore justified. If this preliminary ruling should find an incompatibility between the Italian penalty system, which provides for double sanctioning – both criminal and administrative –, and EU law, which strictly implement the *ne bis in idem* principle, the consequence would be the immediate disapplication of Italian regulations.

### C. Human Rights and the CFREU

The Court of Cassation addressed certain issues which, according to the complainants, were suitable material for a preliminary ruling of the CJEU, as hypothetically related to human rights protected by the CFREU, as well as by the ECHR. The example was provided by a series of decisions made by the Court of Cassation on questions lodged by some public employees concerning extra pay owed to them for working public holidays. A 2005 law had imposed an authentic interpretation (and hence with retroactive effect) for certain previous provisions that had allowed extra pay for public employees who, for service reasons, had worked on public holidays falling on a Sunday. From 2005, the measure – in line with provisions for the private sector – was no longer available and increased pay no longer applied. However, the issue of resolving how to deal with situations that occurred before 2005 remained. The Constitutional Court (judgment 150/2015) had excluded the unconstitutionality of the authentically interpreted law, even considering its retroactive effects. Now a similar question has been raised within the Court of Cassation concerning the possible conflict between the law of alleged authentic interpretation and art. 6 ECHR (right to a fair trial) due to its retroactive nature (which entails interference of legislative power over judicial power) and, due to the contiguity between the ECHR and the CFREU, in contrast to EU law. The Court of Cassation, however, stated that there was no reason to raise the question of constitutionality, as it had already been clarified with the 2015 judgment. It also retained that, as public employment falls outside the scope of EU law, and as the EU is not yet party to the ECHR, the request of a preliminary ruling to the CJEU (art. 267 TFEU) is not viable (Court of Cassation, civil division, labour sec., judg. No. 4433, 7 March 2016, and various others, including judg. No. 7029, 11 April 2016).

## II. Human Dignity: Principles of Biolaw; Immunity of Foreign States and Crimes against Humanity

### A. Living Will: the Non-competency of the Regions to Legislate on the Issue

With judgment 262 of 14 December 2016, the Constitutional Court declared the constitutional illegitimacy of the laws of the Autonomous Region of Friuli Venezia Giulia (No. 4 of 13 March 2015 and No. 16

of 10 July 2015) regarding the establishment of a regional registry for collecting anticipated healthcare declarations, as well as possible voluntary arrangements for organ and tissue donation after death.

The Constitutional Court held that these regional legislations conflicted with the exclusive competence of the State regarding civil law, pursuant to art. 117(2), paragraph m, of the Constitution. In particular, the Constitutional Court highlighted that "given its impact on the essential features of personal identity and integrity, legislation concerning the content of a will related to end-of-life care – and equally for one which governs organ and tissue donation – requires uniform treatment across the national territory, for imperative reasons of equality, this being the ultimate reason why the State retains exclusive legislative competence in matters of 'civil law', as laid down in the Constitution".

## B. Absolute Ban on Clinical or Experimental Research on Embryos

The legislation concerning the absolute ban on any clinical or experimental research on embryos left over from medically assisted procreation procedures, not intended to protect the embryo itself, is the result of a choice of such high discretionary power, due to the axiological profiles that distinguish it, that it cannot be subject to the opinion of the Constitutional Court. That is why, with judgment No. 84 of 13 April 2016, the Constitutional Court declared inadmissible the issue of the constitutional legitimacy of art. 13, paragraphs 1, 2 and 3 of l. 19 February 2004, No. 40 (Medically Assisted Reproduction Law).

## C. Surrogacy

With an important decision intended to guide the courts of merit, the Court of Cassation (joint sec., judg. No. 19599, 30 September 2016) addressed the case of a female couple, one of whom was Spanish, who had married in Spain and were both the mothers of their child, who was born through an assisted procreation procedure. Specifically, the Italian citizen was the genetic mother (egg donor), while the Spanish citizen had carried the pregnancy and given birth to the child. The couple had asked for their child's birth certificate to be transcribed as the child of both (two mothers), according to what was written on the Spanish birth certificate, which had been duly created. The Municipality of Turin rejected the request on the grounds that is was contrary to a principle of public order within the Italian legal system, according to which the mother is only the woman who gave birth to the child. This position was confirmed by a first instance court, but overturned in the appeal judgment, which framed the case as a normal process to recognise in Italy the effects of an act produced abroad concerning a matter that falls within those governed by the foreign law, as the child was a Spanish citizen (his Italian nationality being conditional precisely on the recognition that he was also the son of the genetic mother). The impugnment before the Court of Cassation, however, contested that the civil status legally formed abroad could produce effects in Italy that would be contrary to Italian public order. The Joint Sections of the Court of Cassation therefore gave the current notion of "national public order". The Court held that over the course of the decades there has been a "gradual and comprehensible easing of the opposition traditionally shown by the national legal system to the entry of laws, judicial institutions and foreign values", with the consequence that now the concept of "international public order" prevails over "national public order". This latter should be "understood as a set of fundamental principles that characterise the internal legal system within a certain historic time period, yet are inspired by the need to protect fundamental human rights shared across different legal systems and which come above ordinary law". Therefore, the Joint Sections held that, "Italian judges called to assess the compatibility of a foreign civil status document with public order [...], according to [Italian legislation concerning international private law] must ascertain, not whether the foreign act applies legislation that complies or does not comply with one or more internal regulations (even if imperative or mandatory), but whether it is in conflict with the need to protect fundamental human rights, as found in the Constitutional Charter, the EU Treaties and the Charter of Fundamental Rights, and the ECHR". In this specific case, these principles required the most significant weight to be given to the best interest of the child in particular, for his personal and social identity to be recognised as fully as possible. Rejecting the transcription of the birth certificate in Italy, and thus preventing the child from being identified as the son of the woman who is his genetic mother in Italy (and mother in all respects in Spain), as well as preventing him from obtaining Italian citizenship, would constitute discrimination against the child for an unlawful conduct (the Italian laws exclude heterologous fertilisation with "womb for rent") attributable to others (the parents). The prevalence of the child's best interests was compared to other relevant principles in this case, on the grounds that, as stated by the Court, an atypical form of surrogacy had occurred as the woman who gave birth was not extraneous to the couple and certainly did not act for profit, but rather due to a common motherhood project. In regard to the principle under Italian law that states that the mother is the woman who gave birth (art. 269(3) of the civil code), this "does not constitute a fundamental principle at a constitutional level" that would make impossible the transcription of the foreign birth certificate that contradicts it. The appeal was therefore rejected and the legitimacy of the transcription confirmed.

An "ordinary" case of surrogacy was heard at the Milan Court of Appeal (order 25 July 2016): a heterosexual couple had "commissioned" the gestation and birth of a child from a woman in India (where this practice is not illegal) and proceeded to acknowledge the child as their natural child, yet he was actually the genetic child of the man and an anonymous egg donor. Upon the request of the child's guardian, the mention of the woman as the child's mother was removed from the birth certificate, as it had been transcribed in Italy. At this point the child was recorded only as the natural child of the man and totally unrelated, under Italian law, to the intended mother. The mother contested this measure, arguing the principles of best interest of the child – to which, however, the court countered by raising the principle of protection of a person's dignity, with the defence provided by the absolute ban established under Italian law concerning the so-called "womb for rent" practice, especially in the presence of circumstances such as those occurring in the case in question and admitted by the couple, such as the real purchase of the "service" of carrying the pregnancy and giving birth to the child of completely unrelated parties. However, the court suspended the decision, acknowledging doubt as to the constitutionality of art. 263 of the civil code (action for annulment of the child's recognition for lack of veracity), as the law, also in the light of previous judgments from the Constitutional Court, does not allow for the principle of perfectly matching the legal and the factual data to be tempered in any way by the consideration of the child's best interests. The court held that a law "which does not provide for, and leaves no room – in its unambiguous interpretation – for the assessment of the real interests of the child to preserve, or to lose, his/her relational identity and the status of a recognised maternal relationship" raises well-founded doubts concerning its constitutionality.

With judgment 236/2016, the Constitutional Court declared the punishment (five to fifteen years of imprisonment) prescribed for the crime under art. 567(2) of the criminal code – which sanctions amendments to the civil status of a new-born through false certifications, false statements or other falsehoods – to be illegitimate, as it conflicted with articles 3 and 27 of the Constitution. The event originated from a surrogacy case, which was followed by criminal proceedings against two aspiring parents who were accused of having altered the civil status of their daughter who was conceived via surrogacy, as they falsely declared on the birth certificate that the child had been born from their natural union. Accepting in part the findings of the referring court, the Constitutional Court found that the particular harshness of the sanction of the contested legislation undermined the principle of proportionality of the penalty – and the consequent sacrifice of fundamental rights caused by the same – in comparison to the importance of the objective pursued through the incrimination, as well as rehabilitation function of the penalty. Therefore, the crime in question should see applied the mildest penalty (three to ten years' imprisonment) provided for the other type of amendment to the family status of the new-born, committed by way of substitution, pursuant to art. 567(1) of the criminal code.

## D. Condition of Transgender

Judgment 221/2015 of the Constitutional Court and the rulings of the Court of Cassation on similar matters (see *2016 Yearbook*, pp. 223–226) have been echoed in several decisions taken by local courts in 2016. The Court of Catania (sec. I, judg. 18 November 2016, No. 5662), for example, ordered the civil registrar to amend the gender attributed in the documents regarding the complainant, who was to be considered male to all legal effects despite the fact that he had not undergone gender reassignment surgery, as the surgical route is only one possible path for changing sexual nature to the gender with which the individual identifies and as the psycho-physical well-being of the person is to be considered a priority, which also relies on the consistent documentation of personal data. In another case, the court authorised the male-to-female gender reassignment surgery of a transsexual individual and, with the same provision, the rectification of the individual's name and gender (from male to female) on vital records (Bari Court, sec. I, judg. 11 October 2016, No. 5079).

## E. Immunity of the State and International Crimes against the Dignity of the Person

Once again in 2016 the Italian courts followed the 2014 ruling of the Constitutional Court which declared the incompatibility between the principle of absolute immunity of foreign States before Italian courts, including those related to cases of liability for violating laws for the repression of international crimes, and some inalienable principles of the Constitution, referring to articles 2 and 24 of the Constitution in particular (judg. 238/2014 – see *2015 Yearbook*, pp. 240–241 and *2016 Yearbook*, pp. 218–219). Indeed, the Court of Cassation (joint sec., judg. 29 July 2016, No. 15812) concluded that the judgment of the Bergamo Court, which – pursuant to l. 5/2013 – had rejected the reimbursement claim made to the Federal Republic of Germany must be overturned. As the Italian court's obligation to comply with the ruling of the International Court of Justice of the 3 February 2012, which recognised the immunity of the State, was dismissed, all that remained was to confirm the jurisdiction of the Italian court to recognise reimbursement claims put forward by the many people who were victims of forced labour as an international crime during the Second World War.

# III. Associative and Political Rights; Freedom of the Press

## A. *Italian Citizenship*

The Court of Cassation (sec. I, judg. 3 November 2016, No. 22271) ruled on a case of an Australian woman and her son who had applied for the recognition of Italian citizenship as, in the case of the woman, a person that had acquired Italian citizenship through marriage in the period when Italy was present in territories subsequently ceded to Yugoslavia as part of the Paris Peace Treaty in 1947. She had chosen Italian citizenship in 1951 and then implicitly waived it after acquiring Australian citizenship in 1957 following her moving to that Country. Law 8 March 2006 No. 124, which introduced articles 17-*bis* and -*ter* of the citizenship law (No. 91/1992), permitted individuals who were Italian citizens residing in territories that subsequently passed to the former Yugoslavia, and their descendants who, despite living in the former Yugoslavia, still share the Italian language and culture, to obtain Italian citizenship under certain conditions. Local courts had excluded the applicability of these provisions to the complainants, given that they were Australian citizens residing in Australia and their situation was in no way covered by the aforementioned legislation. However, the Court of Cassation found that, contrary to the findings of the courts, acquisition of Australian citizenship in 1957 – based on the legislation in force in that Country at the time, which entailed the cessation of the former nationality of the naturalised individual – could not have led to the loss of Italian citizenship, neither pursuant to the law in force at the time (l. 555/1912) nor, even less so, under current l. 91/1992. Indeed, the latter in no way prevents dual citizenship for Italian citizens. The former, for its part, entailed the loss of Italian citizenship for persons that acquired another only if the acquisition of the new citizenship occurred spontaneously and was followed by the waiver of Italian citizenship. In the case in question, the loss of the Italian citizenship did not occur through choice, but as a consequence, not desired by the interested party and only imposed by the laws of the State, of acquiring Australian citizenship. The citizenship of the State was essential in Australia for gaining access to the most basic rights and services and therefore indispensable for staying in the Country. The right to a nationality, however, should be understood as a fundamental right which cannot be removed failing an express statement of renunciation. In conclusion, the Court of Cassation concluded that the woman had never lost her Italian citizenship and thus her son should also be considered an Italian citizen, as he was the child of an Italian mother.

## B. Freedom of the Press and Judicial Secrecy

The Court of Cassation confirmed the interpretation of the crime under art. 684 of the criminal code as exclusively intended to protect the proper progress of the criminal proceedings and not as a form of individual privacy protection. Art. 684 punishes with arrest or a fine anyone who publishes, in whole or in part, even in summary, acts or documents of criminal proceedings, of which the publication is prohibited by law. An influential newspaper, and then a book published by another journalist, made known information – albeit reworking it – taken from documents in criminal proceedings against Mediaset, a major TV broadcast network and media conglomerate, concerning the purchase of television rights. The company held that this was a violation of the right to privacy of the persons associated with ownership of Mediaset who were mentioned in the documents that were made public. The merits of the case, however, excluded that Mediaset was entitled to raise the question regarding art. 684 and that there were no damages to be paid for violation of privacy. The Supreme Court confirmed this finding. Art. 684 of the criminal code aims not to compromise the proper process of criminal proceedings during the delicate phase of evidence acquisition and to safeguard the psychological neutrality of the judge. That is why the publication of information covered by investigative confidentiality is completely prohibited, even for journalists, yet the diffusion of information concerning a case is possible – albeit only in summary and without the publication of the texts – after the data has been brought to the knowledge of the accused and used in the hearing. Thus, from the hypothetical violation of art. 684, no obligatory compensation automatically derives for violation of privacy or the reputation of persons mentioned in procedural documents – any damages must be proven with specific evidence, otherwise excessive repression of freedom of information and the right to be informed would occur (Court of Cassation, civil division, joint sec., judg. 25 February 2016, No. 3727).

## C. Ineligibility of Persons with Convictions to Hold Public Office (Severino Law)

With judgment 276/2016, the Constitutional Court ruled inadmissible the questions of constitutional legitimacy raised by the Bari Court of Appeal, the Court of Naples and the Court of Messina, which made reference to certain provisions contained in the law known as the "Severino law") (lgs.d. 235/2012) concerning the ineligibility and ban on holding elected and government positions following final judgments for crimes of intent. In summary, the questions concerned an alleged excess of delegation related to law 190/2012, in violation of art. 76 of the Constitution; the retroactive effectiveness of the laws in question over crimes committed before the law came into force, in alleged violation of the principle of legality and non-retroactivity in criminal matters pursuant to articles 25(2) and 117(1) of the Constitution (the latter in connection with art. 7 ECHR); the alleged disparity between the treatment of elected officials on regional councils and individuals elected to the Italian and European Parliament, in violation of articles 3, 51 and 76 of the Constitution.

The part of the judgment dedicated to examining that second complaint is of particular interest for the emphasis given to ECtHR case-law. Indeed, the Constitutional Court, while concluding that the valid principle of non-retroactivity for the punishments and for the punitive-afflictive administrative measures cannot be predicated in regard to the provisions in question due to their non-punitive nature, found that it had to verify whether the suspension of local government administrators should fall within the notion of punishment, and in so doing it applied the criteria autonomously elaborated by the ECtHR (qualification of the offence under national law; the punitive substance of the measure and the severity of the sacrifice imposed).

## D. Non Justiciability of the Government's Refusal to Enter into State-Religion Discussions

There is no judicial claim that can be used to start negotiations with a religious association in order to conclude a bilateral agreement to govern reciprocal relations under art. 8(3) of the Constitution, as it falls to the Cabinet to assess the opportunity of whether to begin or not such talks. This is what was established by Constitutional Court judgment 52/2016, that accepted the appeal of the Prime Minister's Office against the decision made in the Court of Cassation (16305/2013), which had affirmed the disputable nature of the ruling with which the Cabinet had refused to open up negotiations with the Union of Atheists and Rationalist Agnostics in 2003 to conclude an agreement pursuant to art. 8(3) of the Constitution. Furthermore, the Constitutional Court held that any act of refusal to open up negotiations — insofar as it assumes that the interlocutor is not a religion — would not result in further negative consequences, other than failing to start negotiations, within the legal sphere for the applying association, in accordance with the principles expressed in articles 3, 8, 19 and 20 of the Constitution.

## E. Places of Worship: Prohibition on Different Conditions for Non-Catholic Religious Faiths without an Agreement

With judgment No. 63 of 24 March 2016, the Constitutional Court, ruling on an appeal lodged by the Prime Minister's Office, declared the constitutional illegitimacy of certain provisions in law No. 12 of the Lombardy Region, 11 March 2005 (Law on Territorial Government), as amended by regional law 2/2015, which intervened, inter alia, on principles related to the planning of equipment for religious services. The Constitutional Court held that, while the Region is entitled to dedicate specific provisions for planning and constructing places of worship in the course of governing over the composition of different interests that exist within its territory, it is not permitted to introduce provisions that obstruct or compromise freedom of religion, for example, by providing different conditions for access to the allocation of places of worship. As the availability of dedicated sites is a fundamental condition for the effective implementation of freedom of religion, such legislative intervention would exceed regional competences, as it would interfere with the implementation of freedom of religion by influencing its effective implementation, which is guaranteed by articles 8(1) and 19 of the Constitution. The provisions of the Lombard law concerning the acquisition of opinions regarding public safety and the installation of surveillance equipment in all new places of worship also fall outside of the competences conferred upon the Region, as they pursue clear public order and safety purposes, which are the exclusive competence of the State.

## F. Fascist Manifestations

The Court of Cassation, criminal division (sec. I, judg. 2 March 2016, No. 11038) returned to the crime of fascist demonstrations, punished by the "Scelba law" of 1952, concerning the ban on reconstituting the disbanded fascist party contained in the 12$^{th}$ transitional provision of the Constitution, as reformulated in l. 152/1975 (see also *2015 Yearbook*, p. 296). Based on the law in question, the Italian legal system punishes "anyone who carries out manifestations typical of the disbanded Fascist party or Nazi organisations when taking part in public meetings". In this specific case, Roman salutes and similar gestures were carried out during a public commemoration ceremony for some well-known exponents of neo-fascist groups. The Supreme Court, in agreement with the territorial courts, ruled out the possibility that the crime had been committed, as there was no evidence whatsoever that a real danger of the fascist regime being restored existed. The existence of this real danger is a pre-requisite for the crime in question. Consequently, apart from cases in which the specific context suggests the existence of danger to the democratic order and the values of the Republic, ideological fascist manifestations and the display of its symbols are not, in and of themselves, prohibited, but rather fall within the freedom of expression that is guaranteed by the Constitution.

## IV. Asylum and International Protection

### A. *Appeals against Denial of International Protection*

Once again in 2016, many judgments of the Court of Cassation, civil division, examined appeals lodged by international protection applicants, whose requests had been rejected by both the territorial commissions and courts to which they had applied. The judgments of the Court of Cassation that confirmed the rejection reached this conclusion due to the recognition of the lack of coherence and thus credibility of the statements made by asylum seekers during the various procedural phases (see, for example, Court of Cassation, civil division, sec. VI, judg. 29 December 2016, Nos. 27428 and 27439, on requests of Nigerian nationals).

When processing the case of a Turkish national of Kurdish ethnicity, whose international protection request had been rejected by the Commission and territorial courts as his account concerning the political persecution he had suffered in Turkey was judged to be unreliable, not least due to the democratic nature of the Turkish regime certified by Turkey's alliance with NATO, the Court of Cassation stated that the evaluation of the situation in the Country of origin "cannot be constituted by generic statements, but rather requires assessment, making use of reputable and esteemed international institutions (the High Commissioner of the United Nations for Refugees, various observatories, magazines specialised in analysing judicial-political systems, etc.) which can now be easily accessed by merely consulting the Internet and allow the actual status of liberties and the terms of their hypothetical violation and the risks for discriminated minorities (political, racial, religious, etc.) to be ascertained" (Court of Cassation, civil division, sec. VI, judg. 12 September 2016, No. 17932).

The Court of Cassation, civil division, sec. VI, judg. 22 December 2016, No. 26884 acknowledged the validity of the court's decision – quashed during appeal – which had given international protection to a Nigerian citizen who declared that he feared for his life if he were to be sent back to Nigeria due to the disorder existing in the Country and the fact that he was homosexual (to be considered proven, despite his married with children status).

In the Court of Cassation, civil division, sec. VI, judg. 23 November 2016, No. 23884 the Supreme Court conducted a thorough examination of the reasons that led to the Bologna Court of Appeal's rejection of the international protection application of a refugee from Guinea, after the court had accepted his request for political asylum in 2012 (the Territorial Commission had rejected it on the basis of the time that had elapsed since the events that justified his fear of persecution). The person concerned had stated that he had taken part in some political demonstrations in 2007 – when he was around 15 years old – since which time he had been subjected to persecutory measures by the police. The Court of Appeal, however, encountered a lack of cooperation from the asylum seeker, as it was only in front of the court (and not the Territorial Commission) that certain documents were produced (including an arrest warrant for the events in 2007) which were felt to be relevant to the proceedings. It was the court's opinion that the gradualness of the statements and the lateness in producing the documents should lead to the complainant being judged unreliable. The Supreme Court was not in agreement and accepted the appeal of the asylum seeker given that "gradualness" in producing the documents did not fall within the supposition of failure to collaborate pursuant to lgs.d. No. 251 of 2007, art. 3. Moreover, the overall view did not contradict the findings of the previous favourable decision found for the complainant. The Court of Cassation thoroughly examined the legislation and case-law on the matter and concluded that it was for the court to provide the reasoning for the non-existence of circumstances (first and foremost, the complainant's young age) which could justify the asylum-seeker's failure to highlight the judicial acts from his Country. The rejection of the international protection request was quashed and a new trial was ordered for the case.

The Court of Cassation ruled on the appeal of a Ghanaian citizen whose international protection request had been rejected on the basis of the fact that the described events – concerning the complainant being threatened by a political faction – dated back to 2004 and that generally the alleged political violence in the Country did not appear to be confirmed. The Supreme Court held that such considerations were not supported by adequate analysis of the situation in Ghana and were not sufficient to provide a reason to refuse protection and, in particular, requested that the Italian judicial authorities ascertain the complainant's circumstances regarding the torture and inhuman and degrading treatment imposed by the Ghanaian police on citizens who have committed or have been accused of crimes connected to conflicts between political groups (Court of Cassation, civil division, sec. VI, judg. 14 January 2016, No. 448).

The existence of risk to the safety of family members deriving from usury debt contracted in Nigeria to finance transfer to Europe was not found to justify recognising international protection to a Nigerian citizen, as it was a private circumstance which was not related to persecution or similar situations. Indeed, the person concerned had decided to leave his

Country for purely economic reasons, so much so that he had first applied for a work permit. The Court of Cassation agreed with the territorial court in finding that if his personal situation was so seriously at risk of grave danger in Nigeria, "it is not clear why this was not stated at the time of his entry [to Italy] with the motion of a prompt protection request, while the complainant only turned to this after his request for a residence permit for work purposes was rejected". The overall situation points to the unreliability of the statements made by the complainant. The same holds for the alleged danger arising from the spread of the Ebola virus in his home village (Court of Cassation, civil division, sec. VI. ord. 29 September 2016, No. 19350).

The Rome Court (sec. I, judg. 22 January 2016) recognised the refugee status of a Coptic Christian Egyptian woman, annulling the decision of the Territorial Commission that had, on the other hand, merely granted humanitarian protection. The court found the statements made by the complainant to be credible and supported by sufficient evidence. She was the wife of a public official who had taken part in anti-Morsi demonstrations and was subjected to serious threats from exponents of the Muslim Brotherhood which were aimed at him and his family and were also motivated by their religious affiliation.

However, the appeals of certain individuals who had requested international protection in order to avoid inheriting the role of village chief in their home village were not accepted. This role would have led to, inter alia, polygamous marriage, submission to other tribal rituals, as well as responsibility for managing familial and hereditary conflicts of community members with subsequent exposure to "mortal malfeasance" from people penalised by their decisions (Court of Cassation, civil division, sec. VI, judg. 25 February 2016, Nos. 3755 and 3756).

The Supreme Court (Court of Cassation, civil division, sec. VI, ord. 17 November 2016, No. 23457) found that in some cases the Ministry of the Interior had appealed, before the Court of Appeal, the sentences of courts that recognise international protection for asylum seekers using "serial" appeal acts, namely extremely generic acts that were not calibrated for the specific case tried. This mere fact makes the appeal inadmissible, also in light of the choice taken by the legislator that aims to reduce appeals to the Court of Cassation motivated by a judgment of merit (see *2015 Yearbook*, p. 211).

## B. Application of the Dublin Regulation

Some judgments of the Council of State ruled on appeals that requested the application of art. 3(2) of Regulation No. 604/2013, dated 26 June 2013 of the Council and Parliament. This law provides that a

European State can process the case of an asylum seeker or can transfer the individual concerned to a different EU State instead of delivering them to the authorities of the State that has competence under the Regulation, wherever there are "founded reasons to believe that systematic problems exist in the asylum process and in the reception conditions within that member State, which would lead to a risk of inhuman or degrading treatment under art. 4 of the CFREU". Rulings in this sense were issued in regard to the situation in Bulgaria (Council of State, judg. No. 3998, 27 September 2016) and in Hungary (judg. 27 September 2016, No. 4004).

## V. Discrimination – General Issues

### A. Right to Mother's Surname

With judgment 286/2016, the Constitutional Court declared the constitutional illegitimacy of a group of existing laws within the Italian legal system, which conflict with articles 2, 3 and 29 of the Constitution, as they do not allow spouses, by mutual consent, to also give their children the surname of their mother, either at birth or in the case of adoption. The Constitutional Court held that such limitation prejudiced the right to personal identity of the child and, concurrently, constituted an unreasonable difference in treatment between spouses, which did not find any justification in the aim to protect family unity.

### B. Citizenship and Access to the National Civilian Service

Following on from the Constitutional Court (judg. 119/2015), the Court of Cassation also reaffirmed – in 2016 – that excluding non-Italian citizens from the possibility of gaining access to the national civilian service set out in the notices issued pursuant to lgs.d. 77/2002 (National Civilian Service Regulation) constituted a case of discrimination on the basis of nationality. The anti-discrimination action provided by art. 44 of the Consolidated Law on Immigration (Court of Cassation, civil division, joint sec., judg. 20 April 2016, No. 7951) can be used against this regulation, already declared constitutionally illegitimate through the aforementioned judgment of the Constitutional Court.

## C. Maternity Benefits

The Court of Cassation (civil division, labour sec., judg. No. 8594, 2 May 2016) ruled on the claim of a male self-employed professional who intended to receive maternity pay instead of the mother. The man invoked the principle of non-discrimination and cited judgment 385/2005 of the Constitutional Court in particular, which found articles 70 and 72 of lgs.d. No. 151, 26 March 2001 (Consolidated Law on Legislative Provisions for the Protection and Support of Maternity and Paternity) to be illegitimate for not having treated the father in the same way as the mother for the purposes of access to maternity benefits (the judgment referred to an adoption case). The Court of Cassation rejected the request and concluded that the different treatment between the mother and father, in the case of biological parenthood, did not constitute discrimination. Indeed, the law of art. 70 aims to "protect the health of mothers in the time before and after birth, when it is completely self-evident that, in these cases, the role of the former cannot be compared to that of the father". This is shown by the amendment made in 2015 to article 70, which added the subsequent paragraph 3-*ter*: "The benefits referred to in paragraph 1 are owed to the self-employed father for the period for which it would have been owed to the self-employed mother, or in the remaining amount, in the case of the mother's death or serious illness or abandonment, as well as when the father is awarded sole custody of the child".

## D. "Imputed" Social Security Contributions for Victims of Racial Laws

The conclusion of a process that underwent various vicissitudes regarding the application of l. 96/1955 is worth mentioning here. It granted people who had suffered racial persecution in Italy from 1938 onwards, and those who had lost their jobs in particular, benefits equivalent to the social security amount they had lost due to the racial laws in place in Italy between 1938 and 1945. It was argued that this benefit should also be paid to the complainant, who had been recognised as the victim of racial persecution brought about by the fascist regime, yet who – at that time – had not begun to pay any social security contributions (this was also due to the fact that until 1940 he was below the minimum working age). The Court of Cassation accepted the interpretation that considered the 1955 legislation (and subsequent amendments) as being solely applicable to workers (employees) who had lost their job due to racial laws and thus it could not be extended to anyone who had been victim of such persecution (Court of Cassation, civil division, labour sec., judg. No. 15633, 27 July 2016).

## VI. Rights of Persons with Disabilities

### *A. Ability of Persons with Disabilities to Take an Oath in Order to Acquire Italian Citizenship*

The Court of Modena (sec. II, 6 December 2016) decided to raise the question of the constitutional legitimacy of a series of pieces of legislation, including art. 10 of l. 5 February 1992, No. 91 (New Citizenship Laws), insofar as these include the obligation to swear an oath as a condition for acquiring citizenship through naturalisation, even where this condition cannot be met by a person with disabilities (in the specific case this involved a woman suffering from a serious psychosocial, or "mental", disability"). Indeed, current legislation dictates that citizenship cannot be acquired by a person suffering from a disability that prevents them from understanding the moral commitment that an individual is called to accept in regard to the community when taking the oath. The Court found that the impossibility of completing the citizenship process due to this condition would lead to the violation of articles 2 and 3 of the Constitution and would be incompatible with art. 18, paragraph a) of the International Convention on the Rights of Persons with Disabilities, according to which disabled persons have the "right to acquire and change citizenship and [to not be] deprived of their citizenship arbitrarily or due to their disability". Hence the necessity for the Constitutional Court to intervene on the point of law.

### *B. Architectural Barriers*

The Constitutional Court (judg. 16 December 2016, No. 272) declared the unconstitutionality of certain provisions of Liguria regional law 7 April 2015 No. 12, which specified that where changes are requested for buildings containing businesses open to the public (bars, cafés, restaurants, etc.), such changes "should not lead to the deterioration of the original accessibility features of the properties concerned with the same". The Court held that this law not only intervened on a matter that fell under the competence of the State, as it concerned essential levels of performance regarding civil and social rights (Constitution, art. 117(2), paragraph m), but also appeared potentially capable of reducing the provisions for persons with motor and sensory disabilities as established by art. 82 of presidential decree 6 June 2001, No. 380 (Consolidated Law on Legislative and Regulatory Building Provisions) which imposes, without further specifications, the obligation to remove architectural barriers in all new builds and in existing buildings that are renovated.

The same judgment also censured the aforementioned regional law for excluding, under certain circumstances, the obligation to obtain prior antiseismic authorisation from the competent regional technical office for those who renovate buildings. This authorisation is compulsory before starting building works in all areas of the Country that are at risk of earthquakes and is a fundamental principle of Italian legislation, established in art. 94 of the aforementioned Consolidated Law, which is binding for all Regions pursuant to art. 117(3) of the Constitution.

## C. Discrimination in Schools. Support Teachers

With a series of judgments (2 November 2016, Nos. 371, 372, 373 and 374 and 18 November 2016, Nos. 401, 402, 403, 404, 405, 406, 407, 408, 409, 410, 411, 412, 413 and 414) the Sicily Council for Administrative Justice found the judgment of the Palermo Regional Administrative Court (TAR) – which called for a support teacher to be assigned to a student with disabilities for all school hours – to be insufficiently motivated (and thus repealed it). This ruling was made as the court of first instance had failed to discuss – in any way – the possibility of protecting the educational needs of the student by allocating a number of support hours below the maximum, which could have been specified in the Personalised Education Plan drawn up for the child. The Council also overturned the decision to grant the student's family compensation for non-material damages as, once again in this case, the first instance judgment failed to indicate elements that would objectively demonstrate the prejudice suffered and which could link it to the conduct of the school's administrators as it is not sufficient to merely mention the hypothesis that the failure to assign a support teacher for all school hours may have negatively affected learning. Moreover, according to the Council, it had not been established that the school administration was at fault, which is a prerequisite for the granting of damages. Indeed, the Council held that the failure to assign support in the amount requested by the interested party did not implicate the liability of the school, given the complexity of the legislation and the lack of resources, which would have placed the school in a "state (at least putatively) of need, which conditioned the adoption of the actual provision being disputed". From these considerations, it can be noted how there is the risk of challenging the principle that insufficient resources cannot justify the failure to implement the fundamental right to education to which the student with disability is also entitled.

On a similar matter, one can consider the Council of State, sec. VI, judg. 27 December 2016, No. 5466. The case in question concerned a girl enrolled in a nursery who suffered from an illness that required the daily administration of certain medicines. After her mother found it impossible to personally go to the school to administer her care, the child was forced to forgo attending the nursery for around three months as the competent authority was unable to send a health worker to the school or use school staff to administer the prescribed medications, despite requests. The school staff began to provide the service only after a court order. The Regional Administrative Court (TAR) with which the child's family lodged the appeal also found the school administration guilty for non-material damages resulting from the interruption in school attendance (to the sum of 800 euro). The appeal made to the Council of State focused, inter alia, on the merit of damages, finding that the TAR had not acted adequately to establish the damages as a result of the administration's omission. The Council of State agreed that a hearing was required, as it concerned compensation for loss and not the punishment of conduct for the sole reason that it occurred. However, it also noted the evidence of harm, understood as "suffering resulting from the impairment of a constitutionally-protected right, seen in the dual component of inner suffering and projection in the dynamic-relational sphere of the subject" (Court of Cassation, civil division, sec. III, judg. No. 7766, 20 April 2016), could be given in all manners and even presumptively, and that in these terms the decision of the TAR must be confirmed. Indeed, the failure to attend school constitutes the impairment of a fundamental right that is founded in articles 2 and 34 of the Constitution and on laws that protect the rights of individuals with disabilities, including art. 38(3)(4) of the Constitution and the 2006 United Nations Convention.

### D. Discrimination in Schools. Right to Education of Students with Disabilities and Budget Constraints

With judgment 275/2016, the Constitutional Court ruled on the relationship between the principle of balancing revenue and expenditure, established by art. 81 of the Constitution, and fundamental social rights, including the right to education and school transport for disabled students. In the case in question, the Constitutional Court found the issue of constitutional legitimacy raised by the Abruzzo Regional Administrative Council (TAR) to be founded, inter alia, pursuant to art. 38 of the Constitution, related to a provision of regional law No. 78, 15 December 1978 (Interventions for Access to the Right to Education), subsequently amended in 2004. Specifically, the regional legislation underlying the issue of constitutionality established the fact that the Abruzzo Region's obligation to reimburse the Provinces with 50% of the expenses incurred for the transport service provided to disabled students was limited by the financial availability determined by annual budgets. Consequently, the Abruzzo Region had provided funds, for several years, for amounts below those documented by the Province of Pescara for a total of approximately 1,800,000 euro.

Rejecting the Region's defence, which stated that the effectiveness of the right to education for disabled persons must be balanced against other relevant constitutional rights and, in particular, with the principle of having sufficient funds and balancing revenue and expenditure, the Constitutional Court found that the fundamental nature of the right to education imposes an insurmountable limit on the discretion of the legislator represented by the "respect for an unfailing core of guarantees for the interested parties". According to the Constitutional Court, these included school transport and support for the disabled student, to the extent that the latter constitute an essential component for ensuring the effective implementation of the right to education itself. Indeed, the constitutional judges believed that "it is quite evident that the alleged violation of art. 81 of the Constitution is the result of an incorrect view of the concept of budget balancing, both in regard to the Region and the co-financing Province. It is the guarantee of essential rights that should affect the budget, and not the balancing of the budget that should condition the provision to which they are bound."

## E. Cohabiting Partners and Monthly Paid Leave for Supporting Persons with Serious Disability

With judgment No. 213 of 23 September 2016, the Constitutional Court declared the constitutional illegitimacy of art. 33(3) of l. 104/1992 (Framework Legislation for the Support, Social Inclusion and Rights of Handicapped Persons), as amended by a law in 2010, insofar as it does not include the cohabiting partner amongst parties legitimately qualifying for monthly paid leave to support a person with serious disability, as an alternative to a spouse, or relative up to the second degree of affinity.

Indeed, the Constitutional Court held that the law in question violated art. 3 of the Constitution due to the contradictory reasoning behind the exclusion of the cohabiting partner from the provision of a law for which the *ratio legis* involves protecting the right of disabled persons to psycho-physical health. The latter right, including support and socialisation, must be guaranteed and protected for the seriously disabled, both as an individual and in the community they live in, and cannot be unreasonably restricted to serve a "legal" datum represented by the mere fact of being a relative or spouse. The law in question, therefore, also violates articles 2 and 32 of the Constitution, constituting an inadmissible impediment to the effectiveness of support and integration for persons with serious disabilities.

## F. Cost-sharing Based on the Economic Status of the Family

With judgment No. 2 of 14 January 2016, the Constitutional Court judged ill-founded the question of the constitutional legitimacy of art. 18 of law 13/2007 of the Autonomous Province of Trent (Social Policies in Trent Province), raised in reference to articles 38(1) of the Constitution and 4 of presidential decree 670/1972 (Consolidated Law on Constitutional Laws Concerning the Special Statute for Trentino-Alto Adige) in relation to the United Nations Convention on the Rights of Persons with Disabilities as an intermediate law. The referring court held that the contested law contradicted both the Constitution and international obligations, insofar as it provides that persons receiving welfare benefits are required to share in these expenses based on the financial condition of their family, rather than on the disabled person's income alone, as the latter consider the individual and independent condition of the disabled person as the specific and exclusive object of protection.

The Constitutional Court found, however, that the assumption according to which the disabled person should be considered not in a condition of relative independence from their family, but rather almost totally independent or even relatively isolated, even from a strictly economical standpoint, appears incongruous and out of line with the constitutional and international standards called upon. Moreover, the constitutional judges were of the opinion that it was also contrary to the current trend – favoured by both provincial legislation and, more recently, State law in this area – towards making the family the preferred place in which the needs connected to the difficulties of one of its members were met, configuring the choice of external welfare solutions as merely subsidiary – and in any case secondary and complementary.

## G. Job Placement

A disabled person was dismissed by a private company, despite the fact that the business was required – according to the number of its employees – to have one disabled employee among its workforce pursuant to law 68/1999 (Law for the Right of Disabled People to Work). The point of contention concerned whether employees hired on an apprenticeship contract should factor into the calculation of the number of employees that would trigger the obligation to hire a disabled person. The company held that this was excluded by lgs.d. 276/2003 – which, in fact, established that apprentices should not be counted among the company workforce for certain purposes. The Supreme Court (civil division, labour sec., judg. No. 2210, 4 February 2016), as well as territorial courts, were of the opposite opinion. The conclusions were founded on an interpretation of the laws in question, which place great emphasis on the Convention on the Rights of Persons with Disabilities and art. 26 of the CFREU, as well as the European Social Charter (art. 15) of the Community Charter of the Fundamental Social Rights of Workers (point 26). As a result of this, the law protecting disabled persons must direct the interpretation of provisions that, dealing with other matters, do not establish specific protection for this category of workers. Consequently, the company was required to reinstate the dismissed worker and pay damages.

The Court of Cassation (civil division, labour sec., judg. No. 17867, 9 September 2016) recognised that the obligation to indicate – in the employment contract – the technical, organisational, productive or replacement reasons that can justify a temporary contract in the place of a permanent position also applies to disabled persons hired by a company on the basis of an agreement stipulated with a municipality that aims to foster disabled persons' access to work, implementing l. 68/1999. The company claimed to apply the agreement made with the municipality to hire disabled people on an annual contract (despite the fact that there was no need to hire them for a fixed period) simply so it could then hire others in subsequent years. The Court found that this system constituted a perversion of the facilitation mechanism for disabled people, as it perpetuated the positioning of "socially disadvantaged persons in precarious contexts, and, moreover, took advantage of public funding".

## VII. Social Rights

### A. Minimum Wage and Contracts with the Public Administration

The Calabria Regional Administrative Council (TAR) (sec. I, judg. No. 1315, 15 December 2016) annulled the awarding of a tender by the Calabria Region for private security services, which was allocated to a company that intended to pay its employees wages significantly below those of the competition, making use of "proximity contracts" negotiated by some trade unions. The TAR therefore applied lgs.d. 50/2016 (New Public Contracts Code), based on which the public administration is obligated to exclude competitors that do not comply with obligations concerning the minimum wage in their proposal, as indicated in the specific tables in the same code. Indeed, the Regulation states that economic operators working for the public administration must rigorously comply with occupational, environmental and social rights and that this is regardless of the fact that their compression of costs creates the cheapest offer.

## B. Interventions on the Pension System: Partial Lifting of Restrictions on Automatic Pension Revaluation

With judgment No. 173 of 13 July 2016, the Constitutional Court declared ill-founded the question of the constitutional legitimacy of l. 27 December 2013, No. 147 (2014 Stability Law), which recognised the automatic revaluation of pensions for the three-year period 2014–2016, progressively decreasing from 100 to 40 percent, in line with the pension amount which is, respectively, three to six times higher (only for 2014) than minimum INPS (the main Italian State social security/pension institute – *TN*) payments. Unlike the provisions of judgment 70/2015 (see *2016 Yearbook*, p. 239), in which the challenged law included a wholesale ban on the revaluation for pensions of an amount over three times the INPS minimum, the Constitutional Court held that the contested provision was not illegitimate as it was inspired by criteria of progressivity based on the constitutional values of proportionality and adequacy of retirement pensions. Indeed, the 2013 legislator provided for a remodulation of the application of the automatic percentage equalisation of all pensions, with the zero setting only for the band that is six times higher than the minimum INPS payment and only for 2014.

## C. Pay in Lieu of Leave for Public Employees

With judgment No. 95 of 6 May 2016, the Constitutional Court ruled on the question of constitutional legitimacy raised by the Rome Court acting as the labour court in relation to art. 5(8), l.d. 95/2012 (converted into l. 135/2012), as it prohibits payment to public administration employees for holidays, days off and leave not taken where the failure to make use of these is due to the employee's conduct or choice. In declaring this issue to be ill-founded, the Constitutional Court observed how the law intends to "repress the uncontrolled recourse to monetising holidays not taken and [...] aims to reaffirm the pre-eminence of actually using holiday, in order to incentivise the rational planning of the holiday period and foster virtuous behaviours from the parties within the work relationship". Furthermore, the constitutional judges found that the law did not prejudice innocent employees as extinguishing events within the work relationship which are not attributable to the will of the parties fall outside its scope of application (in the case in question, an employee was unable to take holidays accumulated prior to the termination of the employment relationship due to illnesses he suffered from).

The Constitutional Court (judgment No. 175 of 14 July 2016) held Apulia regional law No. 12, 23 March 2015 (Promotion of the Culture of

Legality, Memory and Engagement), to be legitimate insofar as it generally provides for recruitment via a simple direct and personal call to victims of terrorism and organised crime and people killed in the line of duty for openings (up to the fifth level) in the regional administration and those of bodies and agencies established or, in any case, subordinate to or controlled by the Apulia Region, including companies wholly owned by the region and businesses and local health units. Indeed, the regional provisions merely replicate and specify those of l. 407/1998. On the other hand, regional legislations that extend compulsory employment beyond spouses, children and, under certain conditions, siblings, to cohabiting partners and parents were found to be constitutionally illegitimate. Indeed, State legislation holds exclusive competence in this matter.

## VIII. Immigration

### A. Expulsions, Push-backs

The Court of Cassation confirmed the principle which stated that the family situation in Italy must be taken into account for foreign citizens when ordering their expulsion, even if the person in question has not exercised his or her rights in relation to family reunification. In fact, even if the Consolidate Law on Immigration only provides this for those who have exercised their right to family reunification, the principle of protection of the family unit set forth, inter alia, by art. 8 ECHR, also applies to foreigners who have married and created a family in Italy (Court of Cassation, civil division, sec. VI, judg. No. 14176, 12 July 2016).

### B. Social Rights of Immigrants

With the ordinance of the 1st August 2016, the Genoa Court decided to refer to the CJUE the decision on the compatibility between European legislation concerning equal treatment between European workers and workers from other countries (art. 12(1) paragraph e) of directive 2011/98/EU) and Italian law (l. 448/1998, art. 65) which limit eligibility of foreigners for the care allowance provided for families with three or more minor children and who are legal residents with an income below a certain threshold, to those with a long-term residence permit (excluding holders of the "single work permit"). Indeed, the court doubted that the exclusion of holders of a single work permit constituted discriminatory treatment. It should be noted that with decision No. 472 of 25 February 2016, the Florence Court had resolved this doubt and, ignoring the aforementioned

Italian law, ordered INPS and the municipality to pay the care allowance to a large family of third-Country nationals in financial difficulty.

The Supreme Court held (civil division, labour sec., judg. No. 27557, 30 December 2016) that the limitation contained within law 388/2000, which states that for the payment of an assistance allowance for blind or deaf-mute students (l. 289/1990), the beneficiaries or their parents must hold a long-term residence permit, must be considered overturned by the declaration of the unconstitutionality of the law in 2011 (Cost. Court, No. 329/2011 – see *2012 Yearbook*, p. 323). Consequently, the non-EU minor legally residing in Italy is entitled to the assistance allowance, regardless of whether they hold a residence permit. Indeed, "this welfare allowance has social purposes that involve fundamental rights of the person [...] thus the limiting law is not only in conflict with art. 117(1) of the Constitution, in reference to art. 14 ECHR, but also with the principle of equality and rights to education, health and work".

## IX. Right to a Private and Family Life, Right to Property

### A. *Protection of Confidentiality: Adoptee's Right to Know the Identity of His or Her Natural Mother*

The Court of Cassation (civil division, sec. I, judgments No. 15024, 21 July 2016, and No. 22838, 9 November 2016) established that, due to the case-law of the ECtHR (*Godelli v. Italy*, 25 September 2012) and the Constitutional Court (judg. 278/2013 – see *2014 Yearbook*, p. 278), the right of the adoptee's natural mother to anonymity, who has stated her unwillingness to be named on the birth certificate, ends with the death of the woman, without the need to wait 100 years after the birth certificate or the date the relative hospital records were created, as provided by art. 93(2) of lgs.d. 196/2003 (Privacy Code). Indeed, a "dynamic" balance must be made between these two rights, those of the child (to know his or her origins and define their individual and social identity), and that of the mother (to give birth safely, and then maintain her privacy). This balance must account for changes in the interests and rights involved. The Constitutional Court held, therefore, that the law should be adapted, assuming that the woman can withdraw her declaration of wanting to remain anonymous; if this were no longer possible due to the woman's death, the right of the child to know his or her rights would be wholly compromised. This gave rise to the need for the law to be interpreted in the sense indicated. In any case, access to information concerning the identity of the natural mother must be made without prejudice to the privacy of the deceased (only the data strictly required to ascertain the social identity of the child should be made known) and of any third parties – relatives of the woman, for example. In other words, the laws concerning personal data protection must be applied, pursuant to lgs.d. 196/2003 (Privacy Code).

## B. Right of the "Social Parent" to Spend Time with the Minor Children of a Former Same-sex Partner

With judgment No. 225 of 20 October 2016, the Constitutional Court declared the question of the constitutional legitimacy of art. 337-*ter* of the civil code to be ill-founded, insofar as it does not allow the court to evaluate, in the real case, whether it is in the interests of the minor to maintain a meaningful relationship with the former partner (in this case, a same-sex partner) of the biological parent, in reference to articles 2, 3, 30 and 31 and, as concerns art. 8 ECHR, to art. 117(1) of the Constitution. Unlike the referring court, the Constitutional Court did not find any lapses in the protection of the child within the de facto family, even made up of people of the same sex. Indeed, it specified that the interest of the child in maintaining meaningful relationships with non-relatives is protected by the faculty of the judge, recognised in art. 333 of the civil code, to adopt suitable provisions on specific cases, either at the request of the public prosecutor, even on the request of the unrelated adult involved in the relationship in question.

## C. "Right to be Forgotten"

The Milan Court (sec. I, judg. No. 10374, 28 September 2016) issued an interesting decision concerning the so-called right to be forgotten, referring to a well-known judgment of the CJUE (*Google Spain and Google*, C-131/12, 13 May 2014). The case concerned a businesswoman and politician who had been the subject of an article in a newspaper, which was held to be defamatory and subsequently deleted from the paper's website as part of a settlement between the interested party, the journalist who wrote the piece and the director of the newspaper. The same article, however, had been republished on a blog and, after almost six years, was still found in searches made on Google by entering the name of the complainant. Thus the latter brought a civil lawsuit against Google Italia to protect her right to personal identity. The court held that the "right to be forgotten" is simply one aspect of the right to personal identity and, ultimately, to dignity of the person, including ensuring that information regarding him or her is neither outdated nor incomplete, especially if mediated and "packaged" by search engines such as Google. Google cannot be asked to check the defamatory character of information supplied on certain individuals, however its search engine must de-index articles that are not relevant or up-to-date. This also holds if the interested person is, as in the case in question, a public figure: this circumstance broadens the pertinent criteria, yet does not exclude the right to personal identity entirely. It should be noted that the court in this decision ruled against Google Italia (which must proceed to de-index the contested article) and against the Privacy Authority, which had supported Google's position in this circumstance.

The Court of Cassation, civil division, sec. I, judg. No. 13161, 24 June 2016, also ruled on a matter of right to be forgotten. It confirmed the legitimacy of a judgment which awarded compensation to two restaurateurs who had, for years, seen their names associated with an article published by an online newspaper, which gave information about criminal proceedings involving them in 2008. The indexing of the article was deleted only after the interested parties started court proceedings. The illegal processing of personal data was acknowledged by the tribunal and the Court of Cassation, not in the content and the original modes of online publishing and diffusion of the news article concerning the relevant criminal case that occurred in 2008, and not even in its electronic archiving and storage, but rather "in the maintenance of the direct and easy access [via a simple Google search using the names of the restaurateurs] to that old article published [...] and in its diffusion on the web, at least starting from when the cease and desist order was received [in 2010] for the removal of this publication from the internet".

## D. Right to Privacy and Checks on Employees

The Court of Cassation, (civil division, labour sec., judg. No. 22313, 3 November 2016) ruled on a case of dismissal of a bank employee who was surprised, during an ordinary inspection, using his work computer to save – as emerged subsequently – pornographic material: asked to open the volume that was seen to contain video files, the employee deleted the entire disc content, putting the integrity of company data at risk. However, the Tribunal and Court of Appeal found the dismissal to be illegitimate, due to the way in which the employee was asked to open the saved videos in the presence of strangers, in violation of the dignity of the employee. The courts of merit held that the company had not proven that the deleted volume contained company data and the action of the employee should be considered an excusable reaction given the excessive demand of the person who conducted the inspection. The Court of Cassation considered the evaluation made by the courts of merit on the abusive character of the inspection and the risk to company data deriving from the employee's reaction to be insufficiently detailed and thus deferred the case to another section of the Court of Appeal. From a legal premises perspective, however, the Supreme Court confirmed the opinion of the courts, observing that it is legitimate for the employer to carry out controls intended to check the correct use of IT tools by employees, but that "such prerogative must be exercised while respecting the freedom and dignity of employees, as well as the principles of polite, relevant and moderate behaviour, as it may involve handling sensitive personal information".

## E. Automatic Telephone Marketing Systems

Some large companies have been using a telemarketing process for a long time on landlines and mobile phones which included automatic calls (not from a telephone operator) to verify the presence of the recipient on the telephone; an operator, who in the meantime has finished a previous conversation, comes in later. The mechanism aimed to avoid any downtime for the telemarketing operator, yet translated – from the perspective of the user of the telephone service – into the phenomenon of "silent calls", a source of disturbance and, at times, apprehension. The Privacy Authority intervened to limit this practice, dictating that the same person could not be contacted using this automatic method more than once a month. Some companies that use or supply the software that allows "silent calls" challenged the decision, observing that the practice was founded on the implicit consent provided by the user when they made their telephone number known. The Court of Cassation rejected the appeal and, in addition to confirming the restriction established by the Authority, to protect the privacy of telephone users it also specified that the practice could not cover mobile phones as, unlike landlines, there are no public telephone directories that third parties can obtain, and thus the prerequisite for hypothesising any kind of alleged consent is lacking (Court of Cassation, civil division, sec. I, judg. No. 2196, 4 February 2016).

## F. Confidentiality and the Diffusion of Telephone Numbers on the Internet

The Court of Cassation (civil division, sec. III, judg. No. 14694, 19 July 2016) processed the case of a sentence for the payment of damages deriving from the actions of a representative of an animal-rights association against a research institute accused of practising vivisection. The person was found guilty for abuse of the right of criticism in regard to animal testing, and the Supreme Court confirmed the correctness of the reasoning of the lower courts concerning the fact that the criticism expressed by the activist attacked not the behaviour and opinions, but the persons of the institute's administrators and employees. The most interesting part of the decision, however, regards the proven responsibility of the complainant for having made public contact details and phone numbers of various people who work with the institute. Over the course of years these people were subjected to hostile anonymous phone calls. The complainant rejected the accusations, observing that the personal data were available elsewhere on the internet and that they had been gathered on a different site to that of the association, which only highlighted the link on its site. Above all, the complainant held that there was nothing to prove that she had made the persecutory calls and other forms of harassment: therefore the causal link between the publication of the contact information and the harassment suffered by the institute's employees was lacking. The Court of Cassation rejected these considerations; however it noted that the disclosure of personal data and the facilitation of their retrieval made possible by the action of the activists infringed the right to privacy of the persons whose addresses were made public without their consent and without their personal addresses having any connection with the cause of the anti-vivisection fight or it corresponding to a public interest. In addition to privacy, their reputation was also damaged, given that they were singled out as "vivisectors". As the illegal dissemination of this data made anonymous telephone calls and other persecutory activities possible, albeit by unknown parties, this is sufficient to find the connection of causality between the diffusion of the personal information and the damage to privacy and to the reputation suffered by institute employees. Thus the sentence forcing the complainant to pay a sum of approximately 140,000 euro was found to be justified.

The Court of Cassation also issued an interesting judgment in regard to a large telephone company that had acquired the databases of certain companies, which contained telephone numbers of millions of subscribers that had been gathered up until 2005, the use of which is explicitly forbidden in the personal data protection code, and used them for an intense promotional and publicity campaign, without, however, re-acquiring the consent of the interested parties and also managing an extensive database. The judgment clarified the relationship between the various penalties provided for protecting individuals' personal data and, finally, confirmed the penalty previously imposed by the Data Protection Authority (Court of Cassation, civil division, sec. I, judg. No. 17143, 17 August 2016).

## G. Confidentiality and Internet Banking Procedures

The Court of Cassation reiterated that the internet banking activities promoted by credit institutions – including Poste Italiane – should be considered "dangerous activities" pursuant to art. 2050 of the civil code. Consequently, if any damage should come to the account holder from using the internet banking platform – in the case in question it concerned a bank transfer for over 5000 euro made by an anonymous party who had got hold of the 10-digit secret code of the postal account holder – the company that offers the online service is required to provide compensation "if it cannot prove it had adopted all reasonable measures to avoid the damage". As the same territorial courts had noted, precisely as a result of incidents like those contested by the complainant, Poste Italiane introduced a new protection system of secret access codes for private accounts, which are more secure than the secret code in the specific case that was violated. Indeed, the bank, the personal data holder of its clients, must – in accordance with the Privacy Code – adopt all the most advanced measures made available by IT development to protect this data and avoid any damage to property and non-material damages caused to the private person (Court of Cassation, civil division, sec. I, judg. No. 10638, 23 May 2016).

## H. Confidentiality and Publication of Court Judgments

With certain rulings the Court of Cassation accepted the appeals lodged by individuals who had seen their personal data concerning their state of health and disability made accessible to all through the online publication of judgments regarding them on the Court of Accounts' site. Although it is not clear who should pay the relative compensation for the damaged suffered – without prejudice to the fact that damage must be proved, as finding the violation of a fundamental right is not sufficient to this end – the Court of Cassation confirmed that this was a breach of the right to privacy and control over one's personal data (Court of Cassation, civil division, sec. I, judg. Nos. 10510, 10511, 10512 and 10513, 20 May 2016).

## I. Right to Personal Portrayal

In regard to the right to personal portrayal and surveillance tools installed in commercial businesses (in this specific case, a pharmacy), the Court of Cassation reaffirmed the principle that, according to the Privacy Code, information on the existence of a surveillance system (which depends on the implicit consent given by the individual that his/her image can be collected and processed for legitimate purposes) must be given before the interested party reaches the surveillance area. For example, by posting a sign in an area outside of the radius of the cameras. Consequently, if a camera is located outside the pharmacy, an informational sign inside the pharmacy is not in compliance with the parameters of the law. This also holds for systems installed prior to the issue, in 2010, of a specific directive on the matter from the Privacy Authority (Court of Cassation, civil division, sec. II, judg. No. 13663, 05 July 2016).

Still pertaining to the subject of right to personal portrayal: a well-known coffee company had, for a certain period, used photos of a famous actress in its advertising campaigns. This actress had sold the rights for the sale of her image to an Austrian company. However, the actress had subsequently withdrawn her authorisation and, therefore, requested the removal of her photos from the company's sales communications. Failing to do so within an appropriate time, it was sued for violating the right to personal portrayal. The lower courts rejected the request, stating that the contract with the Austrian company also included consent given in very general terms for the sale of the woman's image to other companies for advertising purposes. The Court of Cassation, also following on from ECtHR case-law, observed that the dissemination of the image of an individual is legal only if and insofar as it meets the needs of public information, not also when it has – as in the case in question – advertising purposes. In this situation, the actress had revoked the consent previously given to the company concerning the used of her image: therefore the company was obligated to immediately suspend any use of the image for commercial purposes. The Supreme Court therefore set the principle that: "consent to the publication of one's image constitutes a unilateral negotiation, the subject of which is not the extremely personal and inalienable right to personal portrayal, but merely the exercising on this right and, therefore, although it may be occasionally included in a contract, this consent remains distinct and independent from the agreement that contains it, with the consequence that this is revocable at all times, whatever termination date may be indicated for the consented publication, and regardless of the agreement on remuneration" (Court of Cassation, civil division, sec. I, judg. No. 1748, 29 January 2016).

## J. "Simplified" and "Indirect" Expropriations

Law 10/1991 of the Autonomous Province of Bolzano (Expropriations of Public Utility for All Provincial Matters), as amended by law 4/2008 (Amendments to Provincial Laws in Various Sectors and Other Provisions), does not disregard the criteria established by the Constitutional Court and the ECtHR on expropriation allowances. This was set forth by the Constitutional Court with judgment No. 90 of 22 April 2016, which declared the issue of constitutionality raised in reference to articles 42(3) and 117(1) of the Constitution – the latter in relation to art. 1, Protocol I ECtHR– to be ill-founded. Indeed, the Constitutional Court held that the contested provision requires the competent body to determine the expropriation allowance by taking due account of the actual characteristics of the area to be expropriated in its quantification and, thus, the actual market value.

Following on from the Court of Cassation (see *2016 Yearbook*, p. 248), the Council of State also agreed that "whatever the form of manifestation (violence, usurpatory occupation, acquisitive occupation), the illegal conduct of the administration over the right to property cannot lead to the acquisition of the land and constitutes a permanent crime pursuant to art. 2043 of the civil code". In order to put a stop to this situation, the administration must return the property, or reach a settlement agreement with the owner or obtain an abdication waiver from the same, which is considered implicit in the request for damages for the monetary equivalent when faced with the irreversible transformation of the land. Another option for acquiring the land for public ownership is to carry out an acquisitive prescription (provided that this is done in an absolutely non-violent manner and the precise moment of the transfer from private hands to the public administration can be defined), yet only from 2003 onwards, from when the Consolidated Law on Expropriations came into effect, which ended the previous regime that allowed acquisitive occupation. Finally, the transfer of property ownership to the public administration may be founded on art. 42 of the Consolidated Law on Expropriations, which gives rise to an extremely special procedure which, in any case, is not a blanket regularisation, as it is premised on the judicial finding of the right of the private person over the asset that was illegally taken by the administration (Council of State, sec. IV, judg. No. 1466, 13 April 2016).

## X. Children's Rights

### A. *Opening of the State of Adoptability as Extrema Ratio*

The Court of Cassation, civil division, sec. I, judg. No. 13435, 30 June 2016 (see above also, section I) repealed a previous decision of the Court of Cassation that had confirmed the declaration of the state of abandonment and the consequent adoptability of a little girl, which was fundamentally motivated by a conviction that was to be imposed on the parents for abandoning the minor (their daughter of only a few months to be exact). The original judgment also made questionable considerations concerning how very late in life the couple had decided to start a family and consequently the "unnatural" gap between the age of the parents and their daughter, thereby suggesting that the parents lacked an appropriate approach to parenthood. The new decision found that the courts were wrong to consider the alleged criminal conviction for abandoning a minor as proof of inadequate parenting skills. After a more careful reading, the decision actually absolved the accusation of having exposed the child to danger by leaving her alone in a closed car for a short time. Indeed, the criminal judgment had excluded that any danger existed for the child in the situation and therefore acquitted the parents as the act was not a crime. The revocation judgment is also based on an analysis of ECtHR case-law on the subject of right to a family life and adoption, concluding that the declaration of the state of adoptability of the child must also be considered by the Italian court as extrema ratio, which should only be resorted to when all the possibilities of activating the resources of the natural parents have been explored (concerning this last point, see also, for example,

Court of Cassation, civil division, sec. I, judgments No. 7391, 14 April 2016; No. 9339, 9 May 2016; some judgments emphasise the fact that "the mere willingness of the parent to care for the child in the future, the simple hope of recovery, if not accompanied by conclusive behaviour, is not sufficient to overcome the state of adoptability": see, inter alia, Court of Cassation, civil division, sec. VI, No. 17316, 24 August 2016). On the other hand, in evaluating the actual parenting capacity, the courts must take due account of all the information properly submitted in accordance with the procedure for their assessment, not only expert opinions: see, for example, Court of Cassation, civil division, sec. I, judg. No. 10708, 24 May 2016.

## B. Adoption "in Special Cases": Stepchild Adoption, Cross Adoption

Italian courts ruled discordantly on the problem of adopting a partner's child in same-sex couples and, in particular, in cases of cross adoption of the respective children by members of an unmarried couple. L. 11 May 2016, No. 76 (Regulation on Civil Partnerships between People of the Same-sex and Cohabitation Legislation) did not intervene on this issue, thus leaving l. 184/1983 on adoptions unchanged. The latter, in addition to the legal adoption of abandoned children, also provides for other special cases of adoption (l. 184/1983, art. 44), which can take place without requiring the child to have been abandoned. According to the interpretation of some courts, paragraph d) of art. 44 (Impossibility of Child Placement for Adoption) allows for the adoption of the child of one member of the unmarried couple by their partner (so-called second child or stepchild adoption), even in the case of a same-sex couple. Specifically, cross adoption, i.e. the adoption of the children of their respective partners, would be possible. In this way, same-sex couples too could have children in common who are biologically born children of just one partner (and thus, until now not recognised as brothers).

This option was held to be viable on several occasions by the Rome Juvenile Court, as well as by other courts, especially after the intervention of the Court of Cassation (sec. I, judg. No. 12962, 22 June 2016), which substantially confirmed the applicability of art. 44, paragraph d) for stepchild adoption on the premise that this is in the best interests of the child. Indeed, in this way the actual family relationship which has been created around the children of the members of the couple is confirmed at the juridical level (on the judgment of the Rome Juvenile Court which initiated the case decided by the Court of Cassation in 2016, see *2015 Yearbook*, p. 300).

The Milan Juvenile Court, however, was of a different opinion, denying – with decree No. 261, 17 October 2016 – that the forms of adoption in the special cases covered by art. 44, l. 184/1983 could apply to situations like the ones considered here. Once again in this situation, two women who had been cohabiting for many years turned to the juvenile court. Each woman had given birth to a child through medically assisted procreation. Both filed adoption requests for the biological child of the partner. The judge criticised the "extensive" reading of art. 44, paragraph d) propounded by section I of the Court of Cassation, stating that the laws in question govern cases, while not of abandonment, of "permanent semi-abandonment" and therefore cannot be applied to the situation in which a child already has a parent (the biological mother – or the father, in the case of a male same-sex couple) who is perfectly capable of taking care of said child. The Court also emphasised that, faced with the best interests of the child, adequate weight must be given to the legislative framework in force (unchanged, on this point, by the entry into force of the law on civil partnerships) and to the principle that the institution of adoption should not be understood as the attribution of a right to adopt by an adult, but the right of a child in a state of extreme familial deprivation to be adopted. Furthermore, it reiterated that the status of the child adopted under art. 44 are not exactly identical to that – fully equated with the natural child – of the child who has been ruled legally adopted (l. 183/1984, art. 7). Therefore, the couples in question would only be allowed a "minor" form of adoption with possible implications in terms of discrimination.

Both the ruling of the Court of Cassation and that of the Milan Court make extensive reference to ECtHR case-law, however the conclusions drawn are non-definitive in regard to Italian law.

In conclusion, the legislator's failure to take a position, despite the timely intervention of the Court of Cassation (yet not, for the moment at least, the joint sections), has led to foreseeable differences between judicial decisions, to the detriment of the legal certainty over an issue which is of no little importance.

## C. Recognition of Foreign Provisions on Coparental Adoption for Same-sex Couples

With judgment No. 76 of 7 April 2016, the Constitutional Court declared inadmissible the questions of constitutional legitimacy raised by the Bologna Juvenile Court in relation to articles 35 and 36 of l. 184/1983 (Right of a Minor to a Family) insofar as – pursuant to the law in force – it does not allow the court to assess how much the recognition of the foreign ruling pronouncing his adoption by the spouse of the biological parent corresponds with the best interests of the child, regardless of whether the wedding itself has produced legal effects in Italy, as in the case of marriages between persons of the same sex. Indeed the Constitutional Court held that the referring judge had incorrectly identified the pertinent legislative context, since it had erroneously believed it should apply the regulation concerning the recognition of judgments for the international adoption of minors to the case in question, and, in particular, art. 36(4) of l. 184/1983, which aims to prevent the circumvention – only by Italian citizens – of the strict national regulation on the adoption of abandoned minors, through the fictitious transfer of residence abroad. However, considering that the minor was still an American citizen at the time of the adoption, the Constitutional Court held that the referring judge should have referenced the legislation concerning the recognition of a foreign judgment.

## D. Child Prostitution. Child Pornography

The Rome Court, with judgment No. 266 of 20 September 2016, in ordering the conviction of certain individuals guilty of crimes pursuant to articles 600-*bis*, paragraph 2 and 602-*ter*, paragraph 5 of the criminal code (Sexual Acts with Minors Under the Age of 16, in Exchange for Money or Other Benefit), resolved the issue of damages for the victims in an unusual manner. The civil claimants had requested, with a generic formula, a sentence ordering the payment of 20,000 euro to each of the two girls (approximately fifteen years old at the time of the events) who had been child prostitutes. At the end of a long examination of the features of the crime and the victims, the judge at the Rome Court ordered compensation in a specific form, consisting not of the payment of an additional sum of money (which would have seemed like an additional offence towards the dignity of the girls, coming – moreover – from the same persons that used to pay them for their sexual services), but of ordering the offenders to purchase and make available a list of books and films that deal with youth and female issues having content which could restore value to the personality of the young women, who had been morally and culturally degraded by their experiences. The judge specified that the measure "has none of the re-educational or imposed value of a model, but is simply [...] a specific means of compensation that appears to be the only one suitable for the case in question".

The Court of Cassation confirmed that the dissemination, over the internet, of pornographic videos made by under-age persons – if it gives rise to the offence pursuant to art. 600-ter, paragraph 3 (which punishes those who distribute, divulge, disseminate or publicise, even electronically, pornographic material containing children under the age of 18) – can lead to the payment of damages to the victim (or their parents) to a lesser extent if it was the victim who filmed the pornographic video within a relationship of reciprocal provocations and solicitations with the offender. In the case in question, the compensation of 100,000 euro decreed in the first instance was reduced during the appeal, with the approval of the Court of Cassation, to 20,000 euro (criminal division, sec. III, judg. No. 6119, 20 January 2016). The filming of the video and its transmission to the person who disclosed it actually constituted the voluntary exposure to the risk of dissemination of pornographic material on the part of the minor, and thus her co-responsibility in occasioning the damage subsequently caused by said dissemination.

## E. Right to be Heard in Judicial Proceedings

The Court of Cassation repealed a judgment that had put a girl up for adoption, despite the fact that the father (who had had a non-continuous relationship with his children and their mother) had declared that he was willing to accept her, as he had, furthermore, with his older son. The decision to sever the relationship between father and daughter was judged to be insufficiently supported by objective data, and particularly deserving of criticism because it was taken without ever having heard the child, who at the time was 11 years old and had sufficient capacity of judgement. This conduct of the Court of Appeal was held to be in conflict with the principle of a child's right to be heard, affirmed in the 1989 Convention on the Rights of the Child and adopted in l. 84/1983 on the right of a child to a family (Court of Cassation, civil division, sec. I, judg. No. 23635, 21 November 2016).

The necessary participation in the adoption proceedings by the parents and the adoptee, who must be guaranteed the advocacy of a lawyer, was reiterated in the Court of Cassation, civil division, sec. VI, judg. No. 11782, 8 June 2016. The child's guardian, if appointed, is the counterpart required in the proceedings, in which he/she is present with unconditional and legal autonomy. If a conflict of interest between the child and his/her guardian is found (the conflict between the child and his/her parents is assumed), it is up to the judge to assign a special carer. The guardian or carer will have to appoint the lawyer that will provide legal assistance to the child.

On the other hand, however, the Court of Cassation reiterated that, whenever the particular circumstances require it, the obligation to hear the minor can also be fulfilled indirectly via a specific delegation to expert third parties (psychologists, remedial educationalists, etc.). This was the case that was presented in the Court of Cassation, civil division, sec. I, judg. No. 9780 12 May 2016, with the consequence that the point of appeal based on the failure to hear the two children for whom the state of adoptability was declared and who were heard only indirectly by the juvenile court was rejected (although nothing was said concerning the particular circumstances that led the juvenile court to not provide a direct hearing).

## F. Abuse of Means of Correction

A teacher, found guilty for the crime of abuse of means of correction (art. 571 of the criminal code) for having used various forms of physical (clips around the ear, pulling of hair, etc.) and psychological violence towards some students, appealed to the Court of Cassation. The defence pointed out, inter alia, that the law presupposes legal means of correction or discipline, subjecting to sanctioning not their use but their abuse. This should consequently rule out that a crime occurred in the cases when modest slaps were used "in well-defined contexts and in cases of necessity". The Court of Cassation rejected the argument. Indeed, it reiterated that the conduct of the teacher included forms of physical violence consisting of smacks and slaps or forceful hair pulling, not to mention psychological violence and humiliating behaviour, such as threatening the children with the arrival of the devil, forcing them to sing or eat and making them keep their tongue out. The Court held that there was no doubt that "such behaviour far exceeds the limits of education respectful of the dignity of the child – which still always implies exercising disciplinary power with permitted and proportional means – and was here transformed into afflictive behaviour against the personality of others". More generally, the Court observed that, in cases of this type, "the pursuit of correctional or educational purposes is entirely irrelevant, since, considering the particular relationships with the recipients of the behaviour, any conduct that takes on the shape of humiliation, of denigration, of [physical or psychological] violence in concrete terms must be considered out of the question" (Court of Cassation, criminal division, sec. VI, judg. No. 9954, 3 February 2016). The Court argued similarly in the criminal division, sec. VI, judg. No. 52542, 27 September 2016.

On this point see also the Court of Cassation, criminal division, sec. VI, judg. No. 2669, 7 December 2016: a woman, found guilty for having hit a child – with a carpet beater – of whom she had been given custody by the juvenile court, lodged an appeal with the Court of Cassation, stating that, as violence could never be considered a legitimate means of correction, art. 571 no longer had a place in our legal system. Rather the law on (mild) personal injury should be applied, which – however – requires the injured party to bring an action for its prosecution. Without the complaint of the injured party, the court would have to rule not to pursue the case. The Court of Cassation rejected the appeal and observed, in regard to the non-prosecution, that the crime of personal injury would – as an alternative to the crime of abuse of means of correction – in any case be prosecutable ex officio as the carpet beater could easily qualify as a "weapon", thus falling within cases that are punishable ex officio pursuant to art. 585 of the criminal code.

## G. Foreign Minors and Residence Permits for their Parents

The Court of Cassation held to be illegal the prefectural expulsion decree issued for a foreigner with minor children located within Italy who had omitted to request, within the legal deadlines, the renewal of the residence permit from the juvenile court due to serious reasons connected with the psycho-physical development of the children, considering their age and their state of health (art. 31 of lgs.d. 286/1998, Consolidated Law on Immigration). It was found to be illegitimate due to the violation of the clause safeguarding family cohesion unless it gives full details of plans for protecting the family of the undocumented immigrant (Court of Cassation, civil division, sec. VI, judg. No. 3004, 16 February 2016).

The Bari Juvenile Court (decree of 20 May 2016) authorised an Albanian citizen without valid documents for his stay to remain in Italy, implementing art. 31 of the Consolidated Law on Immigration, in order to care for a child with serious disabilities. The peculiarity of the case concerns the circumstance whereby the adult authorised to remain in Italy was the maternal grandfather of the child, who – however – had both parents legally residing in Italy. On the advice of the court, the presence of the maternal grandfather contributed to the emotional and sentimental stability of his disabled grandson, as well as his other grandchild. The removal of their grandfather would undoubtedly cause harm for both children (aged two and six), which could place their psycho-physical development in serious danger. The extension to the grandfather of a provision generally reserved only to parents is in line, according to the court, with the provisions of the Convention on the Rights of Children and supports the constitutionally protected right to family unity.

In another case (Court of Cassation, civil division, sec. I, judg. No. 18563, 22 September 2016), the expulsion concerned a family with three children, two of whom were pre-school age and one of whom suffered from albinism. In having considered the tender age as proof of the children's very limited ties to Italy's social context (omitting to consider other elements that show the contrary) and in having considered the condition of albinism as a mere health factor that did not require particular treatment, without assessing the risk of discrimination that this illness would expose the child to in the family's Country of origin, the lower courts did not give correct application to the law pursuant to art. 31 of the Consolidated Law on Immigration. The Court of Appeal, revisiting the initial conclusions, must – in particular – carry out a "serious investigation and assessment of the existence, scope and diffusion of discrimination against albinos in the Country of return, as it is a determining factor in the serious disadvantage for the psycho-physical development of all three children".

# XI. Due Process: Pinto Act

## A. Questions of Constitutionality

With judgment No. 36 of 19 February 2016, the Constitutional Court declared art. 2(2-bis) of l. 24 March 2001, No. 89 (so-called Pinto Act) to be constitutionally illegitimate due to the violation of articles 111(2) and 117(1) of the Constitution, insofar as it sets maximum duration of a claim for fair compensation resulting from the unreasonable duration of (other, previous) proceedings at three years. The Constitutional Court observed that pursuant to well-established European case-law, the State is held to conclude fair compensation proceedings for damages due to delays in other trials within a quicker time period than those allowed for ordinary proceedings, which – in the majority of the cases – are more complex and in any case are not designed to remedy a previous period of inaction in administering justice. In other words, continued the Constitutional Court, art. 6 ECHR prevents the national legislator from allowing an overall duration for proceedings governed by l. 89/2001 equal to that which is acceptable for other civil cognisance proceedings, rather than modelling it on the shorter two-year period indicated by the Strasbourg Court and adopted by Italian case-law, in the case of processing both the degree of merit and legitimacy. Therefore, the contested provision violates the aforementioned parameters, given that the term of three years means that the total duration of the "Pinto" judgment may be longer than the two-year limit adopted by the ECtHR and Italian case-law for proceedings governed by this law.

## B. Application Problems

The number of judgments from the Court of Cassation settling disputes concerning the recognition of fair compensation as the result of the excessive duration of proceedings, as provided by art. 6 ECHR and governed in Italy by l. 89/2001 (the so-called "Pinto Act"), continues to be substantial.

In 2016 the interpretative guidelines, already established in previous years, and recognised as being compatible with the principles identified by the ECtHR, were confirmed. The Court of Cassation, however, raised doubts concerning compliance of l. 208/2015, adopted in accordance with judgment No. 30/2014 of the Constitutional Court, with ECHR standards and the Constitution. The problem regards the possibility of lodging an appeal to obtain compensation for the excessive duration of proceedings, even before a definitive judgment has been reached for the latter (see *2016 Yearbook*, p. 252). Admitting that a similar appeal should be able to be presented as soon as excessive duration has occurred, without waiting for the conclusion of the trial, the legislator intervened in 2015 with l. 208/2015, effectively obliging the parties to give prior notice of the expiry of the reasonable duration and hopefully to thus obtain an acceleration of the proceedings. However, the reform does not eliminate the need, founded on art. 4 of l. 89/2001, to wait for the outcome of the proceedings before being able to begin the fair compensation process for unreasonable duration of proceedings. In the Court of Cassation, civil division, section VI, orders Nos. 26402 and 26403, 20 December 2016, the Supreme Court noted this inconsistency and raised the question of the constitutionality of art. 4 of the "Pinto Act". It should be noted that in some previous judgments the same Supreme Court did not raise any doubts as to its constitutionality and had actually welcomed the approval of l. 208/2015 as a provision that clarified a situation of temporary constitutional incompatibility deriving from the pre-existing legislative framework (See Court of Cassation, sec. VI, judg. No. 13556, 1 July 2016).

The Joint Sections of the Court of Cassation (civil division, joint sec., judg. No. 9142, 6 May 2016) intervened to clarify that the execution stage of a judgment, which has definitively recognised a certain right, can be included in the calculation of proceedings duration. Indeed, what is protected is the right of the individual to see a definitive outcome to proceedings regarding him or her within a reasonable time and up to its final implications. This means that the stage subsequent to the judgment should also be taken into consideration if, for the execution of the same and thus for the tangible satisfaction of the reasons put before the court, other measures are required. In the specific case, the proceedings began in 1975 and ended in 2000, however the judgment, which included the destruction of a building, was not carried out and the execution, begun in 2002, did not lead to useful results (also as, in the meantime, the building adjacent to the one to be demolished, owned by the complainant, was abandoned in unsafe conditions, thus making it impossible to proceed with the ordered demolition of the illegal construction). The point requiring clarification concerned whether the period of six months established by the "Pinto Act" to promote the compensation proceedings related to the unreasonable duration of the legal action had expired when the appeal was lodged, which was presented when the execution procedure was still pending. The complainant held that the execution stage should be included in the notion of the judicial proceedings for compensation, with the consequence that the appeal was filed within the deadline. The State counterpart, however, held that the two proceedings, of cognisance and execution, should be considered as separate, with the consequence that the deadline was well overdue for the cognisance proceedings, while for the execution proceedings the request should be rejected as the delays were due to the behaviour of the complainant. Basing the argument on a thorough analysis of ECtHR case-law – which generally does not distinguish between the stages of cognisance and execution – but also giving due weight to the dictates of the "Pinto Act", where the period of six months takes on a decisive value, the Joint Sections concluded that the proceedings including the cognisance process and executive process should be taken as a single action if there is no more than six months between the final judgment of cognisance and the beginning of the execution stage. If, however – as in the case in question – the beginning of execution proceedings takes place after six months, the two proceedings must be considered as separate and the excessive duration of cognisance proceedings can no longer be invoked for compensation provided by the "Pinto Act". The Court ruled on other similar cases in the same manner. For example, the Court of Cassation, civil division, sec. VI, judg. Nos. 23187 and 23188, 14 November 2016, intervened on a case, which began in 1992, that had been processed up to the Court of Cassation and concluded in 2004. However, the judgment was not carried out due to a series of material errors in identifying an immovable property and the relative owner, until the correction occurred in 2014. The Supreme Court concluded that once again in this case the period of six months for lodging the correction proceedings for the errors present in the last judgment from the Court of Cassation was not respected and that this dismissed the possibility of processing the event unitarily. The Court also observed that the material errors could have been corrected before the judicial decision was passed.

Still in regard to the period of six months from the irrevocability of the decision of the prerequisite proceedings, the Court of Cassation clarified that, in the case of criminal proceedings, the period is calculated starting from when the possibility of appealing to the General Prosecutor's Office expires (thus, from when the judgment is issued, a maximum of sixty days have to be calculated for filing the motion, plus 45 days for the appeal to be processed by the General Prosecutor's Office) and must also take into account the period of weekday suspension of procedural deadlines (Court of Cassation, civil division, sec. VI, judg. No. 22818, 9 November 2016; concerning the correctness of the criterion that also takes account of the holiday suspension period see Court of Cassation, civil division, sec. VI, judg. No. 5423, 18 March 2016).

In regard to the fact that a delay in the public administration executing the decisions of the judicial authorities – which results in an abnormal delay in the case being closed – the Court of Cassation established that "uncooperative conduct [...] of a third authority whose action is required does not exclude the responsibility of the State for the subsequent dilation in the times of proceedings. On the contrary, the State must set up its own judicial apparatus in such a manner that it can meet the demands for justice in a reasonable period, prevailing if necessary even against the fiercest and most unjustified resistance. Undoubtedly these may influence the evaluation of the complexity of the proceedings, and reflect on the judgment of reasonable duration in the real case, however they cannot suspend nor attenuate the obligation of the State to guarantee a reasonably quick trial, making use of the appropriate governmental and coercive tools, any lacking provision of which constitutes a 'systemic violation' pursuant to the applications of art. 6(1) ECHR" (Court of Cassation, civil division, sec. VI, judg. No. 2586, 9 February 2016).

Based on a series of reforms to the "Pinto Act", the latest introduced with l. No. 208 of 28 December 2016, (which introduced art. 1-*ter* of l. 89/2001), the possibility of obtaining compensation for the excessive duration in proceedings is subject to the filing of a "preventative remedy", before the maximum duration of the ongoing proceedings is reached, understood as the stimulus to accelerate the trial under way. In the case of civil proceedings, it entails requesting the summary rite or the oral part of the procedure six months before the maximum duration of proceedings in the stage considered (three years for the first instance, two for the second, one for the judgment of the Court of Cassation); concerning criminal proceedings, on the other hand, an acceleration request must be filed within the same time period; in an administrative trial, however, a withdrawal petition must be lodged (acceleration requests are also required for accounting and pension judgments).

However, problems have arisen in this regard, caused by the succession of amendments that various laws have made to l. 89/2001. The Court of Cassation clarified that the period of time elapsed before the filing of the withdrawal petition in administrative proceedings is held to be relevant in order to calculate the reasonable duration of the proceedings if, in the meantime, the prerequisite judgment has already exceeded the maximum duration, also for proceedings introduced on the basis of the "Pinto Act", after the entrance into force of the regime, on the 16 September 2010, that influences the admissibility of the "Pinto" remedy before the withdrawal petition has been filed (see Court of Cassation, civil division, sec. IV, judg. No. 5434, 18 March 2016; many judgments are in accordance with this). Only for cases established from 2016 onwards does the law apply, which states that the request for fair compensation cannot be presented, not even in regard to the period before its filing, if the "preventative remedy" of the withdrawal petition has not been utilised in the judgment before the administrative court. Furthermore, for proceedings before an administrative court that are still pending as of the 16 September 2016, the rule holds that "without a withdrawal petition the request for fair compensation cannot be filed, neither for the preceding or subsequent period, whereas once the petition has been lodged the request itself can be proposed without any limitation" (Court of Cassation, civil division, sec. VI, judgment No. 13554, 1 July 2016, subsequently reproduced in several other rulings).

For criminal proceedings, see, for example, the Court of Cassation, civil division, sec. VI, judgments No. 23448, 23 November 2016; No. 25564, 13 December 2016; 21 December 2016, Nos. 26627, 26628 and 26629. The rule on the "acceleration request" does not exclude compensation if the prerequisite proceedings had already exceeded the reasonable time period before the reform came into force in 2015. On the matter, see, for example, the Court of Cassation, sec. VI, judg. No. 23449, 17 November 2016.

So as to prevent delays in justice turning into a profitable enterprise, and provided that no tangible elements emerge that are able to show a peculiarly large amount of non-material damages caused by the excessive duration of proceedings, the sum owed has been determined in a fixed amount for every year of delay in relation to the first three years after the reasonable duration and subsequent years respectively (art. 2-*bis* l. 89/2001, recently reformed on the point of l. 208/2015, which reduced the reference values, which now stand at 400 euro for the first three years and 800 euro for subsequent years – they were 500 and 1500 euro respectively). There is some flexibility in these parameters if the process in question is of "extraordinary complexity" (see, for example, the Court of Cassation, civil division, sec. VI, judg. 28 December 2016, No. 27239). In order to prevent overcompensation, the contribution of the law which states that the amount of compensation "cannot in any case exceed the amount in controversy or, if lower, that of the right established by the court" intervenes: this provision was held to be compatible with the Constitution (see, for example, the Court of Cassation, civil division, sec. VI, judg. No. 14047, 8 July 2016; see also the *2015 Yearbook*, p. 303).

The Court of Cassation, civil division, sec. VI, judg. No. 24997, 6 December 2016, established that compensation is not owed for excessive duration of proceedings in the case in which a trial, originally combined with another and regarding the same fact, was subsequently separated, and both were concluded going beyond a reasonable duration. The Supreme Court agreed that the complainant, having already obtained restitution for the first proceeding, could not invoke additional non-material damages for the excessive duration of the "twin" proceedings.

Moreover, the Court of Cassation ruled illegitimate the decision of the Court of Appeal which, due to the particular complexity of the proceedings, had doubled all the ordinary duration periods for the various stages of the prerequisite proceedings, with the consequence that proceedings lasting 22 years were held to be of an excessive duration only by 10 years (with some departures for different complainants). The Supreme Court found that the special complexity of the trial concerned the first instance (the reasonable periods for which were then extended from three to six years), yet not the appeal and cassation levels (respectively of the ordinary duration of two and one years). The excessive time taken to pay compensation must, therefore, be calculated by accounting for the fact that the unreasonable duration is that which exceeds nine years, and not 12 years (Court of Cassation, civil division, sec. VI, judg. No. 13201, 24 June 2016).

The excessive duration of proceedings recognised as being "frivolous", or ones held to be so by the court processing the excessive duration, cannot be compensated. The same holds for abusive proceedings or those brought that are known, or become known through questions and defences, to be unfounded (see *2016 Yearbook*, p. 253). This was also the case before l. 208/2015 came into force, which amended the point of the "Pinto Act", making this limit explicit: see, for example, Court of Cassation, civil division, sec. VI, judg. No. 9100, 5 May 2016 (reproduced in many other rulings of the Supreme Court). On the other hand, the unfavourable outcome of litigation held by the courts to be unfounded does not exclude the right to fair compensation for the delay, except in cases of litigation pursued largely in order to profit, with procedural tactics of various kinds, from the remuneration provided by the "Pinto Law" (see, for example, the Court of Cassation, civil division, sec. VI, judgments Nos. 43, 44, 45, 46, 47, 48 and 49, 5 January 2016; No. 13200, 24 June 2016). The phrase "manifestly unfounded" used by the judge of the prerequisite proceedings in rejecting a request, used does not mean that the excessive duration of the proceedings concluded in this manner cannot be compensated in the same way as l. 89/2001 (Court of Cassation, civil division, sec. VI, judg. No. 1904, 1 February 2016). Furthermore, the right to fair compensation ceases from the moment in which the interested party becomes aware of the impossibility of obtaining a positive outcome to the prerequisite case (Court of Cassation, civil division, sec. VI, judg. No. 26968, 23 December 2016). The fact that a case has been left to draw out for years without solicitation – which is then submitted only starting from when the reform in 2008 made it an indispensable procedural condition for any compensation request in accordance with the "Pinto Act" – is not reason enough to hold the prerequisite proceedings to be "frivolous" and the subsequent request for compensation for excessive duration to be inadmissible (Court of Cassation, civil division, sec. VI, judg. No. 22727, 9 November 2016).

A worthy interest exists in protecting the reasonable duration of a proceeding even when this aims, through the appeal of a criminal judgment of acquittal founded on the remission of the complaint, promoted in order to get an acquittal on the merits. Once again in this case, although the lack of criminal liability has nevertheless been guaranteed, it cannot be denied that an interest in establishing the innocence of the complainant remains. Therefore, there must be scope for compensation for the extreme worry caused by the excessive duration of the court of appeal (Court of Cassation, civil section, sec. VI, judg. No. 26630, 21 December 2016).

The complainant of the crime who was the civil complainant in the criminal proceedings has the right to compensation for excessive duration of proceedings only from the time he or she became a civil complainant, even if the duration of proceedings had already exceeded the limits of reasonableness before his/her entry (Court of Cassation, civil division, sec. VI, judg. No. 26625, 21 December 2016).

The Court of Cassation, civil division, sec. VI, judg. No. 26002, 16 December 2016, clarified that the applicability of the "Pinto Act" also extends to proceedings begun before 1973, the year in which Italy adopted the clause that allowed individual appeals against Italy before the European Commission on Human Rights – subsequently the ECtHR. The right to a reasonable duration of proceedings is actually founded on art. 6 ECHR, and is not connected in any way to the possibility of filing an appeal with the ECtHR.

The Court of Cassation also reiterated that only criminal, administrative or civil judicial proceedings which concern private law and not public obligations can be the subject of an appeal for excessive duration. Therefore, controversies between citizens and the tax authorities dealt with before tax commissions are not covered by the "Pinto Act" as they are related to taxation provisions (Court of Cassation, civil division, sec. VI, judg. No. 25944, 15 December 2016).

Fair compensation can be requested by any procedural party, even by those left in absentia due to irregularities of the proxy given to their defence (Court of Cassation, civil division, sec. VI, judg. No. 26976, 23 December 2016). In calculating the duration of the prerequisite proceedings, the period required to establish the lack of jurisdiction of the first-instance court must be included – of course provided that the stage of the proceedings carried out before a court found to lack jurisdiction in the area is considered excessive in relation to the complexity of the case (Court of Cassation, civil section, sec. VI, ord. No. 262089, 19 December 2016).

## XII. Criminal Matters

### *A.* Ne Bis in Idem

With judgement No. 102 of 12 May 2016, the Constitutional Court declared inadmissible the questions of constitutional legitimacy raised by two different sections of the Court of Cassation relating to the penalties provided for by the Consolidated Law on Finance (lgs.d. 58/1998) in relation to market abuse. Both questions queried the compatibility of the twin-track sanction mechanism (criminal and administrative) – in this case, for abuse of privileged information as per articles 184 and 187-*bis* – with the fundamental right to *ne bis in idem,* as expressed in ECtHR case law, when interpreting art. 4 Protocol VII ECHR (see *Grande Stevens and others v. Italy*, 4 March 2014; *2015 Yearbook*, pp. 308–309). Without going into the merits of the case, the Constitutional Court recalled how, based on consolidated case law from the European Court of Human Rights, the *ne bis in idem* principle is procedural, not substantial, in nature. This therefore allows States "to punish the same deed as part of more than one claim, using different sanctions, but requires this to be done in a single procedure or through coordinated procedures, while respecting the condition that when a definitive ruling is made on one procedure, the other cases are dropped." Given this, the Constitutional Court believes it is primarily the legislator's responsibility to set out which solutions are to be adopted to remedy any conflicts arising between national legislation and the ECHR due to the twin-track sanction system.

With Ordinance No. 112 of 20 May 2016, the Constitutional Court returned acts relating to the issue of constitutionality raised regarding the compatibility between *ne bis in idem* pursuant to article 4 Protocol VII ECHR and twin-track sanctions (criminal and administrative-fiscal) when it comes to fiscal matters, particularly in relation to article 10-*ter* lgs.d. 74/2000 (combating

VAT evasion), in view of legal reforms which took place in relation to tax offences (lgs.d. 24 September 2015, No. 158), to the Court of Bologna. Indeed, the Constitutional judges were of the view that it is falls to the appellate judge to assess the repercussions in the case before the court of subsequent amendments to the law, which fundamentally changed the relationship between the criminal and administrative offences in question, particularly in terms of relevance. Specifically, the referring court must assess whether any new exemptions from criminal liability exist if all taxes and fines are paid before the first level court hearing begins, which would entail an extinguishment of offence if the accused settles his or her debt with the *Agenzia delle entrate* (Italian Revenue Agency).

With judgement No. 200 of 21 July 2016, the Constitutional Court found article 649 of the code of criminal procedure to be unconstitutional in the part where it "limits the application of the *ne bis in idem* principle to the existence of the same "legal act", in its component parts, even if classed otherwise, rather than the existence of the same "historical act"", with reference to article 117(1) of the Constitution, in relation to article 4 Protocol VII ECHR. This question arose during the case known as the Eternit bis trial, during which the owner of the multinational was accused of murdering 258 people through prolonged exposure to asbestos. A new strand of the trial was opened because 72 of these victims had not been taken into account during the previous case (which concluded due to the statute of limitations) for the crimes of aggravated atypical disaster and wilful failure to take precautions against occupational accidents. In aligning itself with ECtHR case law, and thereby opting for the *idem factum* rather than *idem crimen*, the Constitutional Court concluded that the contested legislation is indeed unconstitutional "in the part in which it excludes that the act is the same due to the mere existence of formal concurrence between the crime which has already been ruled on with an absolute judgement, and the crime for which new criminal proceedings have been launched".

## B. *Retroactive Application of* Lex Mitior

Recalling what it stated in judg. 240/2015 (see *2016 Yearbook*, p. 258), the Constitutional Court declared the question of the constitutional legitimacy of art. 464-*bis* (2) of the criminal code to be manifestly unfounded in the part in which it provides that the request to suspend proceedings with probation "may be made until the proceedings of the direct judgement are declared open" – raised, with reference to art. 117(1) of the Constitution, in relation to art. 7 ECHR (ord. No. 207 of 8 September 2016). According to the Constitutional Court, the law being examined in the ongoing cases, for which the proceedings had already been declared open, is not applicable as a consequence not of the fact that the most favourable criminal legislation is not retroactive in nature, but of the fact that the normal temporal arrangements in procedural regulations – to which the reference to art. 7 ECHR relates – was irrelevant.

With judgement No. 193 of 20 July 2016, the Constitutional Court found the question of the constitutionality of art. 1 of l. 689/1981 (Decriminalisation Act) by contrast with article 117(1) of the Constitution in relation to art. 7 ECHR, and article 3 of the Constitution, to be unfounded in the part in which it does not provide for the application of the most favourable successor law to persons who have committed administrative offences. The Constitutional Court recalled, by way of motivation, that when affirming the principle of retroactivity of the most moderate sanction, ECtHR case law has never addressed the administrative sanction system as a whole; rather, it has addressed individual, specific sanctions, and in particular those which – while considered administrative under national law – are best suited to achieving the "punitive" aims under ordinary law. The Court further notes that "in the framework of guarantees given by the ECHR as interpreted by the European Court of Human Rights, there is nothing asserting a conventional obligation with regard to the general provision of the principle of the retroactivity of the most favourable law under the national legal systems of the individual participating States to be transposed into the administrative sanction system".

## C. Relations with the ECtHR and the Crime of External Complicity with Mafia-type Associations

In two judgements, the Court of Cassation, criminal division, took action on a very thorny issue: the alleged discrepancy between the positions of the Italian judiciary and that of the ECtHR relating to the crime of "external complicity" with mafia associations (articles 110 and 416-*bis* of the criminal code), a charge used in Italy to combat types of collaboration with organised criminal organisations, especially those involving political and business circles.

The most significant of these is Court of Cassation, criminal division, section I, judg. 18 October 2016, No. 44193. A well-known Sicilian politician and businessman had requested his definitive sentence for this crime (which he had committed between 1982 and 1992) to be overturned, invoking the precedent of the ECtHR judgement in *Contrada v. Italy* (see *2016 Yearbook*, p. 267). In this judgement, the ECtHR established that as the exact notion of the means of being complicit in mafia crimes which are considered external complicity in mafia-type associations was only established in Italian case law in 1994 (the year in which the Court of Cassation issued an important ruling on the matter), a criminal conviction for this crime issued in relation to events which took place entirely prior to 1994 must be considered retroactive application of criminal law, which contravenes art. 7(1) ECHR (banning retroactive application of criminal law).

In this judgement, the Court of Cassation firstly denies that the precedent set by the ECtHR in the *Contrada* judgement can be applied in this case, though both of them relate to the same crime. The procedural situations in which the problem arises are different (in the Contrada trial the problem was in ascertaining the crime, whereas here a definitive sentence has already been issued, and the question is raised before the enforcement judge: in order to reconsider whether the law on external complicity is applicable, the trial may have to be revisited. Furthermore, while the situations are similar, they are not identical and therefore the principle established by the Constitutional Court in its decision 210/2013, following the ECtHR's 2009 *Scoppola v. Italy* judgement, cannot be applied (the Constitutional Court had admitted that ECtHR precedents may justify a way of failing to apply an Italian legal provision found incompatible in cases different from that to which the ECtHR refers, but only if they are legally identical – see *2014 Yearbook* pp. 312–313)). However, the Court of Cassation's decision is particularly interesting as it explicitly and thoroughly examines the issue raised by the ECtHR's *Contrada* judgement. Rather than solely criticising the ECtHR judge and underlining the foundation of the legislation, nor merely the case law, which punishes external complicity in mafia-type associations, the First Section of the Supreme Court proposes reconstructing national legislation and case law relating to "external complicity" as far back as the 11$^{th}$ century, from which it can be seen that under Italian law this type of complicity in criminal associations has always existed, particularly in laws punishing collaboration with banned political associations. Applying this extended interpretation of the rules of art. 110 of the criminal code on complicity in crime ("When several persons are involved in the same crime, each of them shall be subject to the punishment for this crime"), in force of which actions are punished which, while carried out by subjects "external" to the criminal association, contribute in a way which is objectively relevant to and subjectively responsible for the fulfilment of the punishable action (i.e. the mafia organisation's operation), which was not "unforeseeable" and were not unforeseeable prior to 1994. However, in the *Contrada* case, classifying his behaviour as a sort of aiding and abetting some mafia members rather than as (external) participation in Cosa Nostra was plausible, particularly as the trial was in relation to events which took place in the 1970s and 80s. In the case in question, on the other hand, in which the conviction was for mafia-related crimes which took place shortly before 1994, the accusation of external complicity in mafia-type associations had clearly and unequivocally been ongoing since the beginning and challenged as such by the defence, so that the conviction for this criminal charge could not in any way have appeared unforeseeable.

With this judgement, the Court of Cassation defends the particular "broad" interpretation of the crime of external complicity (which is thereby extended to non-members), but at the same time justifies and supports the ECtHR's decision in *Contrada v. Italy*, taken with particular reference to the individual procedural circumstances in which the criminal conviction was made and which therefore cannot be applied more generally.

In the other case (Court of Cassation, criminal division, sec. V, judg. 12 October 2016, No. 42996), which arose following the Public Prosecutor's appeal against the decision of a judge who had rejected a request to arrest a well-known Sicilian businessman accused of external complicity in mafia-type associations (on the assumption that following the *Contrada* case this crime had been removed from the law), the Court of Cassation reaffirms that "external complicity in mafia-type associations is not contrary to the principles of legality and predeterminedness". The judgement, unlike the one recalled above, directly attacks the ECtHR decision, stating that the latter was based on a fundamentally false assumption, i.e. that the criminal actions recalled were criminal due to case law, while they were in fact criminal, based soundly on article 110 of the criminal code. This law may indeed be used to "cover acts which otherwise would not be punishable, where each accessory has carried out not the entire typical action but merely an 'atypical' portion thereof".

## D. Torture, Prison Conditions, Prisoners' Rights

With judgment No. 204 of 21 July 2016, the Constitutional Court declared unfounded the question of constitutional legitimacy raised in reference to articles 3, 24, 27(3) and 117(1) of the Constitution – the latter in relation to art. 3 ECHR, of art. 35-*ter* of l. 354/1975 (Prison system rules) insofar as it does not provide for economic compensation owed for a sentence served in inhuman conditions, provided for in paragraph 2 of the same article 35-*ter*, in cases of prisoners sentenced to life imprisonment who have already served enough of their sentence to make them potentially eligible for release. The Constitutional Court believes the question of legitimacy, as worded by the referring judge, is based on a false interpretative assumption, under which monetary remedies are merely complementary (and therefore subordinate) to a reduced sentence. The Court believes "it would be outside of the system's logic, and run counter to constitutional principles, to believe that during detention the superintending magistrate should deny economic compensation owed for a sentence served in inhuman conditions to the person sentenced to life imprisonment, solely because no reduction in sentence is to be made".

The Court of Cassation, criminal division (sec. I, judg. 15 April 2016, No. 30804) confirmed its position, which has also been corroborated by the Constitutional Court, according to which the "strict regime" introduced by the Regulation pursuant to art. 41-*bis* of the penitentiary system constitutes neither a sanction nor a preventative measure, but rather is a measure aimed at "neutralising", which may be applied – following an administrative procedure – to convicts of whom there is concern they may continue to communicate with the operational organised crime groups of which they are part, even from inside prison. This makes doubts as to the constitutional nature of the regulation in question manifestly unfounded, as they are based on a claimed characterisation of "sanction" imposed by an authority other than the judiciary.

## E. Slavery, Ill-treatment in the Family

The Court of Cassation clarified that the crime of enslavement and slavery can also be committed in the family (in this specific case, a man was convicted for precisely this crime, committed against his wife and children). The actions punishable under this charge imply by their very nature ill-treatment of the victim, even if the victim is unaware of the position as an "object under ownership" to which they have been relegated, and does not consider it a form of ill-treatment, but not necessarily the form of ill-treatment punished by art. 572 of the criminal code. The crime of ill-treatment in the family indeed implies that the victim has not been reduced to an object of property and economic exploitation (which the crime of slavery requires), but that there is an ongoing practice of ill-treatment which causes the victim to suffer moral and material damages. This of course does not exclude ill-treatment in the family and enslavement from occurring at the same time (Court of Cassation, criminal division, sec. V, judg. 19 February 2016, No. 15632).

The Court of Cassation, criminal division (sec. V, judg. 5 May 2016, No. 23052) excludes that the particular cultural reasons or community traditions of those who committed these acts prevent these actions being considered enslavement. Because of this a judgement which acquitted some individuals who had arranged the illegal entry (trafficking) of a young girl from Kosovo and her underage marriage with the son of one of the accused couples, who had been "purchased" for 20,000 euro, must be quashed. The fact that marriages are traditionally arranged by the spouses' parents does not take away from the fact that a transaction had been made for the purposes of exploitation.

## F. Extradition and Risk of Ill-treatment or Unfair Trial

The Court of Cassation refused to extradite a Chinese citizen to his Country of origin under an Arrest Warrant for organising a "pyramid scheme" fraud. The Supreme Court found that under Chinese law, the sentence for this type of crime in the most serious cases is "more than five years' imprisonment" and a fine, making it not only a far more severe sentence that that which exists in Italy for similar crimes (at least six months' and up to one year imprisonment), but moreover the maximum sentence is not laid down at all. Under these circumstances, extradition could not be permitted as it was incompatible with the principle of legality established by art. 1 of the criminal code and article 25 of the Constitution (Court of Cassation, criminal division, sec. VI, judg. 19 February 2016, No. 6769).

The Court of Cassation, criminal division (sec. VI, judg. 19 December 2016, No. 53741) overturned the extradition of a Ukrainian citizen to his Country of origin where the military judicial authority had requested a custodial sentence on charges of corruption. The Court of Cassation ruled that features of the proceedings in Ukraine raised strong suspicions of persecution against the person to be extradited, who was known for having reported corruption within Ukraine's armed forces. There are also grounds, illustrated in part by reports by international bodies (specifically the Council of Europe's Commissioner for Human Rights) to believe it probable that the person in question would be subject to detention measures which breach of art. 3 ECHR (inhuman or degrading treatment) following extradition. A similar case involving Ukraine is Court of Cassation, criminal division, sec. VI, judg. 28 June 2016, No. 28822.

Failure to consider the risk of inhuman or degrading treatment following the extradition of an individual to Belarus motivated the referral to another section of the same Court of Appeal which had ordered a more in-depth assessment of the case (Court of Cassation, criminal division, sec. VI, judg. 13 June 2016, No. 24475).

## G. Crime of Enslavement

The Court of Cassation (criminal division, sec. V, judg. 29 January 2016, No. 23590) helped to clarify the scope of the crime of enslavement (art. 600 criminal code), specifying that the condition of complete servitude which is a feature of slavery "is not incompatible with a certain freedom of movement which may, in fact, be key to fulfilling this role, as in the case in question relating to begging on the street". The total lack of freedom of movement is on the other hand a typical feature of a different crime, kidnapping (art. 605 criminal code). In the case in question, servitude was facilitated by the fact that the victim was a thirteen-year-old girl when the events took place and, furthermore, was pregnant. The crime of slavery and the no less serious crime of ill-treatment in the family may be used to sanction exploitation of an underage girl for begging, even when the perpetrator is a relative of the victim; in this case, her father-in-law. The sanction is further compounded as the crime was committed against a 16-year-old, i.e. a minor. This aggravating circumstance was introduced along with other measures generally favourable to victims of this crime by law 108/2010, authorising the ratification of the 2005 Council of Europe Convention on Action against Trafficking in Human Beings (known as the Warsaw convention).

## H. Criminal Conviction Based on Testimonies Made outside of Cross-examination

The Court of Cassation reaffirmed its consolidated case law, supported by ECtHR case law, under which "a conviction cannot be based solely or preponderantly on statements made by a person whom the accused was unable to question or have cross-questioned during either the investigative phase or during the debate, unless this inability to carry out cross-examination of the witness was counterbalanced by sufficient evidence, or solid procedural guarantees able to ensure the fairness of proceedings as a whole" (criminal division, sec. II, judg. 21 January 2016, No. 3660). Under the circumstances, testimony given without the opportunity to cross-examine was substantiated by a range of objective findings, which made up for the prejudice thereby caused to right of the accused to defence.

## I. Abandonment of Incapacitated Persons

The Court of Cassation, criminal division (sec. V, judg. 12 January 2016, No. 19448) ruled on a case which led to two police officers being sentenced; they had acted to remove an elderly foreign lady from danger, after she was reported wandering along a street with heavy traffic, but had not taken care of returning her to her home, taking her to the police headquarters, or assigning her to another public service. Almost six months later, after the woman's disappearance was reported to various bodies by her son, including the TV broadcast "*Chi l'ha visto?*" (Who has seen them? – which appeals for witnesses to find missing people – *TN*), her body was discovered close to the area where the police officers had left her. The Court confirmed that the crime of abandoning an incapacitated person had been committed (art. 591 criminal code), specifying that a duty of care can arise not only as an outcome of formal legal obligations, but also simply due to circumstance. The assumption is therefore different from that of a failure to fulfil a duty of care, which implies a formal commitment to performing support duties for a person. Consequently, to honour their duty of care, the agents should therefore have ensured that the woman was left in a safe situation, rather than simply distancing her from the road and abandoning her far from a residential area, and where it was blatantly obvious that an elderly person in a confused state and who did not even speak Italian was unlikely to be able to get herself out of trouble.

## J. The Crime of Stalking as a Criminal Act of Violence against Persons

The Joint Sections of the Court of Cassation have ruled that the obligation to notify the victim of a crime if a prosecutor applies for *nolle prosequi* in crimes involving "violence against persons" (art. 408, para. 3-*bis* criminal code) must also be applied to the offence of stalking (Court of Cassation joint crim. sect. judg. 29 January 2016, No. 10959). The joint sections debate the point with abundant references to international norms which in recent years have given more weight to the figure of the "victim" in criminal proceedings. Specifically, they mention Directive 2012/29/EU (Minimum standards on the rights, support and protection of victims of crime) and the other related directives on human trafficking, sexual violence, etc., as well as the 2007 Council of Europe Lanzarote Convention on Protection of Children against Sexual Exploitation and Sexual Abuse and the 2013 Istanbul Convention on Preventing and Combating Violence against Women and Domestic Violence. D.l. 14 August 2013, No. 93, containing "Urgent provisions regarding safety and security and to combat gender violence, as well as on civil defence and placing the Provinces under administration", converted, with amendments, by law 15 October 2013, No. 199, also to implement the principles affirmed in the aforementioned European instruments, provided that, in order to encourage the participation of victims of crimes of femicide and more generally, of crimes involving "violence against persons", any applications made by the prosecution for *nolle prosequi* should also be notified to the victim of the crime. It is the opinion of the Joint Sections that crimes involving violence against persons refer both to physical violence and moral violence, and therefore also the offence of stalking. Indeed, both have in common the violation of the fundamental rights of the person. Moreover, as regards the condition of women, the Istanbul Convention specifies, for example, that "'violence against women' is understood as a violation of human rights and a form of discrimination against women and shall mean all acts of gender-based violence that result in, or are likely to result in, physical, sexual, psychological or economic harm or suffering to women, including threats of such acts, coercion or arbitrary deprivation of liberty, whether occurring in public or private life". The conclusion that the Court of Cassation draws from these provisions and from other international and EU laws is that "the notion of violence adopted in the international and European Community arena is broader than that specifically regulated in our criminal code and certainly includes all forms of gender-based violence, violence against women and in the context of affective relationships, expressed through violence, whether physical or only moral, such as to cause suffering even only of a psychological nature, to the victim of the crime. The offence of stalking, on a par with that of ill-treatment, falls wholly into this category", and therefore the obligation to notify the victim of an application for *nolle persequi* is also applicable to such cases. In the absence of such notification, which infringes the adversarial principle, a *nolle persequi* granted may be challenged.

The Court of Cassation, ruling on an appeal relative to a guilty sentence on a rape charge, reconfirmed the consolidated case-law by which forcing one's wife to have sexual intercourse against her will does not constitute the offence of ill-treatment within the family (art. 572 of the criminal code), but the more serious offence of rape. The latter "does not distinguish between rape of a stranger and rape perpetrated within a marital relationship… the existence of a marital relationship, or cohabitation, does not authorise any violent use of the other's body, nor limitations to the liberty of the person or humiliation of their dignity. Not even the unjustified and persistent refusal of sexual relations legitimates the recourse to any sort of moral or physical coercion in order to have sexual intercourse" (Criminal Court of Cassation, sez. III, judg. 19 January 2016, No. 18937).

## K. Racist Propaganda and Instigation to Racial Hatred. Aggravating Circumstance of Racial, Ethnic and Religious Discrimination

The Court of Cassation (Criminal Court of Cassation, sez. I, judg. 16 February 2016, No. 34713) has provided some clarification on the subject of the offence of propaganda of ideas based on racial or ethnic superiority or hatred (art. 3, l. 654/1975 and subsequent reforms; the appeal was specifically about flouting the ban on setting up any organisation, association, movement or group whose aims include incitement to discrimination or violence on racial, ethnic, nationalistic or religious grounds: sanctions are applicable both to those who run such groups and to those who simply take part or lend support to their actions). The ruling being challenged had found against the members of an informal group which spread messages of clear neo-Nazi inspiration, mainly using the Internet, on forums, blogs etc. In the first instance, the Court confirmed that the case fell under Italian jurisdiction, although the website used by the defendants to manage their forum was hosted by a non-Italian subject and used servers outside Italy: however it was indisputable that the defendants had used Internet points in Italy. As concerns the identification of the territorially competent Italian judge, since it was not possible to ascertain the physical location where the online offence should be considered to have been committed, the rule to be applied is that which assigns competency to the first public prosecutor who recorded the alleged crime. Concerning the characteristics of the "group" of which membership brings liability for criminal charges, the Court specified that it does not necessarily have to be a structured group, so long as it is proven that said group incites racial discrimination. Moreover, the Court found a substantial continuity between the notions of "spreading" and "propaganda" of ideas based on racial or ethnic hatred: the term "propaganda", introduced in 2006, expresses more clearly the notion of "dissemination" contained in the text of the Convention against Racial Discrimination that was being introduced to the Italian criminal code. Finally, the Court rejected all attempts to have the criminal offence of racist propaganda considered incompatible with the right to freedom of expression defended by the Constitution. The Court of Cassation, recalling the provisions of the CFREU and the ECHR and the case-law of the ECtHR, observed that "the penalty set out by law refers to behaviours which infringe the rights of others and their equal dignity and right to social protection [...] and that, by justifying and promoting racial hatred, xenophobia, religious intolerance and justifying and exalting violence used for racial or religious discrimination [such behaviours] also automatically bring an international obligation to press charges". Sentencing some of the defendants to custody in prison is justified, in the view of the Court, since "here it is not a question of mere 'opinions' but of propaganda of illegal behaviours and instigation to material violence, in addition to the instigation to racial hatred, which is in itself a form of moral violence, both for the same reasons of racial hatred". Part of the judgment appealed against, which awarded damages to the civil parties, including UNAR (Prime Minister's Office), was also confirmed as legitimate.

# Italy in the Case-law of the European Court of Human Rights

## I. Torture, Right to Liberty, Right to Life

On 23 February 2016, in the case of *Nasr and Ghali v. Italy*, No. 44883/09, the European Court of Human Rights (ECtHR) unanimously found that articles 3 (prohibition of torture), 5 (right to liberty and security), 8 (right to respect of private and family life) and 13 ECHR (right to effective remedy) read in conjunction with articles 3, 5 and 8 ECHR, had been violated in regard to the complainant Osama Mustafa Nasr (better known as Abu Omar). The same findings, with the exception of those concerning article 5 ECHR, were also established for Nabila Ghali, the wife of the complainant.

The case concerned the "extraordinary rendition", carried out by CIA agents in collaboration with Italian agents (five military secret services agents and one *carabiniere* – militarised police), of the Egyptian imam Abu Omar (who had been granted political asylum in Italy). The applicant was abducted from Milan, transferred to Egypt and detained there in secret and tortured for several months on the grounds of his alleged involvement with terrorist groups. The criminal proceedings brought in Italy established the responsibility of the American agents (for whom, with the exception of one case, extradition was not sought or the clemency of the President of the Republic intervened) and of the *carabiniere*. The criminal convictions regarding the four Italian secret services agents (one agent having passed away in the meantime) were annulled for reasons pertaining to state secrecy.

Despite the assertion of the Italian Government, which stated that the operation was organised and carried out in its entirety by the CIA agents, with the assistance of the Italian *carabiniere* who acted in an individual capacity, the ECtHR established that the Italian authorities were aware that the applicant was the victim of an extraordinary rendition operation and that they had substantially contributed to said operation. Specifically, as regards the complaint founded on art. 3 ECHR concerning the first applicant, the Strasbourg Court established substantial and procedural infringements. In regard to the substantial infringement, the ECtHR held that the Italian authorities were aware, or should have been aware, that the complainant had been the victim of an extraordinary rendition operation that was carried out with the specific intent of delivering him to the Egyptian authorities, with the related probability that he could be subjected to harsh interrogations involving acts of torture prohibited by art. 3 ECHR. In regard to the procedural violation of the same provision, the Court concluded that while the Italian investigation and criminal proceedings had led to the identification of the persons responsible and convictions for some of them, they had not led to the natural outcome, which, in this case, was "the punishment of those responsible". Indeed, the Court found that the investigation conducted by the Italian authorities lacked any effect due to the Italian executive, which exercised its power to oppose on the grounds of State secrecy, and to the President of the Republic who granted clemency.

Both the substantial and procedural violation of art. 3 ECHR were also established for the wife of Abu Omar. Indeed, the Strasbourg Court found that the disappearance of her husband and the prolonged deprivation of news pertaining to him, deeds that were previously attributed to the Italian authorities, caused mental suffering and a state of distress that was sufficiently serious so as to constitute a treatment prohibited by art. 3 ECHR.

Furthermore, by allowing the CIA to abduct the first applicant on Italian territory, Italy's liability also emerged in regard to articles 5 and 8 ECHR relating, not only to the complainant's kidnapping, but also to the entire duration of his detention in Egypt. Finally, as the Italian criminal proceedings could not be considered "effective" and the applicant was unable to use domestic legal remedies in order to seek compensation, the Court found a violation of art. 13 ECHR, read in conjunction with the provisions mentioned above. The ECtHR granted the sum of 70,000 euro to the complainant and the sum of 15,000 euro to his wife in non-material damages.

With the judgment of 15 December 2016, the Grand Chamber of the ECtHR found Italy guilty in part for the *Khlaifia* case, concerning the detention and expulsion of a group of foreign citizens who arrived in Lampedusa in 2011 and were detained in the Rescue and Reception Centre (CSPA) and aboard Italian military ships anchored off the coast of Palermo, which had been converted into detention centres. Italy, found guilty by the Chamber on the 1 September 2015 (see *2016 Yearbook*, pp. 265–266), had lodged an appeal requesting the Grand Chamber to reconsider the case.

While the violations of art. 3 ECHR (prohibition of torture and inhuman or degrading treatment) concerning the detention conditions within the Lampedusa reception centre and of art. 4 Protocol IV ECHR (ban on the collective expulsion of foreigners) were not upheld, the

17 judges of the Grand Chamber confirmed the violations of art. 5(1) ECHR (right to liberty and security), 5(2) ECHR (right to be informed of reasons for arrest and charges brought) and 5(4) ECHR (right to a prompt decision by a court on the legality of detention).

Indeed, the Grand Chamber established that, considering the structures in which the complainants were held were under constant surveillance by the police and that they were not allowed any outside contact, hosting the applicants in the Lampedusa CSPA and on the ships constituted a deprivation of their personal freedom. Secondly, having ascertained that the complainants were not informed of the reasons for their detention and under which law they were being held, the Court concluded that they were completely deprived of their rights to examine the lawfulness of detention.

Finally, the Grand Chamber also upheld the violation of art. 13 ECHR (right to effective remedy), read in combination with art. 3 ECHR (however, not in relation to art. 4 Protocol IV ECHR) because the complainants could not benefit from any legal remedy under Italian law to report the reception conditions in the CSPA and on board the ships.

Case No. 30474/14 of 4 October 2016, *Jihana Ali and Others v. Switzerland and Italy*, regards the application of the so-called "Dublin Regulation" to the four applicants, Syrian citizens of Kurdish origin. The complainants arrived in Italy and then travelled to Switzerland, the Country in which they formally requested asylum. While the Swiss authorities established that Italy was responsible for their request, the complainants stated that their transfer would have constituted treatment contrary to art. 3 ECHR due to the general poor reception conditions for asylum-seekers in Italy.

The Strasbourg Court considered this part of the appeal to be manifestly ill-founded. Even having taken into account the fact that some of the complainants belonged to a particularly disadvantaged and vulnerable population group with special protection needs (single mothers with minors), the ECtHR excluded that the situation of asylum-seekers in Italy was comparable to the situation in Greece at the time of the *M.S.S. v. Belgium and Greece* judgment and that the structure and overall situation of the reception arrangements in Italy could not, in themselves, act as a bar to all removals of asylum-seekers to that Country. Finally, the Court did not find any basis that would lead it to assume that the complainants would not have access to the resources available in Italy for a single mother with an under-age daughter requesting asylum, or that, in the event of health problems or other difficulties, the Italian authorities would not respond in the appropriate manner.

With the judgment of 6 October 2016 in the case of *Richmond Yaw and Others* (Nos. 3342/11, 3391/11, 3408/11 and 3447/11), the ECtHR found Italy guilty of violating art. 5 ECHR (right to liberty and security) in not complying with the principle of the right to a fair hearing in the case of detention measures being extended. The applicants, four Ghanaian citizens, were the recipients of an expulsion decree and, following the validation by the Justice of the Peace in Caserta, had been assigned to the Ponte Galeria Centre for Identification and Expulsion (CIE) for thirty days before a removal order was to be carried out. Once this period had lapsed without the identification process of the complainants being completed, the Justice of the Peace extended their detention for a further thirty days, upon the request of Police Headquarters. However, this was done without informing the applicants or their lawyer and without holding any hearings, thereby making an effective right of defence impossible. The complainants had lodged an appeal against the extension of their detention in the Court of Cassation, which acknowledged its invalidity due to its infringing the right to a fair hearing.

It was the view of the Strasbourg Court that the failure to summon the parties and their lawyer, as well as the failure to schedule a hearing constituted a "serious and manifest irregularity", such as to make the extension of the complainants' detention a deprivation of liberty contrary to art. 5 (1) ECHR. Furthermore, considering that the complainants had no means to obtain, with a sufficient degree of certainty, compensation for the "unjust" detention they suffered, the Court ascertained that art. 5(5) of ECHR had also been violated.

The case of *D.A. and Others*, decided on 14 January 2016, grouped 19 applications lodged to the ECtHR by 889 Italian citizens (and their heirs) who had been infected by various viruses (HIV, hepatitis B or hepatitis C) following on from blood transfusions related to illnesses or surgeries that they had undergone. Specifically, the applicants filed a complaint regarding the introduction of new criteria established by the law (decree 162/12) that prevented them from reaching a settlement for the actions brought in civil proceedings that aimed to obtain compensation for the damages endured as a result of post-transfusion infections (alleged violation of articles 2, 6(1), 8 and 13 ECHR, as well as art. 1 Protocol I ECHR). Furthermore, some complainants reported the excessive length of the compensation proceedings (art. 2 ECHR, procedural limb), and others the State's failure to carry out judicial decisions made in their favour (articles 6(1) and 13 ECHR, as well as art. 1 Protocol I ECHR).

In regard to the complainants awarded a settlement due to final judgments that granted them compensation for damage caused to their health as a result of a post-transfusion infection, the Strasbourg Court established that the impossibility of enforcing these judgments constituted a violation of not only art. 6(1) ECHR, but also art. 1 Protocol I ECHR, as it interfered with their right to respect of their possessions. Furthermore, as there was no effective legal remedy available to report the violation of the aforementioned provisions, the ECtHR also established a violation of art. 13 ECHR.

Regarding the procedural limb of art. 2 ECHR concerning the excessive length of the compensation proceedings brought by another group of complainants, the ECtHR accepted the grievances of this group, reprimanding the conduct of the Italian authorities for failing to provide an adequate and rapid response in compliance with the procedural obligations that arise from the provision invoked.

In regard to all the other reasons for the complaint, the ECtHR declared the grievances inadmissible due to the failure to exhaust internal remedies. Indeed, the judges of Strasbourg held that the procedure introduced with law decree 90/2014, which grants the damaged parties a sum of money determined in the amount of 100,000 euro as fair satisfaction, constituted an available internal remedy pursuant to art. 35 ECHR.

The case of *Duilio and Giuliana Rasman and Maria Albina Veliscek v. Italy*, No. 55744/09, was declared inadmissible on the grounds that it was manifestly ill-founded. The applicants filed a complaint – in several respects – concerning the incompatibility with the procedural obligations of art. 2 ECHR of the criminal proceedings brought after the death of their relative. The latter suffered from paranoid schizophrenia and died from asphyxiation when being immobilised by police officers following on from a violent scuffle. The officers intervened as the man appeared to be in a state of high mental alteration (he was naked on the balcony of his home and was throwing firecrackers). When sent to trial, three of the four police officers involved were sentenced, by way of an abbreviated trial, to six months of imprisonment and ordered to pay a provisional sum to the relatives of the deceased. The Strasbourg Court found that the grievances brought by the applicants concerning the superficial natural of the investigations, the failure to consider certain elements regarding the prior state of the victim's health in the trial and the allegedly overly light sentence imposed were all ill-founded. In fact, the ECtHR held that the internal decisions had been duly motivated and thus could not be considered arbitrary. In conclusion, the complainants did not present any evidence that would suggest that the investigations conducted by the national authorities lacked the effectiveness required by art. 2 ECHR.

The case of *Patitucci v. Italy*, No. 22783/13, was declared inadmissible as internal legal recourses had not been exhausted. The complainant, and his heirs after his death, invoked articles 2 and 3 ECHR, complaining about the insufficient and inadequate medical treatment provided by the Italian authorities during the period in which he was detained, as well as the condition of prison overcrowding to which he was subjected. Concerning the grievance related to inadequate medical treatment, the ECtHR observed that civil liability proceedings brought by the complainant and his heirs for the negligent conduct of the Italian authorities were still pending. Furthermore, the heirs did not have *locus standi* in regard to the grievance concerning prison overcrowding, as this was a plea that was strictly related to the applicant and therefore could not be transferred to his heirs.

## II. Fair Trial

In the case of *Ben Moumen*, decided by the ECtHR with the judgment of 23 June 2016, the applicant, a Moroccan citizen, complained of a violation of art. 6 ECHR (right to fair trial) on the grounds that, within the criminal proceedings that saw him accused of crimes of sexual violence and injury, he was unable to cross-examine an eyewitness that – after having made a statement against him during the investigation – had disappeared.

While observing that the Italian courts had not made every effort that it was reasonably possible to expect from them in order to guarantee that the witness would appear at the hearing, the ECtHR concluded that the complainant had received a fair trial. Indeed, on the one hand, the deposition of the absent witness was neither the sole nor the determining basis for finding him guilty. On the other, it established that there were a series of compensatory elements that were sufficient to counterbalance the difficulties caused to the defence by the impossibility of cross-examining the witness.

In the case of *Huzuneanu v. Italy*, decided on 1 September 2016, the applicant complained of the violation of art. 6 ECHR (right to fair trial) on the grounds of having been sentenced *in absentia*, without being given the opportunity to present his own defence to the Italian judicial bodies. Convicted in absentia on the charge of voluntary manslaughter pursuant to the legislation prior to the reform of law 67/2014, the applicant was not notified within the time limit to put forward an appeal against his conviction. Although the competent Assize Court established that he had not been fully aware of the proceedings brought against him, the second-instance judgment had already been filed after the appeal lodged by a publicly-appointed counsel. A new request was lodged by the applicant to reopen the period for an appeal on the grounds that former art. 175(2) of the code of civil procedure was in breach of the constitution (judgment No. 317 of 4 December 2009). This was also rejected as the competent court held that the complainant had become aware of his conviction on 25 January 2007, thus the period of thirty days had expired and the applicant himself should have been able to raise a complaint, deducing the unconstitutionality of the disputed provision.

In considering the applicant's grievance, the Strasbourg Court maintained that although proceedings conducted in the absence of the accused are not necessarily incompatible with the ECHR, the fact remains that a denial of justice exists when an individual convicted in absentia cannot subsequently obtain a new deliberation from a court on the validity of the accusations, after having been heard, where it has not been established that he has waived his rights to appear or defend himself, or that he intended to evade justice. In the case in question, the applicant did not have the possibility to obtain a new decision on the validity of the accusation, both on the facts and the point of the law, even though his absence from the trial was due to no fault of his own, as the publicly-appointed lawyer had already exhausted all available legal remedies. In this circumstance, the Court held that the right to defence of a defendant – who had not evaded justice and had not unequivocally waived procedural guarantees – cannot be reduced to the point to render them inoperative with the justification of guaranteeing other fundamental trial rights, such as the right to a "reasonable period" or that of double jeopardy. On the basis of these elements, combined with the fundamental importance that the appearance of an accused carries in criminal proceedings, the ECtHR concluded that art. 6 ECHR had been violated.

In the case *Trevisanato v. Italy* (No. 32610/07), decided on 15 September 2016, the applicant complained about the Court of Cassation's interpretation of the provisions concerning the conditions for lodging an appeal in cassation. The complaint specifically concerned the provision of art. 366-*bis* of the code of civil procedure (repealed by a reform in 2009), which required complainants to conclude their appeals with the point of law that had been breached. The applicant stated that the decision by the Court of Cassation to declare his appeal inadmissible for failure to comply with the aforementioned provision would have deprived him of his right to a tribunal set forth by art. 6(1) ECHR.

While the ECtHR found the appeal admissible, it excluded the violation of the conventional provision invoked. Indeed, the Strasbourg judges held that the rule of the point of law pursuant to art. 366-*bis* of the code of civil procedure had pursued a legitimate aim, namely to protect the complainant's interest in obtaining, if appropriate, the quashing of the decision appealed against and, at the same time, preserving the Court of Cassation's role as judge in ensuring a uniform interpretation of the law. This was held to be a proportionate measure in regard to the aim pursued. Indeed, it was the opinion of the ECtHR that the request to conclude the grounds for appeal with a paragraph summing up the reasoning and explicitly identifying the legal principle allegedly breached did not entail any particular additional effort on the part of the applicant. The Court also observed that the disputed rule of inadmissibility was not judge-made, but had been introduced by the legislature over a year before the appeal in cassation was lodged by the complainant.

The case of *Capriotti v. Italy*, No. 28819/12, of 23 February 2016, was rejected as being manifestly ill-founded. The complainant stated that the wiretapping conducted within criminal proceedings against him had violated his right to respect of private and family life guaranteed by art. 8 ECHR. Considering these interceptions to be illegal, the complainant also disputed the fairness of the criminal proceedings under art. 6 ECHR as it was his belief that his conviction was based directly on these interceptions. Given the fact that the measure to which the complainant had been subjected was provided by the law and that it pursued legitimate and necessary aims within a democratic society, the ECtHR did not hold that there were elements that would constitute a violation of art. 8 ECHR. Consequently, the use of wiretapping as evidence against the complainant cannot be considered a violation of art. 6 ECHR.

In the case of *Olivieri and Others v. Italy*, 22 February 2016, the applicants complained of the excessive length (over eighteen years) of the proceedings initiated by them to obtain the correction of the calculations concerning their length of service at the Campania Regional Administrative Court (TAR). Furthermore, they complained about the impossibility of obtaining compensation within the "Pinto law" remedy due to the introduction of a new admissibility condition, namely the need to request an urgent hearing, applicable to judgments before the administrative court.

The Italian Government argued that legal recourses had not been exhausted as the applicants had not correctly followed the "Pinto law" remedy. The Court, however, excluded that this internal procedure for complaining about the excessive length of a ruling before an administrative court could be considered an effective remedy pursuant to art. 13 ECHR. Specifically, the Court noted the automatic inadmissibility of "Pinto" appeals, based solely on the grounds that the applicants had not requested an urgent hearing, the effect of which on the length of proceedings appeared to be uncertain, deprived the complainants of the possibility of obtaining adequate and sufficient redress. The Court therefore rejected the exception and found a violation of articles 13 and 6 ECHR.

## III. Private and Family Life, Freedom of Expression

In the case of *Cincimino v. Italy*, No. 68884/13, the applicant was a mother who had lost her parental responsibility and had also been prohibited from meeting her under-age daughter. Based on a series of psychological assessments, the national authorities considered it appropriate and in the interests of the child to adopt such measures as the applicant appeared to hinder her healthy and harmonious development. Invoking art. 8 ECHR (right to a private and family life), the applicant complained that the national authorities had not adopted all the measures necessary to allow her to maintain a relationship with her daughter. In particular, the applicant declared that the last decisions concerning her custody rights were adopted on the basis of assessments made seven and eight years before, respectively, without any consideration at all of the improvements she believed she had made.

Although art. 8 ECHR does not contain any explicit procedural indications, the ECtHR emphasised that the decision-making process that results in an outcome that leads to the application of measures which interfere with the parent-child relationship must be fair and adequately respect the interests protected by said provision. In view of the need to adopt appropriate measures to maintain the relationship of the applicant with her daughter during the proceedings, when examining whether the Italian authorities had acted in compliance with their positive obligations arising from art. 8 ECHR, the Court found that the lack of a recent, independent assessment on the applicant had deprived the decision-making process of those procedural requirements under art. 8 ECHR. In addition to the payment of non-material damages of 32,000 euro, the Italian authorities were invited to review the complainant's request to restore her parental responsibility, taking account of the applicant's current situation and the best interests of the child.

With the judgment of 23 June 2016 in the case of *Strumia v. Italy*, (No. 53377/13), the ECtHR found a violation of art. 8 ECHR by Italy due to the failure to protect the father's right to visit his daughter for seven years. Despite his constant requests and the many decisions made on the matter (which show the negative influence of his ex-wife and the need to intervene to preserve his relationship with his daughter), the applicant was only able to exercise his visitation rights in an extremely limited manner due to the opposition of the child's mother. While it recognised that the authorities found themselves faced with an extremely difficult situation in this specific case, which arose, in particular, from the tension existing between the minor's parents, the ECtHR highlighted the fact that a lack of cooperation between separated parents cannot excuse the competent authorities from implementing all the means that could allow family ties to be maintained. In this case, the national courts did not adopt, from the beginning of the separation when the minor was only three years old and had a positive attitude towards the applicant, useful measures aimed at establishing effective contact and subsequently tolerated the mother's behaviour for around eight years, which prevented a real relationship between the complainant and the minor from being consolidated. The

ECtHR observed that the way in which the proceedings were conducted in court showed a series of rather automatic and stereotypical measures, such as numerous information requests and the delegation of monitoring to social services, who were ordered to enforce the visitation rights of the applicant. In doing so, the authorities allowed the existing situation to consolidate by a lack of compliance with judicial decisions. In conclusion, the Court held that the national authorities had not made adequate and sufficient efforts to enforce the applicant's visitation rights and that they had violated his right to respect of private and family life. The applicant was awarded the sum of 15,000 euro in non-material damages.

The ECtHR came to largely the same conclusions in the case of *Giorgioni v. Italy* on 15 September 2016. As in the *Struma* case, the Court held that the national authorities had not carried out adequate and sufficient efforts to enforce the visitation rights of the applicant for a period of approximately four years (from August 2006 to November 2010), thus violating his right to respect of family life. Once again in this case, the authorities did not show the diligence that the case in question required and underperformed vis à vis what they could be reasonably expected to do. In particular, the national courts did not adopt adequate measures to create the conditions necessary to fully realise the father's visitation rights, tolerating the mother's behaviour for approximately four years which prevented a real relationship between the applicant and his son from being established. On the other hand, there is no violation in the time after November 2010 given that, despite serious misunderstandings between the two parents, starting from this time the authorities adopted the necessary measures to encourage them to cooperate and restore the relationship between the applicant and his son.

In the case of *Taddeucci and McCall v. Italy* (No. 51362/09), decided on 30 June 2016, the ECtHR found that Italy had violated the rights of the applicants to not suffer any discrimination on the grounds of sexual orientation in the enjoyment of their rights pursuant to art. 8 ECHR. In the case in question, the applicants were a same-sex couple, formed by an Italian citizen and a New-Zealand national, who were unable to achieve family reunification due to the homosexual partner (non-EU citizen) being refused a residence permit for family reasons.

The Italian Government stated that the refusal was legitimate in that the same treatment was reserved for unmarried heterosexual couples. The Court, however, found that, on the grounds that there was a lack of provision at the time of the events of any judicial recognition for same-sex couples, treating the applicants in the same manner as a heterosexual couple, who, on the other hand, had access to a means of making their union official, must be considered unjustified. In this regard, the ECtHR found that the Italian Government had not indicated other legitimate reasons justifying the fact that, in examining the request for a residence permit for family reasons, they had treated the applicants in the same way as they would a heterosexual couple that had not made their situation official. In particular, in the sector concerned, the Court held that the argument invoked by the Italian authorities, namely the protection of the traditional family, cannot constitute a "particularly sound and convincing" reason as to justify, within the circumstances of the case in question, discrimination on the grounds of sexual orientation. In conclusion, the Court was of the opinion that the restrictive interpretation of the notion of "family member" applied to the second applicant did not take proper account of the applicants' personal situation and, in particular, the impossibility for them to obtain legal recognition of their union in Italy.

The case of *Gueye v. Italy*, No. 76823/12, decided on 31 May 2016, was rejected as being manifestly ill-founded. Invoking articles 8 and 14 ECHR, the applicant, a Senegalese citizen, complained that, on the basis of art. 250 of the civil code, he was prevented from acknowledging his biological son and from creating family relationships with him. Specifically, this provision provides that "the acknowledgement of a child under the age of fourteen cannot be carried out without the consent of the other parent who has already acknowledged the child. Consent cannot be refused when acknowledgement is in the best interests of the child". While the complainant declared that his acknowledgement request was rejected on the grounds of incorrect conclusions by experts and the fact that he was an undocumented foreign citizen in Italy, the Strasbourg Court concluded that the imposition of the measure in question pursued legitimate purposes to protect the minor and that the reasons provided by the national courts for rejecting the paternity acknowledgement request were sufficient and relevant.

The applicants in the case of *Brambilla and Others v. Italy*, No. 22567/09, decided on 23 June 2016, were three crime journalists found guilty, during a search of their vehicle and newspaper office, of possessing radio equipment capable of intercepting the communications of law enforcement with the purpose of getting to active crime sites quickly, and subsequently reporting on them in print articles. Invoking art. 10 ECHR (freedom of expression), the applicants declared that their sentence and the measures imposed upon them constituted a disproportionate interference with their freedom of expression, in particular in regard to their access to information as journalists.

In excluding the violation of the invoked provision, the ECtHR first observed that the applicants were not prohibited from disclosing news on crimes to the public. Rather, their sentence was based solely on their possession and use of radio equipment to obtain information on such events more quickly, intercepting the communications of law enforcement, which were confidential in nature according to Italian law. Furthermore, it was the opinion of the Strasbourg Court that not only did the measures disputed by the applicants pursue legitimate purposes, such as protecting the rights of others, as well as the protection of national security, the defence of public order and crime prevention, but they were also proportionate to the latter.

With the ruling of 8 March 2016, the case of *Gatto v. Italy*, No. 19424/08, was rejected due to a failure to exhaust internal remedies. Invoking art. 8 ECHR, the applicant complained about the disclosure of information regarding his alleged connections with the mafia, via the publication of the – confidential – content of meeting minutes from the Parliamentary Commission on the issue of organised crime, mafia or otherwise. However, as the appeal for damages in regard to the same complaint was still pending appeal in Italy, the ECtHR declared the claim inadmissible.

The case of *Petrache and Tranca v. Italy*, No. 15920/16, was also rejected due to a failure to exhaust internal recourses. It related to the alleged violation of articles 3, 8, 13 and 14 ECHR on the grounds of the eviction measure of which the applicants, belonging to the Roma ethnic group and settled in the Roman camp of "Ex Cartiera", were the recipients. In particular, contrary to the declarations of the applicants, the Court concluded that they had an effective internal remedy for obtaining both the suspension and repeal of the eviction order. In the first case, recourse to articles 55 and 56 of the code of administrative procedure; in the second, lodging an appeal with the Regional Administrative Court (TAR). No exceptional circumstances were found by the ECtHR to relieve the applicants of their obligation to exhaust the legal recourses in question.

# Italy in the Case-law of the Court of Justice of the European Union

## I. The Principle of Retroactivity in Most Favourable Criminal Law

Case C-218/15, decided by the Court of Justice of the European Union (ECJ) on 6 October 2016, was lodged within criminal proceedings brought against several Italian citizens accused of facilitating the illegal immigration into Italy of Romanian citizens before Romania joined the EU (crime pursuant to art. 12, paragraphs 3 and 3-*bis* of lgs.d. 286/1998). Specifically, the referring judge asked whether, given art. 6 TEU, art. 49 CFREU, and art. 7 ECHR, Romania's joining of the European Union abolished the crime of facilitating, by Italian citizens, the illegal immigration of Romanian citizens, which was committed before membership and, on the other hand, if the principle of retroactive application of most favourable criminal law would apply to the accused in the criminal proceedings.

The ECJ held that the criminal case in question was not aimed at third-country nationals that enter Italy illegally and remain without a residence permit, but rather the people who facilitate the entrance and illegal residence of these citizens within the territory of the State. The mere fact that, subsequent to their illegal entrance, these persons became citizens of the European Union by way of their State of origin joining the European Union should in no way influence the way in which criminal proceedings are carried out against the parties who facilitated illegal immigration. It follows that art. 6 TEU and art. 49 CFREU must be interpreted as meaning that one State joining the European Union does not preclude another member State from imposing a criminal penalty on anyone who, prior to said membership, committed the crime of facilitating illegal immigration of citizens from the former State.

## II. Equal Pay for Men and Women

In case C-335/15, decided on 14 July 2016, the ECJ ruled on the Ministry of Justice's refusal – with reference to the compulsory maternity leave periods taken before 1 January 2005 – to allow an ordinary magistrate to benefit from the special job-related allowance compensating the workload encountered by ordinary magistrates in conducting their professional activities. The Luxembourg court was of the opinion that, provided that, during the aforementioned period, this employee had received income at least equivalent to that for service, as laid out by national social security legislation, which she would have received in the event she had been unable to work due to health reasons, the national legislation in question is not contrary to EU law on equal pay between male and female employees, or the regulations governing health and safety in the workplace for pregnant employees, new mothers and those entitled to reduced working hours for infant feeding.

# Index

# Table of Cases

## Constitutional Court

## Court of Cassation, Civil Division

## Court of Cassation, Criminal Division



## Supreme Administrative Council

## Ordinary Tribunals

## European Court of Human Rights (in alphabetical order)

## Court of Justice of the European Union (in chronological order)



## European Committee of Social Rights, decisions on collective complains

## Research and Editorial Committee

**Andrea Cofelice**, MA in Institutions and Policies of Human Rights and Peace, University of Padova. PhD in Political Science – Comparative and European Politics, University of Siena.

**Pietro de Perini**, MA in Institutions and Policies of Human Rights and Peace, University of Padova. PhD in International Politics, City, University of London.

**Paolo De Stefani**, Aggregate Professor of International Protection of Human Rights in the Degree Course in Political Science, International Relations and Human Rights at the University of Padova. At the same University, he also teaches International Criminal and Humanitarian Law. He is National Director for Italy of the European Master in Human Rights and Democratisation (E.MA).

**Marco Mascia**, Associate Professor of International Relations and Jean Monnet Chair in Political System of the European Union at the University of Padova. At the same University, he is Director of the University Human Rights Centre and Director of the Master's Degree Programme in Human Rights and Multi-Level Governance.

**Antonio Papisca**, Professor Emeritus of the University of Padova and UNESCO Chair "Human Rights, Democracy and Peace", in 1982 he promoted the establishment of the Human Rights Centre within the University of Padova. In the period between 1994 and 2002 he was a member of the Italian Inter-ministerial Committee of Human Rights at the Ministry of Foreign Affairs and of the Italian Human Rights Commission at the Presidency of the Council of Ministers.

**Claudia Pividori**, MA in Institutions and Policies of Human Rights and Peace, University of Padova. PhD in International Order and Human Rights, University of Rome – La Sapienza.

# Peter Lang – Italian Yearbook of Human Rights Series

The legal and political significance of human rights has increased enormously at the international and European levels. Awareness has risen that the respect and the promotion of human rights must be at the centre of States and local communities' public policies and that human rights are at the basis of civil society initiatives and movements. There is a large machinery monitoring, at all the levels of governance, the way in which States implement the obligations assumed toward each person under their sovereignty.

The **Italian Yearbook of Human Rights Series** provides year by year, a dynamic and up-to date overview of the measures Italy has taken to adapt its legislation and policies to international human rights law and to comply with commitments voluntarily assumed by the Italian Government at the international level. The Series thus intends to contribute to the continuous monitoring activity on the situation of human rights in Italy undertaken at the local, national and international levels by relevant intergovernmental and civil society actors.

Each volume of this series surveys the activities carried out, during the year of reference, by the relevant national and local Italian actors, including governmental bodies, civil society organisations and universities. It also presents reports and recommendations that have been addressed to Italy by international monitoring bodies within the framework of the United Nations, the Council of Europe and the European Union. Finally, each Yearbook provides a selection of examples from international and national case-law which cast light on Italy's position vis-à-vis internationally recognised human rights.

The Yearbook is edited by the Human Rights Centre of the University of Padova, in cooperation with the UNESCO Chair in Human Rights, Democracy and Peace of the same University, and with the support of the Region of Veneto. The Centre, established in 1982, carries out research and education following a global and interdisciplinary approach. It hosts the Jean Monnet Centre of Excellence on intercultural dialogue, human rights and multi-level governance.

**www.peterlang.com**